THE FLEURY *PLAYBOOK*:

ESSAYS AND STUDIES

Scene from the *Play of Herod* in the original production by the New York Pro Musica as staged at the Rockefeller Chapel, University of Chicago. Photograph by Henry Hartmann. Courtesy of the Music Division, New York Public Library at Lincoln Center, and *The University of Chicago Magazine*.

THE FLEURY *PLAYBOOK*

ESSAYS AND STUDIES

Papers by C. Clifford Flanigan, Fletcher Collins, Jr., Clyde W. Brockett, David Bevington, Thomas P. Campbell, Kathleen Ashley, Miriam Anne Skey, and Cynthia Bourgeault

Edited by Thomas P. Campbell and Clifford Davidson

Early Drama, Art, and Music
Monograph Series, 7

MEDIEVAL INSTITUTE PUBLICATIONS
Western Michigan University
Kalamazoo, Michigan
1985

ISBN 0-918720-66-4 (Paperbound)
ISBN 0-918720-65-6 (Hardbound)

Printed in the United States of America

Contents

Preface • vii

Introduction
Thomas P. Campbell • xi

The Fleury *Playbook*, the Traditions of Medieval Latin Drama, and Modern Scholarship
C. Clifford Flanigan • 1

The Home of the Fleury *Playbook*
Fletcher Collins, Jr. • 26

Modal and Motivic Coherence in the Music of the Music-Dramas in the Fleury *Playbook*
Clyde W. Brockett • 35

The Staging of Twelfth-Century Liturgical Drama in the Fleury *Playbook*
David Bevington • 62

Augustine's Concept of the Two Cities and the Fleury *Playbook*
Thomas P. Campbell • 82

The Fleury *Raising of Lazarus* and Twelfth-Century Currents of Thought
Kathleen M. Ashley • 100

The Iconography of Herod in the Fleury *Playbook* and in the Visual Arts
Miriam Anne Skey • 120

Liturgical Dramaturgy and Modern Production
Cynthia Bourgeault • 144

Appendix: Introduction to Orléans, Bibliothèque Municipale, MS. 201 • 161

Index • 165

Plates

Frontispiece. Scene from the *Play of Herod* in the original production by the New York Pro Musica.

1. Triforium capital at Fleury.
Hugues de Sainte-Marie kneeling before the Virgin and Child and offering a gift of one of his books.

2. Custer LaRue in role of Mary Magdalene in the Fleury *Visitatio Sepulchri* as performed in 1979 at the Abbaye St. Benoit-de-Fleury. Theater Wagon production.

3. Scenes from the story of the Magi and the Nativity.
Leaf from English Psalter. British Library Add. MS. 37,472.

4. Scenes from the early life of Christ.
Psalter. Paris, Bibliothèque Nationale MS. lat. 8846.

5. Magi meet Herod (seated, at left).
Cambridge, Emmanuel College, MS. 252², fol. 8ʳ.

6. Massacre of the Innocents, with Herod (seated, at right) looking on. Cambridge, Emmanuel College, MS. 252², fol. 9ʳ.

7. Death of Herod.
Detail of Paris, Bibliothèque Nationale MS. lat. 8846.

8-74. The Fleury *Playbook*.
Orléans, Bibliothèque Municipale MS. 201.

Preface

This collection had its inception with a symposium on the Fleury *Playbook* at the Fifteenth International Congress on Medieval Studies at Western Michigan University in May 1980. Several additional essays have also been added to the collection, and these have been solicited from scholars whose special interests were not represented at the original symposium in Kalamazoo. The purpose of our book is to present a series of interdisciplinary studies on the most important single document containing the medieval music-drama, the Fleury *Playbook*. By a special arrangement with *Comparative Drama*, the papers were first published in that journal and are reprinted here with the permission of that journal.

Naturally, all possible approaches to the Fleury *Playbook* cannot be covered in a single volume, but we have attempted at least to present studies which show the different ways in which the medieval Latin music-drama may be fruitfully approached. Each essay thus takes up a unique topic which has not previously received sufficient attention in scholarship, and each utilizes a specific analytic method. Because study of the music-drama, often known as liturgical drama, has received new impetus in the last two decades, particularly since the publication of a wonderfully controversial book by O. B. Hardison, Jr., twenty years ago, the editors have sought to choose contributions from established scholars in several academic areas which address issues of the greatest significance in the field.

The presentation of such a book as this cannot be seen as a mere scholarly exercise. The revival of the music-drama, especially the Fleury plays, as living theater owes much in America to Noah Greenberg and the New York Pro Musica as well as to Fletcher Collins, Jr., and in England to E. Martin Browne and William L. Smoldon. Current practice in the production of such plays has, to be sure, reached a much higher level than was possible in some of the pioneering productions of Greenberg or Browne, and we are now able to combine a sense of historical accuracy in staging and musical performance practice with a theatrical liveliness that does not undermine the liturgical meaning of a play. It is also possible to adapt these plays in conscious ways to modern audiences of non-medievalists, e.g., through the use of such modern English translations as those provided by Crown Light Editions. However, we need to remember that in its own time this drama was never popular in the sense of being available for the ordinary folk of, say, a parish, but rather was associated with an ecclesiastical center such as Fleury—though, as we shall see in the essays which follow, even the matter of the "home" of the Fleury *Playbook* has been a matter of some controversy.

We are indebted to a large number of friends and colleagues in the pursuit of the present project to study the Fleury *Playbook*. Without the encouragement of Fletcher Collins, Jr., and C. Clifford Flanigan, the original symposium would never have taken place. The participants in the symposium, especially Diane Dolan Bennett, Paul Hildebrand, Jr., and Marcie Epstein, demonstrated an enthusiasm for the Fleury plays in their presentations which, although not represented in our collection, contributed strongly to the overall shape and emphasis of the present volume. John H. Stroupe and C. J. Gianakaris gave assistance with the essays at their first stage of publication in *Comparative Drama*, and to them we are particularly grateful since without their agreement to participation in this project the present book could not have come into existence. We would also like to acknowledge the support and encouragement of M. Dominique Grandon, Conservateur-Adjoint, Bibliothèque Municipale, Orléans, for allowing us to reproduce photographs of the manuscript, and to Julian Plante, Director of the Hill Monastic Manuscript Library at St. John's University, for making possible the acquisition of a quality microfilm of Orléans, Bibliothèque Municipale MS. 201. Most importantly, we would like to express our gratitude to Wabash College and especially Mr. William Sword, a trustee of the college, for the financial support which made possible the inclusion of illustrations of the entire *Playbook* in the plates. Our deep-felt thanks are extended to Lewis Salter, President of Wabash College, for his long hours in the laboratory producing the glossy photographs which were used for the plates illustrating the *Playbook*.

Permissions to use the other illustrations in this book were granted by the Music Division of the New York Public Library at Lincoln Center, Astor, Lenox, and Tilden Foundations, and the *University of Chicago Magazine* (for the frontispiece, a photograph by Henry Hartmann of the historic production of *Herod* by the New York Pro Musica at the Rockefeller Chapel of the University of Chicago); the Bibliothèque Nationale, Paris; the Master and Fellows of Emmanuel College, Cambridge; the British Library, London; Dom Jean-Marie Berland, Abbaye de St. Benoît de Fleury; and Theater Wagon. Also, we wish to acknowledge the assistance of

LaNoue Davenport, who helped to locate the photograph which appears as a frontispiece to this book.

Thomas P. Campbell
Clifford Davidson

Introduction

Thomas P. Campbell

A volume based upon a single collection of Latin music-dramas—i.e., those contained in Orléans MS. 201—deserves justification, for it has not been the usual practice thus to issue together a number of studies which focus specifically on an individual manuscript containing liturgical plays. Recent scholarship has made it clear, however, that the history of the drama of the medieval period is far more complex than we realized, and a necessary result must be a more rigorous and more complete examination of related plays. Further, *interdisciplinary* approaches to the "drama of the medieval Church" have proved extremely fruitful and have broadened the scope of critical questions concerning such drama. We know that liturgical drama is not a uniform phenomenon, but that it varies significantly from one locale to another, from one century to the next. While purely formal studies continue to be published, scholars frequently are turning instead to various aspects of the whole context in which a play might have been presented. Contributions from fields as diverse as liturgics, history, and art have revealed much about the motives for the composition and presentation of the plays, the conditions under which they were prepared and staged, and their relationship to their age or their locale. Musical analyses, previously neglected (as Karl Young's *Drama of the Medieval Church* demonstrates[1]) except among a small circle of musicologists, have now become a major concern because of their usefulness to all students of the early drama.

Because the Fleury plays are uniquely preserved in a single manuscript, they cannot be treated in quite the same way as other early medieval plays might be treated. It was not usual for a collection of dramas to be prepared; almost always, plays are found scattered through various service books. For instance, of the many examples of the Type III *Visitatio Sepulchri* play edited by Young, all but the Fleury version are embedded in the services of the Easter liturgy.[2] Represented are ordinaries, graduals, responsories, antiphonaries, and processionals. The plays in the Fleury manuscript, on the other hand, bear a less obvious relationship to liturgical services, and, it should be noted, there is no connection at all between the plays and the other texts bound in the same manuscript. In fact, the particular gatherings containing the Fleury plays seem to have once been bound separately prior to their insertion in the manuscript which now contains them.[3]

Strange as it may seem, we do not know with exactitude why such a collection as the Fleury *Playbook* should have been assembled. Given the predominantly monastic context in which the early plays were composed and presented and also their close relationship to the liturgical services in which they usually appear, a collection which brings together plays in a volume separated from the usual context of the liturgy is all the more remarkable. Some may even wish to argue that certain of the Fleury plays as collected in the *Playbook* may not have been *primarily* intended for liturgical presentation. Surprisingly, the rubrics do not point clearly and unequivocally toward specific liturgical feasts, as we would expect to be the case in each instance. Further, seven of the ten plays end with the rubric "sic [hic] finit[iatur]." The recently-published edition of the Fleury monastic Constitutions from the early thirteenth century contains no reference to dramatic presentations; only two quasi-dramatic tropes (on Easter and Ascension) are designated, and neither is very sophisticated.[4] The order of the plays in the *Playbook*—a series of St. Nicholas miracles, Christmas and Easter dramas, St. Paul's Conversion and the Raising of Lazarus—roughly suggests the chronology of the Christian calendar, but the Christmas plays and the two New Testament plays are presented in a dramatic, rather than liturgical, order.[5] On the other hand, the rubrication often, as we would expect, indicates performance within a monastic church: four plays refer to ecclesiastical locations, most of them end with the *Te Deum*, and a liturgical chorus of singers is required in all of them. Internal evidence in the St. Nicholas plays also suggests close association with the liturgy. The antiphon *O Christi pietas*, which ends the *Tres Filiae*, is part of the Vespers liturgy for the feast of St. Nicholas,[6] while *Statuit ei Dominus* likewise potentially connects the *Iconia* with the liturgy for this day since it is the Introit for the Mass of a Confessor Bishop. Finally, the closing of the *Tres Filiae* with the *Te Deum* would seem to suggest a link with the Matins service for the same day.

As the above comments would seem to suggest, we simply do not know the exact conditions under which these music-dramas were *staged* (if, indeed, we may use such a word to designate their production). It is most likely, of course, that they had in fact been written to expand the liturgy for special feasts, as was the custom of Benedictine monasteries in the eleventh and twelfth centuries. Nevertheless, so little attention has been given to the question of liturgical performance and setting in the Fleury *Playbook* that one must speculate about other possibilities.

The medieval liturgy was a musical event, and the daily life of the medieval monk was centered almost exhaustively upon the performance of chant. Because the melodies and the techniques of singing formed so integral a part of monastic education, the composition of pieces which were not primarily intended for liturgical performance, or which were ancillary to the plainchant of Mass and Office, could easily have been a common practice. The tremendous outpouring of rhythmic conductus and sequence, of strophic hymns and *versus* in the tenth through twelfth centuries certainly supports such a hypothesis. The community at St. Martial of Limoges, for instance, produced a number of significant manuscripts which contain far more musical compositions than could have been sung on any one feast day.[7] Is it not possible that dramas were also composed under similar circumstances? The fact that the Fleury plays reflect nearly every important form of religious music, from plainchant through rhymed, strophic verse, certainly suggests that such experimental composition could have been a factor in their creation.[8]

Yet the primarily monastic setting of liturgical plays does not necessarily argue against the possibility that they might even have been written for purposes other than liturgical presentation. The tradition of monastic education encouraged the imitation of many literary forms, including drama. As we well know from the example of Hrosvitha, these imitations were submitted to a student's teachers for correction and emendation.[9] The manuscript context of several plays—e.g., the Beauvais *Daniel* and the works of Hilarius—points to a student hand, and while the Fleury texts themselves do not present overt evidence of a scholarly context, such a possibility has been proposed in recent scholarship.[10]

Finally, the omission of references in the rubrics to specific liturgical contexts may indicate that at least some of the plays might not have been intended as adjuncts to a particular service, but rather the dramas might have been written to be performed independently, though not, of course, at inappropriate times in the calendar. The processional nature of nearly all liturgical plays and their seemingly relative independence from the liturgy itself may suggest that in fact the more successful compositions re-create the liturgical domain while in some sense remaining apart from it. The Fleury plays in particular employ an alternation between processional movement and static, iconographic moment which closely parallels that of the typical liturgical service. Might this not suggest that they *imitate*, rather than *exemplify*, such services?[11] The overtly symbolic use of gesture, location, and musical quotation points to a conscientious employment of well-known liturgical forms by a scholarly author or authors whose interests may well have been primarily dramatic and literary rather than liturgical.

It appears that we cannot hope to identify the author or redactor whose work appears in this collection. We know that all of the plays for which there are analogues differ substantially from other versions and that two of them are completely unique; what has not been established is the uniqueness of the collection as a whole. C. Clifford Flanigan, in his contribution to this volume, tackles this very issue in a wide-ranging and authoritative essay which compares the Fleury *Playbook* to all other major collections of medieval Church drama. His criteria for comparison as well as his use of reception theory for understanding audience expectation provide a new and useful approach to the study of liturgical drama. His analysis also evidences an increased appreciation of the importance of the Fleury collection in the history of literature.

If we are to believe recent scholars who have questioned whether these plays actually belong to St. Benoît-sur-Loire,[12] the Fleury *Playbook* would seem to be misnamed. The manuscript itself contains an attribution to this monastery, but in a much later hand; and the evidence derived from the notation system of the music and the script point to other possible locations.[13] The neumes, on four-line staves with clefs, exhibit specific idiosyncrasies, especially the single-pitch punctum drawn with traces of the virga. These characteristics, to which may be added the slant of the writing—often an ambiguous criterion—suggest the conclusion that the neumes are of the family known as "French." This type of notation was widespread between Sens, the area northwest of Bourges, and Orléans, including the Loire area. Nevertheless, the neumes are not of the types found contemporaneously at Fleury.[14] With regard to the notation, definitive conclusions are likewise impossible, for evidence is altogether too sketchy. Nevertheless, Fletcher Collins' examination of the historical context at the monastery of St. Benoît de Fleury makes a case against Solange Corbin's well-known claim that the manuscript was not written at Fleury. Rather than depending solely upon internal evidence derived from the manuscript, Collins argues that the cultural milieu at Fleury would have been most appropriate for the composition of such a wide variety of plays. His close acquaintance with the monastery itself and his experience in producing all of the plays in this manuscript give added authority to his arguments.

The very diversity of the collection indicates that several sources were consulted in the course of its composition. There are, however, strong arguments for believing that this work was done by a single person—i.e., that a single hand composed all of these plays—and that all of them were produced for a single locale.[15] In this regard, perhaps the most important evidence will be found in the analysis of the modal structure of the music as this musical characteristic suggests relationships among the plays. Clyde W. Brockett's study of modal and motivic correspondences therefore marks the beginning of a new approach to compositional methods in these plays. Focusing on the music as phenomenon rather than in terms of performance practice, he outlines the ways in which mode and motif coincide, interlock, and repeat within individual plays or from one play to another. By isolating the techniques by which each musical piece is tied to its companion pieces (whether original or borrowed from another musical source) as well as by indicating the ways in which coherence within each play is attained through motivic and modal formulae, he supplies a necessary overview of the music in the Fleury plays. While his notation system, based on the naming of pitches rather than on the usual kinds of musical notation, may to some seem unfamiliar at first, it proves to be most useful in providing a visual picture of the many striking musical correspondences which appear throughout the plays.

The question of artistic coherence in the Fleury *Playbook* may be approached from other perspectives as well. The answers suggested in the papers by David Bevington and myself are derived from the tracing of dramatic and literary techniques within the ten plays. Professor Bevington's important study of staging conventions, guided by both the rubrics and the text, suggests that the Fleury plays represent a new departure in medieval dramaturgy in which ritual and communal drama are becoming separated. He discusses the ways in which the drives toward liturgical function and dramatic presentation often seem to contradict or interact with each other. My essay on the philosophical coherence of the plays attempts to show that all of the dramas employ an Augustinian interpretation of man's relationship to God and to his fellow man. Drawing upon *The City of God* as both document and model, I argue that the evidence of unique additions to every play indicates a unified treatment of men and their works which requires indebtedness to St. Augustine's thought, perhaps modified by twelfth-century historical writing.

More particular studies of individual plays, such as Kathleen Ashley's analysis of philosophical themes in the *Lazarus* and Miriam Anne Skey's discussion of the iconography of Herod in the Christmas dramas, lead one further to appreciate more fully the artistic accomplishment and complexity of the Fleury plays. As both of these studies demonstrate, the Fleury plays can be shown to be at once more humane and more innovative, yet more cautious and conservative, than other dramas of the period. Professor Ashley, drawing upon twelfth-century philosophy and theology, argues that seemingly incompatible currents of thought find a resolution in the very structure of the Fleury *Lazarus*. Dr. Skey demonstrates that the depiction of Herod in the *Playbook* is at once more wide-ranging and yet more decorous than in certain other medieval examples of the iconography presented in the visual arts and in drama. Both studies suggest that systematic analysis of individual plays from carefully focused perspectives can be extremely rewarding; their methodologies are indicative of routes which future scholarship might wish to follow for other plays in Orléans MS. 201.

Cynthia Bourgeault's concluding essay expands our awareness of the Fleury drama's importance by reviewing some important aspects of dramatic performance in both medieval and modern times. Because of her experience in staging these dramas within a liturgical setting, she is able to translate their religious experience into practical advice; hence, she can indicate directions for understanding the dramatic achievement of the liturgical drama in ways which translate into effectiveness for modern audiences. Her comparison of dramatic resources in the Fleury dramas to those of other plays in the genre provides an appropriate conclusion to this volume.

We offer these essays as a beginning, as a suggestion of the usefulness of interdisciplinary scholarship for broadening our understanding of a complex and demanding subject. To be sure, more particular and elaborate interdisciplinary studies of the Fleury plays remain to be done. For example, the liturgical associations of the plays, with special regard to the Norman Benedictine tradition, need further specification; we need to have a somewhat better idea than at present of the relationship between the music and texts of these plays and the individual liturgical items available to a monastic worshipper in this region.[16] Study of this material should also identify other ways in which the individual plays are related to the liturgy of, for example, particular feast days; and the musical forms also promise to be even better understood through such study. However, separate attention also needs to be given to the performance practice of the music of these plays: what effects are appropriate, what singing styles are required, and, indeed, what rhythmic practice is right in each case. This last is, of course, a thorny question, as Dr. Bourgeault's comments in this volume will indicate. Many philosophical and theological issues, of course, remain to be explored, especially, I would think, in the plays of St. Nicholas and St. Paul; and further work must certainly be done on the relationships between the plays and the iconography of the contemporary visual arts.[17] Certain larger questions of aesthetics and structure as well as exact locale may never, in fact, be totally settled, no matter how sophisticated our approaches. These may, however, be useful rather for suggesting possible limits to our theories than for settling such controversial issues once and for all.

Finally, these studies ought to affirm our admiration for the artistic achievement of the Fleury plays as supreme examples of twelfth-century Latin music-drama. Subjected to interdisciplinary analysis, the dramas reward us with unexpected depth and complexity. Nevertheless, in performance they continually surprise us with their power and dramatic skill. Appropriately, these essays are presented here with illustrations that include for convenience photographic reproductions of the Playbook pages of Orléans MS. 201. While the collection has received previous transcriptions, the only reproduction of the manuscript, in the edition by Giampiero Tintori, is nearly impossible to obtain and is difficult to read. Further commentary on the manuscript is reserved for the Appendix, which also includes some important remarks by Père Lin Donnat of the Abbaye St. Benoît de Fleury concerning the Fleury Playbook.

NOTES

[1] See Karl Young, The Drama of the Medieval Church (Oxford: Clarendon Press, 1933), 2 vols. For Young's lack of expertise with regard to the musical dimension of the medieval music-drama, see his own admission (ibid., I, xiii-xiv) and the comments by William L. Smoldon, "The Melodies of the Medieval Church-Dramas and Their Significance," Comparative Drama, 2 (1968), 185-89.

[2] Young, The Drama of the Medieval Church, I, 369-410, 663-81. See also the study by C. Clifford Flanigan in this volume. Flanigan is able to draw upon the late Walther Lipphardt's recent edition of the texts of the Easter music-dramas, an invaluable resource for research on certain of these plays.

[3] Even the examination of photographs of the manuscript (Orléans, Bibliothèque Municipale, MS. 201) shows clearly that the gatherings containing the plays were marked with small pricks on the outer margins, that the sermons which immediately precede them in the manuscript are not so marked, and that the sequences which follow the plays, although marked, are in a different hand and a different (campo aperto) system of musical notation. It is not, however, clear whether the pricks were intended to be guides for writing other materials, since they do not correspond with the musical staves or the texts of the plays. Perhaps the copyist used vellum which had been originally intended for writing, as the pricks roughly correspond with the lines of earlier sermons. First-hand examination of the manuscript itself has revealed substantial differences in the type and quality of vellum upon which the plays and the other items are written; see the comments of Père Lin Donnat, as quoted in the Appendix to this volume, below. The Appendix also gives further information about the manuscript and is additionally intended as an introduction to the plates, which include a photographic facsimile of the manuscript of the Fleury Playbook.

[4] Consuetudines Floriacenses Saeculi Tertii Decemi, ed. D. Anselm Davril, Corpus Consuetudinum Monasticarum, 9 (Siegburg: Schmitt, 1976), pp. 133, 166.

[5] Instead of following the liturgical placement for the feasts of Holy Innocents (December 28) and Epiphany (January 6), the Fleury collection employs a chronological or scriptural organization in which the Ordo ad Representandum Herodem is followed by the Ordo Rachelis. Although there is no feast for Lazarusin the calendar of Fleury, his commemoration (in March) should follow that of St. Paul (in January).

[6] See Young, The Drama of the Medieval Church, II, 321n.

[7] For a convenient summary of the remarkable musical activity at St. Martial in the eleventh and twelfth centuries, see Jacques Chailley, L'École Musicale de Saint Martial de Limoges (Paris: Les Livres Essentials, 1960), esp. pp. 73-118.

[8] A summary of the musical styles represented in the manuscript may be found in the edition by Giampiero Tintori and Raffaele Monterosso, Sacre Rappresentazioni nel Manoscritto 201 della Biblioteca Municipale di Orléans, Instituta et Monumenta, Serie I: Monumenta, No. 2 (Cremona: Athenaeum Cremonense, 1958), pp. ix-xxix. See also the summary in Solange Corbin, "Le Manuscrit 201 d'Orléans, drames liturgiques dits de Fleury," Romania, 74 (1953), 22-24. William L. Smoldon's discussion of the various musical styles in the Playbook in The Music of the Medieval Church Dramas, ed. Cynthia Bourgeault (London: Oxford Univ. Press, 1980), represents the most comprehensive analysis to date. It is, however, strongly colored by Smoldon's prejudices toward thematic and musical variety and against the subtler effects of strophic and musical repetition, though such effects are artistically employed in innumerable sequences, conductus, and hymns.

[9] Hrosvitha, "epistola . . . ad quosdam sapientes huius libri fautores," in Hrotsvithae Opera, ed. H. Homeyer (Munich: Ferdinand Schönigh, 1970), pp. 235-37.

[10] See especially Smoldon, Music of the Medieval Church Dramas, p. 265, and Charles W. Jones, The Saint Nicholas Liturgy and Its Literary Relationships (Berkeley: Univ. of California Press, 1963), pp. 90-117. However, see also the comments of C. Clifford Flanigan, below, p. 12.

[11] Particular plays in the Fleury corpus clearly indicate an attempt to recreate a liturgical milieu. Most obvious is the Filius Getronis, in which a church is part of the set, a solemn procession and service are enacted, and bread and wine are distributed among the brethren and the poor (Young, II, 352). Other plays employ similar devices—e.g., communal devotion around the crèche in the Christmas plays, the use of liturgical chant at moments of iconographical significance in the Easter plays, or the quotation from appropriate hymns and antiphons at the conclusion of the St. Nicholas plays. The "liturgical" nature of a Latin play is a complex question; the presence of liturgical elements in a play may indicate borrowing rather than incorporation, and, lacking any specific reference to presentation within the context of a particular feast, I feel nevertheless that it is safest to assume that a drama optionally may be given on the appropriate day. The Fleury plays are ambiguous in this regard; for example, the Lazarus play is preceded by hymns for the Christmas or Easter seasons (possibly, therefore, reflecting the two commemorations of Lazarus in December or March), but no specific directions are given for presentation in either season. See also the essays in this volume by Flanigan and Campbell, where the issue is discussed in more detail.

[12] The most important discussion is that by Solange Corbin, "Le Manuscrit 201 dit d'Orléans," pp. 1-43. For a discussion of her conclusions, see the contribution by Fletcher Collins, below, pp. 26-34. Also important is a recent study by Kassius Hallinger, "Die Provenienz der Consuetudo Sigiberti," in Mediaevalia litteraria: Festscrift für Helmut de Boor, ed. Ursula Hennig and Herbert Kolb (Munich: C. H. Beck, 1971), pp. 155-76.

[13] See Diane Marie Dolan, "The Notation of Orléans Bibliothèque Municipale, MS 201," Studia Anselmiana, 85 (1982), 279-88.

[14] See the thorough study by Dolan, pp. 285-86, for the assertion that the Playbook's system of notation bears no relation to any examples from that monastery and for the localization of that type of notation inside an area "between Sens, Massay-Cher, and Orléans, including (approximately) the Loire area." I am also grateful to Clyde W. Brockett, Jr., for suggestions with regard to the comments on the music in my introduction.

[15] The text and the rubrics are obviously the work of a single scribe, who also certainly drew the staff-lines. It was common practice for a separate scribe to draw in the musical notation after the text had been entered into the manuscript. Typically, rubrics were written between or at the end of musical staves, separated from the music by a bold vertical line. There seems to be no evidence of erasure, indicating that the copyists responsible for the text and the music had originals before them when they wrote. Additional scholarly analysis of the music and text in the manuscript may, admittedly, reveal further evidence concerning the authorship and copying of these plays. Certainly, as several papers in this volume argue, there are strong possibilities that one person, as lyricist and composer, altered or adapted texts from several sources for inclusion in the Playbook.

[16] Such study will build upon the work of Smoldon, whose Music of the Medieval Church Dramas is not exhaustive in this regard. See the review by Gerard Farrell in the EDAM Newsletter, 4, No. 1 (March 1982), 17.

[17] The pioneering work of Fletcher Collins, Jr., on the iconography of the medieval music-drama deserves notice here; see his Production of Medieval Church Music-Drama (Charlottesville: Univ. Press of Virginia, 1972). Though it treats a drama which is not part of the Fleury Playbook, Clifford Davidson's article "On the Uses of Iconographic Study: The Example of the Sponsus from St. Martial of Limoges," Comparative Drama, 13 (1979-80), 300-19, should also be consulted.

The Fleury *Playbook*, the Traditions of Medieval Latin Drama, and Modern Scholarship

C. Clifford Flanigan

The Fleury *Playbook*, containing verbal and musical texts for ten plays and now a portion of MS. 201 in the Orléans Municipal Library, is the most extensive surviving collection of medieval Latin music-dramas. Four of these plays have as their subjects episodes from the St. Nicholas legend, while the remaining six include the Herod and Innocents plays made famous by the New York Pro Musica productions, a Lazarus play, extensive *Visitatio* and *Peregrinus* plays, and a play about the conversion of St. Paul. All have received a great deal of previous attention. Five of them are included in David Bevington's anthology *Medieval Drama*, and Fletcher Collins has edited all ten plays in his book of performing versions of seventeen plays from the music-drama repertory. Similarly, Gustave Cohen devoted more than forty percent of his collection of French liturgical drama to plays from the Fleury collection. Indeed, among the anthologists of the Latin music-drama of the past half-century, only Karl Langosch, with his evident bias for German culture, has chosen to omit the Fleury dramas from his book. Clearly these plays are among the most favored of all medieval dramas.[1]

This predisposition for the Fleury plays is understandable; by any standard they are extraordinary creations. The very excellence of the individual plays has in fact tended to draw attention away from the collection as a whole. It is true that Giampiero Tintori edited the collection in 1958, and that a continuing controversy had grown up around Solange Corbin's claim that the manuscript was not written at the monastery at St. Benoît-sur-Loire.[2] But these scholarly works are only exceptions that point to the relative lack of attention to the collection as a whole. The present essay seeks to redress this imbalance. I shall argue that the Fleury *Playbook*, when understood in context, is one of the most significant documents in the history of European drama not only because of the quality of its contents, but also especially because of what it teaches us about at least one twelfth-century scribe's understanding of the nature and character of drama.

Medieval Latin music-drama has long been the object of intense scrutiny by musical and literary historians, and it may seem an act of critical hybris on my part to argue that the *Playbook* has great historical significance which has eluded earlier scholarship. There is, however, a readily available explanation for this omission—an explanation which stems from the way that the study of medieval Latin music-drama has traditionally proceeded. In Karl Young's *Drama of the Medieval Church* as well as in its predecessors and successors, plays have been edited and discussed according to their subject matter. However different their contents, musical and literary forms, and places of origin, all Christmas plays, for example, have been lumped together in the standard histories. This practice has several unfortunate results. In the first place, the plays' textual histories have been obscured. Young found it impossible to construct textual stemmae for the Easter plays.[3] Happily, this deficiency in Young's work has been corrected by Helmut deBoor's study of the *Osterfeiern* in which the broad lines of the textual dissemination of this enormous mass of material are sketched.[4] Other scholars have also contributed to our understanding of the manuscript tradition.[5] Such studies have now culminated in Walther Lipphardt's magnificent six-volume edition of the Easter *ordines* and plays.[6] These important developments make necessary a complete revaluation of our knowledge about Latin music-drama, including the plays in the Fleury collection—a fact that seems not yet sufficiently recognized by Anglo-American scholars.

At least with Lipphardt's edition a beginning has been made which will take seriously questions of textual relationships and manuscript study. But another difficulty arising from the persistent tendency to edit and study these texts according to their subject matter has yet to be addressed. Without exception the modern editions of these works utterly divorce them from the words and music which surround them in the surviving manuscripts. The impression that students have often drawn from this procedure is that these pieces are independent entities, much like the modern dramas that we read in published editions. This impression is seriously mistaken. The so-called "Drama of the Medieval Church" is almost always contained in service books. Thus its context is wholly liturgical; it is an inseparable part of the much larger annual ritual practice of specific religious communities. Usually it is impossible even to say with certainty where the "play" under discussion begins or ends. Is the singing of the *Te Deum* which comes at the end of the Easter *Visitatio Sepulchri*, for example, part of the dramatic office or does it mark the resumption of the usual liturgy of Matins? No unambiguous answer could possibly be given to such a question. Yet in every edition of the dramatic offices known to me the larger liturgical context is not represented. Nowhere, for example, are we allowed to see the relationship between a *Visitatio* text and the Easter rites which form its larger context. The result has been a failure to recognize that nearly all of the *Visitatio Sepulchri* offices were not originally regarded as plays in our sense of that term but as dramatic rituals.

That the *Visitatio* offices can best be understood as rituals rather than as dramas is a claim that I have defended elsewhere; my arguments need not be repeated here.[7] But because my assumptions about the characteristic differences between drama and ritual have an important place in this study of the Fleury *Playbook*, it will perhaps be useful to spell out some of these differences. Rituals are communal events centered on paradigmatic actions in the history of salvation. The words and gestures of a ritual are thought to be charged with a power of reactualization so that the event imitated is believed rendered present in the community's midst and for its welfare. The officiants of a ritual are not mere actors; for the duration of the cultic action they are thought to become the divine figures whom they imitate. Strictly speaking, there are no audiences for rituals, since the entire congregation thinks of itself as participating in the divine actions rendered present. Dramas, on the other hand, including those performed within a church as part of a service, are not regarded as cultically efficacious. They seek to imitate past actions, not, as rituals do, to render past events present. Hence dramatic performance entails a clear-cut distinction between audience and players, who represent actions and characters but are powerless to re-present them. Dramas are usually more realistically conceived than rituals (though this is only a matter of degree), and they draw on their audience's experience of the world and of human nature for their effect. Frequently they seek to involve spectators in their action by emotional identification with certain of the leading characters. Some dramas are more appropriately performed at one season than another, but they have no necessary relationship to the sacred calendar. Rituals, on the other hand, can only be performed at the one moment in the liturgical calendar that is appointed for them, since only that time is thought to be charged with cultic power. I do not mean to suggest that these distinctions are absolute and unalterable, and I certainly would not claim that these few sentences offer even a point of departure for developing comprehensive definitions of ritual and drama. But we can use them as guides that will help us to characterize some essential generic differences between the two principal forms of enactment in the Middle Ages.

These remarks about the differences that separate ritual from drama can provide us with a convenient starting point for our characterization of the Fleury *Playbook*. Scholarship has paid surprisingly little attention to the fact that the Fleury plays—including those similar to dramatic rituals in liturgical manuscripts—lack a liturgical context. The Fleury *Playbook* is a self-contained collection of plays; it is not a service book in any sense of the word. Its *Visitatio Sepulchri* play, to cite a striking example, is not taken from the Easter section of an office or mass book, nor is the Innocents play, a work profoundly liturgical in spirit, explicitly connected to the rites of Holy Innocents Day. To see how unusual this situation is, we need only compare the plays in the Fleury manuscript having traditional liturgical subjects with their counterparts elsewhere. Of the six other examples of the *Officium Stellae* given by Young, all are taken from liturgical books—tropers, evangelaries, and ordinals of various kinds. Similarly, all other surviving plays concerning the Slaughter of the Innocents have tropers or lectionaries as their sources. Most striking is the comparison of the Fleury *Visitatio Sepulchri* with other Type III *Visitatio* plays in Lipphardt's edition: twelve are contained in processionals, nine in customaries or similar books, four in antiphonaries, two in choir books, one in a breviary, and four others in liturgical miscellanies. There is only one manuscript containing a Type III *Visitatio* play which is in any way similar to Orléans 201, and that is a collection of three Easter offices and a *planctus*

Mariae made by the Czech school teacher Stephan Roth, apparently for use in his school in Jáchymov, in the second decade of the sixteenth century.

The unusual character of the Fleury manuscript as a non-liturgical book containing plays is maintained even when we compare it with manuscripts preserving dramas that are not, strictly speaking, liturgical. The most striking example is British Library MS. Egerton 2615, which contains the famous *Danielis Ludus* from the cathedral school at Beauvais.[8] As a figure in what medieval Christians regarded as Old Testament history, Daniel cannot be the subject of liturgical celebration in the way that the central actions in the Christian myth are; there is no festival of Daniel in the ecclesiastical calendar. Yet the Beauvais play survives in an elaborate manuscript which sets out the entire liturgy for the first day of January, the Festival of the Circumcision of Jesus; the drama is only a small part of a larger non-dramatic whole. The Fleury *Playbook* stands in sharp contrast to such a manuscript. It consists of a collection of dramatic texts and only dramatic texts.

Of course, the Fleury plays could be and probably often were performed as part of a liturgical celebration. Indeed, some of them seem to make such a context obligatory. The *Visitatio Sepulchri* drama and the plays about Herod, the Innocents, St. Paul, Lazarus, and the three students all conclude with the singing of the *Te Deum*. The *Peregrinus* and *Tres Filiae* end with the singing of a hymn, and the *Iconia* seems to require for its conclusion the chanting of the introit for the Feast of St. Nicholas. Furthermore, like most of the dramatic *ordines*, many of the Fleury plays are partially constructed out of pre-existing bits of liturgical text and music. But the inclusion of portions of the liturgy does not insure that a text was performed as part of the liturgical cursus. Neither does the singing of the *Te Deum* clearly mark a play for performance at matins; that venerable chant was, of course, used on many other occasions. In any case, the presence of these liturgical elements cannot obscure the important point that the Playbook is in no sense a liturgical book, and that whatever liturgical context might have been provided for the performance of these plays came from other books with which it has no necessary connection.

Since the need to supplement dramatic texts with liturgical books is a subject that will be touched on several times in this essay, it will perhaps be useful to comment on this issue here.

Any communal celebration of the liturgy in the Middle Ages required several different kinds of books—some for the choir, others for the soloists, and still others for the various officiants.[9] Indeed the appearance of the missal in the tenth century and the breviary in the eleventh marks a turning point in liturgical history in that these books enabled worshippers to use only a single manuscript, one which often included only the verbal text and not the accompanying chant. This new kind of book was used, at least in the earlier centuries, primarily for private masses and recitations of the office. In pointing to the need to supplement the texts in the Fleury *Playbook* and in the other collections discussed here, I do not mean to suggest that the performance at the night office of the version of the *Visitatio Sepulchri* in the *Regularis Concordia,* to name perhaps the best-known traditional dramatic office, did not require the use of other liturgical books; it clearly did. But the ritual use of the collections discussed here—if they were ever used in this way—would necessarily be different from this usual practice. Within individual religious communities the various ritual books needed for the mass and office were commonly regarded as being related to each other; the use of one implied the use of the others. The Fleury *Playbook* and the other manuscripts discussed here lack such a connection to a set of liturgical books. These dramatic manuscripts have no intrinsic relationship to other books in use in a specific liturgical community.

This difference points to another way in which the Fleury manuscript differs from medieval service books. Unlike these texts, the Fleury *Playbook* cannot be identified with a specific liturgical community. Our difficulties in locating the place of its origins partially stem from this circumstance. Obviously the book was produced and probably first used at some specific institution, at St. Benoît-sur-Loire or St. Lomer or at some other place not yet suggested by modern scholars. But the self-evident fact that it originated somewhere cannot allow us to overlook one of the salient observations to be made about this collection—i.e., that its plays are not embedded in the larger context of a single community's annual liturgical cursus. They could therefore readily be performed at many different places without concern for relating them to the details of local cultic practices. What is most to be desired in the study of other so-called liturgical dramas—the investigation of how a text relates to the larger ritual, intellectual, and social contexts of the community in which it was performed—can never be undertaken with the Fleury plays, unless, of course, the collection's place of origin could be indisputably identified. Even then the connections would not be as close as in the usual case where dramatic office and non-dramatic rite stand side by side on the same manuscript page. This liturgical independence of the Fleury collection is a fact of utmost importance, but we need to consider the textual transmission of other collections of medieval Latin plays before we can recognize its full significance.

Aside from the Fleury *Playbook* there are three surviving medieval manuscripts which, though they are not service books, contain more than one dramatic text. Each of these collections shares certain similarities with the Fleury collection, yet each is significantly different as well. One of these collections is a manuscript apparently from the monastic school at Hildesheim and now at the British Library, MS. Add. 22,414. It has been variously dated from the early eleventh to the twelfth century. The manuscript contains two St. Nicholas texts, one concerning his rescue of three women whom poverty had consigned to the proverbial fate worse than death (the *Tres Filiae*) and another about the saint's resuscitation of three murdered students *(Tres Clerici)*.[10] Both of these writings have marked parallels with plays on the same subjects in the Fleury collection, yet the corresponding texts in the two collections are quite different. Neither Hildesheim piece is set to music, nor is space left for musical notation. The assignment of parts to the various appropriate speakers in both Hildesheim works is apparently haphazard and incomplete. There are no rubrics or stage directions of any kind. In all these details, the Nicholas plays in the German manuscript differ greatly from their counterparts in the French collection.

Like the Fleury *Playbook*, the Hildesheim manuscript is not tied to the cultic life of a specific liturgical community. As is the case with the plays in Orléans 201, if the Hildesheim texts were performed as part of the mass or office, they would need to be supplemented by ritual books with which they have no intrinsic connection. But the relationship between the liturgy and these pieces is even more tenuous than is suggested by this lack of a specific cultic context. Karl Young, drawing on a knowledge of liturgical manuscripts that few of his present-day critics could match, recognized that these texts, unlike the *Visitatio Sepulchri* or the *Officium Stellae*, were liturgical in neither source nor intention.[11] He saw that their *raison d'être* is literary rather than cultic, and that they are based on the saint's *legenda* rather than on the words and music of the Nicholas liturgy. Compromising these views, however, he asserted that the plays were sung and that they ended with the chanting of the *Te Deum*. This claim was largely based on an exceedingly enigmatic rubric at the end of the *Tres Filiae* which may not even be part of that piece. In any case, Young's reading of the rubric is by no means the only or, it seems to me, the most likely interpretation of these truly unintelligible lines. In fact, there is only meager evidence for supposing that music was ever supplied for these texts or that they authentically belong to the genre of Latin music-drama.

Ever since Ernst Dümmler edited the *Tres Filiae* nearly a century ago, it has been customary to regard the Hildesheim pieces as fully developed dramas.[12] Such a view seems to me extremely dubious—at least if this assertion suggests that these works made the same generic claims on their original audiences as the Easter or Christmas plays, or that they were directed toward the horizons of expectations which the Fleury collection seeks to arouse and meet. Certainly the Hildesheim pieces are generically far removed from vernacular miracle plays like Jean Bodel's *Li Jus de Saint Nicholai*. Young remarked that both of the Hildesheim pieces give "the impression of a hymn-like poem, rather than a play."[13] No careful reader of these works is likely to dispute this claim. It is based primarily on the observation that both pieces are written in uniform stanzas of four rhymed lines of ten syllables each, with regular concluding refrains of four syllables. Both texts consist entirely of dialogues three or four strophes in length; a change of speakers occurs only at the beginning of a new stanza. Taken together with what we know about the scholastic origins of the Hildesheim manuscript, such characteristics suggest that these works are school exercises written in dialogue form, and this is precisely the way that Charles W. Jones, the scholar who has studied them most intensively, views them. For him, their tradition is "scholastic hymnographical" rather than dramatic, and their function was didactic, not cultic.[14] Their constituent elements and patterns of organization are literary, poetic, and rhetorical.

In his recent book on the St. Nicholas cult and legend, Jones develops his characterization of these texts further. He claims that they are the product of a school tradition of writing hagiographical poetry in a modified form of Horatian sapphics.[15] Thus they are similar in form and purpose to the imitations of Terence that Hrosvitha wrote for her nuns at Gandersheim. Indeed, for Jones both the Hildesheim pieces and the works of Hrosvitha are typical products of a common German school tradition. There is much to be said in favor of such a view. It is perhaps not incidental that the Hildesheim *Tres Filiae* is thematically similar to three of Hrosvitha's works, her *Gallicanus*, *Dulcitius*, and *Sapientia*.[16] Like the works by the Ottonian nun—and in sharp contrast to those in the Fleury manuscript—the Hildesheim pieces were almost certainly intended for recitation, study, and private reading rather than for enactment. Actually the only reason that Young and Jones give for regarding these texts as dramas is that they seem to them incomprehensible unless one envisions their enactment—a very weak argument indeed. But whether the Hildesheim pieces are authentic dramas, performed choral compositions, or mere rhetorical exercises is not crucial to the claims of this paper. The point is that, enacted or not, these works were originally school exercises; they employ an identical verse pattern, and they are written on a single subject, the life of the patron saint of *scholares*. In these characteristics the Hildesheim manuscript is markedly different from the Fleury collection, which has neither its formal unity nor its sameness of subject matter.

The Fleury *Playbook* is not, however, the only medieval manuscript to contain plays on several subjects. Bibliothèque Nationale Latin MS. 11331, edited by John Bernard Fuller in 1927, is a case in point.[17] This manuscript consists of seventeen octavo pages entirely devoted to works by the scholar and poet Hilarius, apparently a protégé of Abelard. It contains a drama of the *Suscitatio Lazari*, the *Historia de Daniel Representanda*, and a *Ludus super Iconia Sancti Nicolai*.[18] Among its non-dramatic contents are three student songs (one directed to Abelard, another to a teacher apparently named "Papa," and a third praising a school at Chalaustre), a versified *vita* of a nun, and eight verse letters of friendship or love to boys. Thus the dramas are part of a larger literary corpus of works by a single scholar-poet. Unity of authorship is the principle that accounts for the placing of these plays with the non-dramatic materials. It is important to notice that the codex interleaves the dramas with the non-dramatic poems; the plays are items 11, 12, and 15 in the manuscript. Here, then, diversity of generic form is balanced by singleness of authorship. In fact, the Bibliothèque Nationale manuscript is unique in that it offers us the only surviving collection of medieval music-dramas by a single identifiable author, unless one wishes, mistakenly in my view, to include in this tradition the school works of Hrosvitha or the quasi-dramatic *Ordo Virtutum* of Hildegard of Bingen.

It is instructive to compare the Hilarius manuscript with the other dramatic collections under discussion here. Unity of authorship sets it off from the Hildesheim manuscript, though probably both Hildesheim texts come from the same school and could conceivably be by the same author—or, more likely, could have been written by different students under the direction of the same teacher. Similarly, the mixture of lyric and dramatic forms and the varied subject matters of the plays distinguish the Hilarius collection from the Hildesheim manuscript. Yet the Hilarius codex is similar to the German manuscript in some respects. Both come from a scholastic tradition, though the purpose of the one seems to have been primarily pedagogical, while the other exhibits a poetic sensibility and artistic self-consciousness characteristic of the twelfth century. Certainly by twentieth century critical standards Hilarius' work seems to have achieved a higher level of literary achievement. Like both the Hildesheim and Fleury collections, the Hilarius manuscript lacks a liturgical context, even though both the Lazarus and Daniel dramas end with rubrics which require that if the play is performed at matins the *Te Deum* should be sung and if at vespers the *Magnificat* should be chanted. These rubrics might seem to mark the plays as liturgical creations. In fact, such a latitude makes clear that they are not a part of a specific community's regular cultic life; if Hilarius' plays were performed at matins or vespers, other unrelated books would have been required. Furthermore, the notion that plays could be performed on arbitrarily chosen occasions in the liturgical cursus is markedly different from the way that the dramatic *ordines* were tied to a single moment in annual celebration. Like the student writings in the Hildesheim collection—and in contrast to the dramas in Orléans 201—the manuscript contains no musical notation, though the texts themselves seem to indicate that they were intended for sung performance. It is clear, then, that the primary interests of the Hilarius codex are literary, not liturgical or pedagogical. This characteristic distinguishes it both from the service books in which most "liturgical dramas" are found and from the Hildesheim collection.

The Hilarius collection has many similarities with the famous *Carmina Burana*, Latin MSS. 4660 and 4660a in the Bavarian State Library at Munich, the last collection of music-dramas to which we must turn our attention.[19] Here too several Latin plays are part of a greater—and primarily non-dramatic—literary manuscript. Indeed, in this codex the huge number of lyrics, sacred and secular, Latin and German, dwarfs the few pages given to dramas. These plays, like the lyrics, have a great diversity of subjects; there is a Christmas Play, two Passion plays, an Easter play, a *Peregrinus* play, and a fragmentary *Ludus de Rege Aegypti.* In some respects this collection is similar to the Fleury manuscript. Both collections are composite works, apparently derived from several sources. In this regard both the Munich and Orléans manuscripts can be contrasted with the Hilarius codex. Yet unlike the Hilarius and Hildesheim collections—and like the Fleury *Playbook*—musical notation is provided for some of the plays in the *Carmina Burana.* For some of them there is further a suggestion of possible performance as part of the liturgy. Yet, as is the case with the Hilarius and Fleury collections, the *Carmina Burana* cannot be linked with the ritual life of a specific community. Liturgical performance of these plays would require the use of unrelated books, since, like the other collections described here, the manuscript contains nothing of the liturgy itself. Yet, despite these similarities between the Fleury collection and the *Carmina Burana* plays, there are significant differences. The most important is that the Fleury manuscript contains only plays, while in the Benediktbeuern codex (as in the Hilarius manuscript) the dramas are part of a larger literary collection. The redactor of the *Carmina Burana,* like the redactor of the Hilarius collection—and unlike the Fleury redactor—apparently believed that music-drama belonged generically with lyric poetry in a category consisting of sung and performable texts.

Having briefly characterized service books and considered each of the non-liturgical manuscripts that contain more than one dramatic text, we are in a position to make some cogent comparisons. When held up against these other collections, the Fleury manuscript is easily distinguished by its astonishing diversity. It includes several genres of performable texts, unlike the other collections which keep these genres separate. Service books contain dramatic offices like Fleury's *Visitatio*, but exclude non-liturgical works like the *Getron*. The Hildesheim collection consists of school exercises like the Fleury's *Tres Filiae*, but its principle of organization excludes liturgical plays like the *Ordo Rachelis*. The Bibliothèque Nationale's manuscript of Hilarius' works eschews both dramatic *ordines* and rhetorical exercises in favor of artistically conceived works similar to the Fleury collection's *Getron*. And, of course, the Fleury redactor drew on materials of widely diverse origins, in contrast to the Hilarius scribe, who limited himself to a single author, and to the editor of the Hildesheim collection, who included only pieces about St. Nicholas. If we were to consider only its dramas, the *Carmina Burana* would seem to come closest to the Fleury collection. However, the kind of simple school exercise which we find in the Hildesheim manuscript and in the Fleury *Tres Clerici* is unthinkable in the Benediktbeuern collection. The Munich manuscript seems to have biblical subject matter and literary virtuosity as criteria of inclusion of its dramas, but the Fleury redactor allows for a greater variety in both respects. If we put these observations together, it is easy to summarize the result: Orléans 201 is generically much less selective than any of the collections which we have considered. Here dramatic offices of the liturgy, school exercises, and works of consciously conceived literary artistry stand side by side. Generic heterogeneity is, in fact, not just one characteristic of the Fleury *Playbook*; it is the chief characteristic which sets it off from every other manuscript containing plays in the music-drama repertory.

This generic heterogeneity has its parallel in the Fleury manuscript's bringing together of different performance conventions, conventions which suggest diverse origins for these dramas. The rubrics in the *Stella* play, for example, explicitly mention the doors of a monastery, the *Ordo Rachelis* calls for the actors to travel across the *monasterium*, and the *Visitatio Sepulchri* and *Peregrinus* plays identify the actors as *fratres*. Such terminology indicates that these plays stem from a monastic tradition, the source of most of the dramatic offices of Easter and Christmas. On the other hand, *Getron* mentions *clerici*, suggesting perhaps that it and the other plays about the patron saint of clerics were originally performed by and for students, possibly in a non-monastic setting (or in the section of a monastic school set aside for boys who were not oblates) and in a non-liturgical context. In contrast, the *Peregrinus* play calls for performance in a manner "ut videtur a populo," an expression that suggests parochial usage or at least performance in a monastery or school where lay visitors were present. The *Visitatio* play also envisages a performance before the *populum*.

This diversity of performance conventions finds its counterpart in a diversity of musical styles.[20] The *Tres Filiae*, the *Tres Clerici*, and the Lazarus play are each sung to a single repeated melodic line, although some slight variation is employed. This simple style might reasonably be associated with school drama, though it also has ties to the sequence and other forms of strophic lyric which were sung in sophisticated circles and which are important elements in medieval sacred and secular music. On the other hand, the more cultically conceived plays about the Magi, the Innocents, the Resurrection, and the Emmaus story employ a richly varied musical style which draws on the melodies of the liturgy. As Willem Elders has shown, these melodies are often reworked, and newly-composed material has been written to supplement them.[21] Frequently the melodies seem to follow the rhythm of the words, and new textual ideas are given new melodic counterparts. Similar (though less elaborate) is the musical style of the *Conversion of St. Paul.* Here the music varies with each textual exchange; Dominus' melodies have a recurring leitmotif, while St. Paul's music constantly changes. Finally, *Getron* and the *Iconia* dramas, plays which we might associate with the artfully conceived and self-conscious poetic tradition which characterizes the plays by Hilarius, have, as we might expect, an elaborate musical expression. In the *Iconia*, the Jew sings his lament on a *planctus* melody made up of repeated musical formulas which never occur twice in the same sequence. Throughout the play there is an attempt to match melody to the verbal text. In *Getron* each character has a recognizable leitmotif, but the mother alters her musical theme when she discovers her long-lost son, and then her companions imitate her musical change. This melodic shift forcefully serves to mark the peripety of the play. Such a practice contrasts sharply with the repeated and unchanged melodies in the *Tres Filiae* and *Tres Clerici*. It is not possible in the scope of this study to comment extensively on the musical styles in the Fleury manuscript. My purpose in alluding to them briefly is merely to emphasize that the *Playbook* contains a great diversity of musical materials, and that this diversity complements its variety of subject matters, performance conventions, and generic traditions.

Diversity, it is clear, is the hallmark of the Fleury collection. Yet it should be equally clear that our manuscript is not an indiscriminate catch-all. If it includes genres, musical styles, and performance conventions that other collections keep separate, it also excludes materials that they bring together. It does not mix dramatic *ordines* with non-dramatic liturgy the way that conventional service books do. In contrast to the *Carmina Burana* and the Hilarius manuscript, it excludes non-dramatic literary works. First impressions to the contrary, there is a principle of selection that can account for the materials in Orléans 201. That principle is easy to discern, but it is not less revolutionary for its being so. Every text in the collection is capable of being enacted. And since these texts cannot all be regarded as rituals or school exercises or dialogues whose chief interest is their literary virtuosity, there is only one category which generically encompasses them in all of their diversity: drama, or a form of mimetic activity carried out for the sake of affecting an audience by means of physical enactment. Whatever unity the collection possesses depends on the fact that everything in it can be regarded as a play. On first consideration this observation seems so obvious that it is hardly worth articulating. Closer investigation will demonstrate, however, that it points to a significant turning point in the history of Western literary culture.

For nearly a century one of the most troubling issues in the study of medieval Latin drama has been the question of whether these dramatic texts are plays in the modern sense of that term. In Karl Young's great opus, *The Drama of the Medieval Church*, this concern was expressed in his persistent but misleading dichotomy between liturgy and drama, a dichotomy which turned on the criterion of impersonation. More recently, O. B. Hardison, Jr., in his *Christian Rite and Christian Drama in the Middle Ages* rightly rejected Young's distinction only to arrive at the related categories of ritual structure and mimetic content.[22] From a somewhat different perspective, this concern with making a distinction between that which is a dramatic ritual and that which is authentically a drama has dominated German scholarship with its categories of *Feier* and *Spiel*.[23] The Fleury *Playbook* provides an important perspective on this discussion, for it demonstrates that at least one twelfth-century redactor had a deep interest in texts that could be enacted, whether he found them in the liturgy or in literary works or in school exercises. The diversity of materials in this collection suggests that our editor came to the realization that materials highly differentiated in origin, function, and generic tradition could be lumped together and perceived as dramas. It is clearly an interest in drama as drama and in the dramatic potential of starkly different kinds of materials which unifies the liturgical, scholastic, and literary materials in Orléans MS. 201. And it is an interest in drama as drama which sets our collection off from all other collections of Latin music-drama where the principle of organization is either a generic one that does not distinguish between the dramatic and the non-dramatic (service books or collections of texts that can be performed with music) or singleness of authorship (the Hilarius manuscript) or unity of subject matter (the Hildesheim manuscript). To grasp the full significance of this observation, we need to consider it both in the light of contemporary literary theory and medieval dramatic history.

When Young, Hardison, and the German historians of the medieval drama attempted to distinguish between dramatic liturgy and liturgical drama, they did so on the assumption that the genre of a work is forever fixed, that from the moment of its creation a ritual is a ritual and a play a play and ever will be so. In the introduction to his textual history of the *Visitatio* offices, Helmut deBoor hesitatingly suggests that genre is not quite as fixed as earlier critics had thought. For deBoor, dramatic rituals are always "in danger of" becoming plays, of crossing the line from one dramatic form to another. DeBoor thought of this process as moving in one direction only, from ritual to play.[24] In this regard he was not able to escape the notions of evolution and development which shaped the thought of his generation. Furthermore, deBoor apparently believed that this crossing over from *Feier* to *Spiel* was produced by the writer or reviser of a text. For him, the moment of origin determined a work's subsequent history. Like other traditional literary historians and students of the Latin music-drama, he seems not to have considered the possibility of a text's changing genre long after it has taken leave of its author and the context and audience for which it was originally intended.

Here a brief excursus into literary theory is necessary.[25] Traditional conceptions of literature and drama are concerned primarily with authors, their backgrounds, and the texts which they wrote. Just as the visual effect or spectacle of the performance is ignored in much scholarship, so too the reader or audience of the work is almost entirely neglected. This neglect overlooks a fundamental fact about literature and drama—that rather than being static artifacts, books and plays set in motion communicative actions. These actions are directed toward readers and audiences who apprehend them in terms of their own life situations. A ritual or play (to turn now to the objects of this study) can only be apprehended by a viewer when he or she approaches it with certain expectations or prejudgments about the nature of what is being communicated—expectations or prejudgments that are, to be sure, affected not only by the text but also by the visual effects or spectacle involved. Meaning is the product of the relationship between the message that is transmitted—in our case the performance of a dramatic ritual or a play—and the way that the audience understands it on the basis of its expectations and previous experiences. The message may confirm or frustrate its audience's expectations; often it does both. But without these expectations, which incline the audience toward one interpretation of the message and away from another, no message can be understood at all.

When the author or redactor of a medieval dramatic ritual or school exercise or artistic *versus* created a work, he naturally attempted to influence the way that his intended audience would understand it. In order to do so he drew on shared generic codes or conventions of interpretation which he knew, if only intuitively, on the basis of his past cultural and social experiences—experiences which he had in common with his intended audience. As far as we know, tenth-century audiences and writers had no conception of dramas as enacted mimesis devoid of ritual power. Hence from both author's and audience's perspectives the early *Visitatio Sepulchri* offices were regarded as purely cultic phenomena; they were appropriated by the shared generic codes of ritual. This understanding of the dramatic action was fostered by the time (a specific moment in the annual liturgical cursus) and place (within a monastic church) in which its enactment occurred. But because meaning is the product of the interchange between a message and its receivers, the same message—in our case the performance of a liturgical *ordo*—presented to a second audience will almost always have a different meaning for that audience than it had for the first. Thus a later medieval audience, living perhaps in the fifteenth century and possessing the experience of the vernacular drama, might well apprehend a tenth-century *Visitatio* office in a non-liturgical manner. Without so much as a change of a word or a note of music, what was once a ritual could easily become a play. Similarly a rhetorical exercise written in dialogue, produced by and for students in an eleventh-century classroom, would be perceived as such by its original audience largely because of the shared generic codes that it evoked and the pedagogical environment in which it was produced. But if that same text were enacted at matins on St. Nicholas Day and if it concluded with the singing of the *Te Deum*, it might appear to an audience of monks as a ritual.

These theoretical observations lead us directly to an appreciation of the historical significance of the Fleury collection. The existence of this manuscript demonstrates that at least one person living in France in the late twelfth or early thirteenth century appropriated a number of what had once been generically disparate works into the single all-encompassing category of drama. He approached a heterogeneous body of texts with his horizons of expectations dominated by a sense of drama as enacted mimesis. For him, whatever the original function and intention of these diverse creations, they could be understood as dramas, could function as dramas, could be performed as dramas. No other collection of plays in the entire corpus of medieval Latin drama witnesses so directly to such an understanding. It would be entirely too much to claim that our redactor was the first person in post-classical times to perceive the dramatic potentiality in such diverse materials—or that he was the first person to be interested in dramatic enactment for its own sake instead of as an aid for teaching advanced composition or as a means for enriching liturgical celebration. But it is not too much to claim that of all the surviving monuments from the medieval period, it is only the Fleury *Playbook* which testifies so clearly to an interest in the dramatic possibilities of disparate traditions, some of which were customarily performed liturgical texts with few literary pretensions and others of which were literary and scholastic texts that were not usually afforded fully enacted performances.

Thus far I have emphasized the revolutionary manner in which the Fleury redactor perceived the diverse traditions which he inherited. But the possible result of his perception also deserves attention. His understanding of drama may well have had an effect beyond the mere writing of the *Playbook*. By gathering generically disparate texts within the covers of a single manuscript, the Fleury redactor may have encouraged those who came in direct or indirect contact with his collection to view these materials from the same unifying perspective that marks his work. If he did affect his readers in this way, his achievement is an enormous one. By the simple act of placing these disparate works side by side, he helped create and enforce an understanding of a literary form that had been absent from the consciousness of Europe for almost a millenium.

We cannot, of course, prove that the Fleury collection played such an important role in dramatic history. There is another (opposing) trajectory of reception for the *Playbook* that can be sketched. According to it, the manuscript had no effect on the subsequent apprehension of the plays it contained or on the understanding of the Latin music-drama repertory in general. If such were the case, the collection could only be regarded as the work of an idiosyncratic individual without influence. Such a view, unlikely as it first seems, is not beyond the realm of possibility. Perhaps better than the scenario offered here, it accounts for the uniqueness of the collection. At our present state of knowledge, in which no one has traced the reception of Orléans 201, we cannot decide which of these positions is historically more correct. This essay has opted for the first trajectory, but the main strands of my argument, which concerns the redactor's horizons of expectations more than his audiences' apprehension of his work, would not be greatly affected if the second turned out to be a more likely account of the collection's reception.

Considering the Fleury *Playbook* from the perspective of contemporary critical theory can obviously help us to understand the significance of this manuscript. But this innovative perspective only complements and confirms observations about the collection that can be made from the more traditional perspective of literary history. Many recent studies have suggested that the twelfth century is the period when a full-fledged dramatic consciousness first appeared in post-classical Europe. One of the most comprehensive surveys of this subject is the second chapter of Rosemary Woolf's study of *The English Mystery Plays.* Having argued that "liturgical drama . . . arose through a complex of chances and decisions remote from literary thought," she goes on to ask "to what extent this development was itself stimulated by a conscious knowledge of and reflection upon the art of drama." To deal with this question she considers "a rag-bag of scraps of evidence of widely different kinds."[26] She points, for example, to a proliferation of Terence manuscripts in the post-Carolingian period and to the rediscovery of Plautus in the twelfth century. Special attention is given to writers of *comoediae* like Vitalis of Blois who claimed—quite questionably, it seems to most modern critics—that Plautus' *Aulularia* and *Amphitrio* were the sources for his own literary creations in Latin dialogue.

Woolf relates this new popularity of Roman comedy to an equally new understanding of theater and drama, an understanding attested to in the learned literature of the century, especially in encyclopedias and glosses. It seems certain that some twelfth-century schoolmen, in contrast to their predecessors, understood that Roman drama had originally been enacted and not merely recited. But Woolf does not limit herself to the school tradition in considering the question that she raises. She gives attention to the use of metaphors for the stage. She takes account of the work of twelfth-century professional entertainers and of the possible influence of folk drama on twelfth-century literature and on the dramatic *ordines*. And most interestingly, she considers non-religious terminology used to characterize religious plays. A drama performed in Riga in 1204, for example, was described by an almost contemporary chronicler as a "ludus prophetarum . . . quem Latini comoediam vocant."[27] This designation of a sacred Latin drama as "comoedia" is, as far as we know, unique. Far more widespread is the use in twelfth-century books, including liturgical ones, of the term *ludus*, obviously of antique secular origin, where earlier such words as *ordo* or *officium* would have been employed. Woolf further argues that the terms *miraculum* and *miracula*—which significantly first appear in reference to a dramatic writing in the Fleury *Playbook*'s *Iconia Sancti Nicholai*—were originally terms for secular entertainments.[28]

Whatever the truth of this claim, there can be little doubt that, in Woolf's words, "the reasonable conclusion to be drawn from the scattered and sometimes ambivalent pieces of evidence" which she surveys "is that in the twelfth century there was some understanding of drama as a secular literary form."[29] I would only add to this conclusion that such an understanding grew up in schools and apart from the two-centuries-old tradition of the dramatic enactment of portions of the liturgy. Thus the recognition to which, I have argued, the Fleury *Playbook* attests—that disparate enacted traditions could be understood as dramas—should not be regarded as surprising or unlikely, given this twelfth-century context. Yet before we proclaim that this new understanding of drama was widely shared in the twelfth century and that the Fleury redactor should be recognized as one of its heralds, there are two caveats to be sounded, again one from the perspective of the theoretical concerns expressed earlier and the other from the viewpoint of traditional literary history.

Reception theory has shown us that dramaticality cannot be solely determined by qualities that intrinsically inhere in a text. As we have seen, whether a work is regarded as a *Feier* or a *Spiel* is largely due to such conditions of its enactment as time and place and to the horizons of expectations which its audiences bring to it. Even if the St. Nicholas *Iconia*, to take perhaps the most striking example, was regarded by its Fleury redactor as a play rather than as a school exercise or liturgical office, he had no means to enforce that understanding on contemporary or subsequent audiences. I have already suggested that, performed as part of the St. Nicholas liturgy, the play's enactment might well have been regarded as a ritual. If this is the case for such an apparently unliturgical play, would it not be much more so for a play such as the *Ordo Rachelis* which seems even to our twentieth-century sensibilities charged with the power of cultic stylization and reactualization?[30] The most that we can claim about the Fleury *Playbook*, then, is that it testifies to one individual's recognition of the dramatic potentialities in liturgical *ordines*, school exercises, and literary creations in dialogue. To this extent the manuscript is an important document in the history of Western drama, but its existence does not authorize unqualified and overgeneralized statements about the subsequent history of that drama.

Perhaps this claim appears unduly cautious. Given the evidence assembled by Rosemary Woolf, it seems safe to assume that the Fleury redactor's understanding of the dramatic was shared by some of his contemporaries. In fact, this is a reasonable assumption. Yet if literary history encourages us to think that such an understanding was shared, it also encourages us to be modest in our claims. The Fleury *Playbook* is, after all, unique. Almost every Latin manuscript contemporary with it or posterior to it that contains drama-like texts is either a collection of a literary nature (e.g., the *Carmina Burana*) or a liturgical book. Indeed, the majority of Easter *Feiern* edited by Lipphardt post-date the time of the Fleury redactor, and yet, aside from a few insignificant exceptions, they are all taken from liturgical books. Of course, *ordines* performed as part of the office or mass no doubt were sometimes regarded by their audiences as plays, especially in the later Middle Ages. But their preservation in service books demonstrates that for many scribes and the communities for which they labored, these dramatic pieces continued to be regarded as belonging to a liturgical tradition and were perhaps viewed as rituals in the narrowest sense of that term. Thus it is not possible to claim that the understanding of the dramatic to which the Fleury *Playbook* points dominated the production and reception of all drama-like creations in the later Middle Ages, especially those written in Latin. The surviving manuscript tradition, in fact, suggests just the opposite. Any broad claim about the abiding historical significance of the Fleury redactor's perspective needs to be carefully qualified.

The course of this essay has been necessarily complex and dialectical. In conclusion, it will perhaps be worthwhile to survey briefly the territory we have traversed. When compared with all other books containing medieval Latin music-drama, the Fleury *Playbook*'s revolutionary character is apparent. It is the only surviving collection which unambiguously testifies to an understanding of drama as enacted mimesis, as drama, in the ancient and modern sense of that term. In all likelihood this new understanding and interest in drama marked our redactor as a man of the twelfth century, and this fact tends to confirm much that we know about the twelfth century as a turning point in dramatic, literary, and cultural history. Yet even if we can demonstrate with reasonable certainty that the Fleury redactor's collection was a product of the newly recovered understanding of drama, there is no reason to believe that every reader of his collection or every performer of the plays contained within it understood his dramatic pieces in this way. In fact, there is good evidence that thirteenth-, fourteenth-, and fifteenth-century audiences for these plays often continued to understand them and similar plays in ways that might seem old-fashioned to us—i.e., as liturgical offices or school exercises or displays of literary virtuosity. Be that as it may, none of these trajectories of reception detracts from the aesthetic values that twentieth-century critics have perceived in the Fleury plays or from the historical significance of the collection as the record of at least one twelfth-century writer's horizons of expectations concerning drama.

Beyond these immediate concerns, such observations have

broad ramifications for the study of medieval Latin drama. As a *coda* to this essay, it may be useful to point to a few of them as possible avenues for future exploration. Perhaps the most important of these is the recognition that we still have a long way to go before we completely purge ourselves of the evolutionary paradigm which still dominates so much of the writing of literary history, especially on medieval subjects. One cannot emphasize too strongly that there are no intrinsic lines of demarcation that differentiate one form of literary production or reception from another. Nor is it possible to point to a definite moment in history in which dramatic action ceased being liturgical and became enacted mimesis devoid of ritual power. This fact has escaped Young's critics at least as much as it did Young himself. It is an exercise in futility, one that is based on the most serious of misunderstandings about the practice of cultural history, to engage in arguments over whether a given text is or is not intrinsically a play. The mere production of a drama, as opposed to a dramatic *ordo*, by a twelfth-century author does not preclude the apprehension of his text at a later time as *Feier* rather than *Spiel*. Of course, the reverse is true as well. Nor is it correct to say that such subsequent acts of reception are mistaken ones. The meaning of a work is subject to constant alteration; it is always the product of the interplay between the text itself and the varying horizons of expectations that different audiences bring to it. This single sentence offers us a program for rewriting much of the history of medieval Latin and vernacular drama.

Equally important, and closely connected with this insight, is the realization that the study of medieval Latin drama must once again regard history with utmost seriousness. Above all, manuscript study, including both a concern with the community for which the book was originally written and the subsequent history of the use of the manuscript by that community or other contemporary and later communities, needs to regain the importance that it has lost in the past half-century. But this new concern must be granted to a kind of historical writing that differs markedly from the older traditions of positivistic literary history—traditions unfortunately still as evident in the writings of O. B. Hardison, Jr., and our generation as they are in the works of Karl Young and his contemporaries. The new literary history that the study of the Latin drama now demands must afford the place of eminence to readers and audiences, whose roles in determining the meaning of specific performances and written records of these performances was at least as crucial as that of the author or scribe. The attempt to determine the horizons of expectations out of which each drama grew, to which it was directed, and by which it was constantly in the process of transformation must be afforded the highest priority. Such a history is always complex and invariably dialectical. Because this is so, concentration on the context of a work, on the received and transmuted horizons of expectations implied by a body of texts, and on the reconstruction of its subsequent reception will both direct us to larger "extrinsic" concerns and turn us back to a consideration of individual creations and creators. That, at least, is what I hope this essay has demonstrated. For whether seen from the perspective of manuscript study, traditional literary history, or recent literary theory, the redactor of the Fleury *Playbook* stands out as a central figure in the history of Western drama. If his position in that history has not been fully appreciated, this is surely because the nature of the traditions he inherited and the varied and conflicting horizons of expectations of medieval audiences have not received the serious consideration they deserve.

NOTES

1 David Bevington, ed., *Medieval Drama* (Boston: Houghton Mifflin, 1975; Fletcher Collins, Jr., ed., *Medieval Church Music-Dramas: A Repertory of Complete Plays* (Charlottesville: Univ. of Virginia Press, 1976); Gustave Cohen, ed., *Anthologie du drame liturgique en France au Moyen-age* (Paris: Editions du Cerf, 1955); Karl Langosch, ed., *Geistliche Spiele* (Darmstadt: Wissenschaftliche Buchgesellschaft, 1957).

2 Giampiero Tintori and Rafaello Monterosso, eds., *Sacre rappresentazioni nel manoscritto 201 della Bibliotheca municipale di Orléans* (Cremona: Athenaeum Cremonense, 1958); Solange Corbin, "Le Manuscrit 201 D'Orléans: Drames Liturgiques Dits de Fleury," *Romania,* 74 (1953), 1-43.

3 *The Drama of the Medieval Church* (Oxford: Clarendon Press, 1933), I, 239-41.

4 *Die Textgeschichte der lateinischen Osterfeiern* (Tübingen: Max Niemeyer, 1967).

5 See especially Diane Dolan, *Le Drame Liturgique des Pâques en Normandie et en Angelterre au Moyen-Age,* Publications de Université de Potiers, Lettres et Sciences Humaines, 16 (Paris: Presses Universitaires de France, 1975), and also David Bjork, "On the Dissemination of the *Quem Quaeritis* and *Visitatio Sepulchri* and the Chronology of Their Early Sources," *Comparative Drama,* 14 (1980), 46-69.

[6] *Lateinische Osterfeiern und Osterspiele* (Berlin and New York: Walter de Gruyter, 1975-81), 6 vols.

[7] C. Clifford Flanigan, "The Liturgical Context of the *Quem Queritis* Trope," *Comparative Drama,* 8 (1974), 45-62, and "The Roman Rite and the Origins of the Liturgical Drama," *University of Toronto Quarterly,* 43 (1974), 263-84. Cf. James M. Gibson, "*Quem queritis in presepe*: Christmas Drama or Christmas Liturgy?" *Comparative Drama,* 15 (1981-82), 343-65.

[8] There is an excellent edition and study of this manuscript by Wulf Arlt, *Ein Festofficium des Mittelalters aus Beauvais in seiner liturgischen und musikalischen Bedeutung* (Cologne: Volk, 1970), 2 vols.

[9] A useful reference book for the study of medieval liturgical books is Andrew Hughes, *Medieval Manuscripts for Mass and Office: A Guide to Their Organization and Terminology* (Toronto: Univ. of Toronto Press, 1982).

[10] These texts are edited by Young, *The Drama of the Medieval Church,* II, 311-14, 325-27.

[11] Young, II, 307-11.

[12] *Zeitschrift für deutsches Altertum,* 35 (1891), 402-05.

[13] Young, II, 315.

[14] *The Saint Nicholas Liturgy and Its Literary Relationships (Ninth to Twelfth Century)* (Berkeley: Univ. of California Press, 1963), p. 93.

[15] *Saint Nicholas of Myra, Bari, and Manhatten: Biography of a Legend* (Chicago: Univ. of Chicago Press, 1978), p. 133.

[16] The works of Hrotsvitha can be conveniently consulted in Hrotsvitha, *Opera,* ed. Helene Homeyer (Munich: Schöningh, 1970).

[17] *Hilarii Versus et Ludi* (New York: Henry Holt, 1927).

[18] Texts in Young, II, 212-18, 276-86, 338-41.

[19] The standard edition is *Carmina Burana,* ed. Otto Schumann and Bernhard Bischoff (Heidelberg: Carl Winter, 1930-70), 2 vols. There is a facsimile edition of the manuscript also edited by Bischoff, *Carmina Burana,* Publications of Medieval Musical Manuscripts, 9 (Brooklyn, New York: Institute of Medieval Music, 1970). The dramatic texts are also edited by Young. Both Bischoff and Walther Lipphardt have suggested that the manuscript was written at a southeast German Augustinian house, possibly at Seckau, and not at the Benedictine monastery at Beuern as has generally been thought. Obviously, the provenance of the manuscript does not affect the argument of this essay.

[20] See the study of the music of the Fleury plays by Corbin, "Le Manuscrit 201 d'Orléans," which I have freely drawn on for the information in this paragraph.

[21] "Gregorianisches in liturgischen Dramen der Hs. Orléans 201," *Acta Musicologica,* 36 (1964), 169-77.

[22] *Christian Rite and Christian Drama in the Middle Ages* (Baltimore: Johns Hopkins Press, 1965).

[23] The best discussion of this distinction is in deBoor, *Die Textgeschichte der lateinischen Osterfeiern,* pp. 5ff.

[24] DeBoor, pp. 12ff.

[25] For the theoretical basis for what follows, I have drawn on several studies in reader-response theory and especially on the work of the Constance school of reception aesthetics. I have been greatly influenced by the work of Hans Robert Jauss, above all by his essays "Literary History as a Challenge to Literary Theory" and "Theories of Genres and Medieval Literature." Both are now available in English in

Hans Robert Jauss, *Toward an Aesthetic of Reception*, trans. Timothy Bahti, Theory and History of Literature, 2 (Minneapolis: Univ. of Minnesota Press, 1982), pp. 3-45, 76-109. The first of these studies is the programmatic essay for reception aesthetics and should be read in the translation by Bahti or in the original German edition, *Literaturgeschichte als Provokation* (Frankfort am Main: Suhrkamp, 1970), pp. 144-207, and not in the abbreviated English translation which appeared in *New Literary History*, 2 (1970), 7-38. A second volume of Jauss' work is also available in English: *Aesthetic Experience and Literary Hermeneutics*, trans. Michael Shaw, Theory and History of Literature, 3 (Minneapolis: Univ. of Minnesota Press, 1982). Another essay by Jauss which has great relevance for the study of medieval drama is "The Alterity and Modernity of Medieval Literature," *New Literary History*, 10 (1979), 181-230. In many ways the present study comes closest to issues raised by Rainer Warning, *Funktion und Struktur: Die Ambivalenze des geistlichen Spiels* (Munich: Wilhelm Fink, 1974), and especially his essay "On the Alterity of Medieval Religious Drama," *New Literary History*, 10 (1979), 265-92. His concerns and conclusions, however, are ultimately quite different from the ones offered here.

26 *The English Mystery Plays* (Berkeley: Univ. of California Press, 1972), p. 25.

27 This quotation can be most conveniently studied in Young, II, 542; for Woolf's discussion of it, see her *English Mystery Plays*, pp. 34-35.

28 Woolf, pp. 39-40. For another discussion of terms for dramas in medieval manuscripts, see Erwin Wolff, "Die Terminologie des mittelalterlichen Dramas in bedeutungsgeschichtliches Sicht," *Anglia*, 78 (1960), 1-27.

29 Woolf, p. 29.

30 Robert Guiette, "Réfexions sur le drame liturgique," *Mélanges offerts à René Crozet*, ed. Pierre Gallais and Yves-Jean Riou (Potiers: Société d'Etudes Médiévales, 1966), I, 197-202, offers a reading of the *Ordo Rachelis* sensitive to its liturgical overtones. For a different view which seeks to balance the liturgical with other elements in the play, see C. Clifford Flanigan, "Rachel and Her Children: From Biblical Text to Music-Drama," in *Metamorphosis and the Arts: Proceedings of the Second Lilly Conference*, ed. Breon Mitchell (Bloomington: Indiana Univ. Comparative Literature Program, 1979), pp. 31-52.

The Home of the Fleury *Playbook*

Fletcher Collins, Jr.

The late and revered Professor Solange Corbin seems to have intended her 1953 *Romania* article to be controversial.[1] She wished to challenge the presumed origin of the famous Fleury *Playbook*[2] as the Abbaye St. Benoît de Fleury at St. Benoît-sur-Loire, to proclaim indeed that "Le manuscrit [of the *Playbook*] ne provient pas de Saint-Benoît," and that the Abbaye St. Laumer[3] in Blois was a preferable location. In her challenge were echoes of Baconian and other Shakespearean lost causes that took a hundred years to run their courses and return us to a conviction that William Shakespeare of Stratford-on-Avon is the best candidate for the composition of the plays attributed to him.

Questions of place and authorship are often more difficult in respect to medieval religious plays than to those of the Elizabethans, for a manuscript containing liturgical material was in mortal jeopardy from the time of the Reformation, and frequently survived destruction only by going underground. In that process its origin was often deliberately obscured and its authorship unacknowledged. Hence any strong skepticism in these matters, particularly from a highly respected scholar, is likely to result in discrediting the existing assumption. For this reason the thirty-two years since the Corbin article appeared have not been filled with rejoinders and counter-claims; indeed, the Fleury stronghold of nearly two centuries fell with hardly a shot fired in its defense. Most scholars in the field apparently believed that Professor Corbin knew more than they did, impressively paleographical and bibliographical as her presentation was. Several scholars—among them Grace Frank, Jean LaPorte, and Richard B. Donovan[4]—were not intimidated by the article. The present writer, while more cautious in 1972 than he now would be, even then dissented: "Her hypothesis does not work any better than the assumption she disturbs."[5] But the Abbaye St. Benoît de Fleury, as soon as it became aware of Corbin's attack on the assumption, withdrew from guide book and guided tour all mention of the plays, formerly a bright jewel in Fleury's medieval crown.

The purpose of the present re-appraisal of Corbin's argument is to foreshorten the winter of our disbelief by carefully scrutinizing her evidence, and by offering additional circumstantial evidence for renewed acceptance of the Fleury abbey as the most probable home of the *Playbook* in the twelfth and thirteenth centuries. From the forty-three pages of Corbin's article can be sifted five major points on which she based her statement that the *Playbook* came not from Fleury but probably from St. Laumer de Blois. I propose to give a fair summary of each point and to attempt to dispose of it.

1. Bibliothèque Municipale, Orléans, MS. 201, a total of 251 pages, is in anyone's eyes a compilation. The bulk of it is Marian homilies (pp. 1-175), the remainder the *Fleury Playbook* (pp. 176-243) and sequences to the Virgin and to St. Laumer (pp. 244-51). Of these three sections, only the latter two have musical notation, though such notation is lacking in the sequence to the Virgin in the third section. Corbin finds fault with the notation of the plays as being "légèrement négligée"[6] in its confusion of *punctum* and *virga* symbols, and correctly observes that the style of the notation is unlike that of other liturgical manuscripts in the same library. Orléans MS. 129, for example, can be traced to a Fleury origin in the early thirteenth century.[7] The presumption therefore is that because MS. 201 cannot be so traced some other abbey in central France must be proposed as the source of that manuscript, including the *Playbook*. So runs her first argument.

The section of MS. 201 containing the plays was, as Corbin herself states, bound into a volume with the other sections of that manuscript in the sixteenth century, four hundred years later than the date of the *Playbook*. Thus the nature of this total manuscript, a post-medieval compilation, is quite different from that of two entirely musical manuscripts from Fleury, Orléans MS. 129 and Paris, Bibliothèque Nationale Latin MS. 1020. Both of the latter are acknowledged by all, including Corbin, to have originated at Fleury, and their contents are recognized as directly and entirely liturgical; one is an Ordinary-

Customary, the other a Missal. Corbin describes the *Playbook* notation as less "advanced" than that of the Ordinary and Missal, and therefore older. In this event one may legitimately posit that the *Playbook* was notated in the twelfth century, while the other two Fleury manuscripts were scored a century later, in the then current notational style. There is thus no reason to exclude the *Playbook* section of MS. 201 from attribution to Fleury merely because its notation is different from that of other known Fleury manuscripts.

2. In her attempt to associate the plays with the St. Laumer sequence in Orléans MS. 201, Corbin reiterates that the parchment is identical from one end of the manuscript to the other: "identique d'un bout du livre à l'autre," "le parchement est le même."[8] Père Lin Donnat, however, describes the manuscript quite otherwise in a hands-on examination of it. In remarks prepared for publication and authorized for me to report here, he indicates that the plays are written on a very different kind of parchment from that of the preceding homilies and the following hymns. The parchment of the play section of the manuscript is much finer, more supple, and white, and compares in quality with that of the best illuminated manuscripts of the period. The parchment of the final pages of the book, including the St. Laumer sequence, is comparatively crude, brittle, and yellowed with age. My own perusals of the manuscript confirm these findings. Corbin's acquaintance with MS. 201, on the other hand, was apparently limited to published paleographic studies (1924-41) by V. Leroquais, cited by her,[9] and to single-page facsimiles in Coussemaker, Young, and Albrecht.[10]

3. Four of the *Playbook* dramas are St. Nicholas miracle plays. To Corbin this fact suggests that only an abbey with a strong cult of St. Nicholas would have produced four such plays in a single manuscript. Her requirements for an "active cult" of a saint are that the service books show an office of that saint, or at least an octave, and that in the abbey there exist relics or a chapel or an altar to the saint. None of these can be shown to have existed at the Abbaye St. Benoît de Fleury: no office, not even an octave.

The present church at Blois, called "St. Nicolas, Abbaye de St. Laumer" in a pamphlet available in 1979 at the church, was apparently called St. Laumer in the twelfth century, and another, smaller church on the cliffs above, next to the great

Château de Blois, was St. Nicolas. The association of the two names dates from sometime after the French Revolution, during which time the St. Nicolas church was destroyed, and after which St. Laumer was re-established and re-named. Corbin stresses the coincidence in MS. 201 of the sequence to St. Laumer and the four St. Nicholas plays. She concludes that St. Laumer is therefore the more suitable central French abbey to have originated the *Playbook.*

Corbin admits that no twelfth-century service books remain from St. Laumer with notation to compare with that of MS. 201, or indeed any documentary evidence of an active cult of Nicholas at St. Laumer on the terms she requires. One would imagine that whatever cult of Nicholas there was at Blois would have been more active at the little church of St. Nicolas than at St. Laumer, but of this activity we have no record. If, moreover, the four St. Nicholas plays were indeed the possession—and possibly the creation—of Fleury in the twelfth century, the fact that they were performed at Fleury would itself represent a strong expression of interest in St. Nicholas. Centered as that abbey was on St. Benedict, it could hardly have been expected to maintain relics of importance or chapel or altar to another major saint. The two main altars in the Fleury chancel at that time were to the Virgin and to St. Benedict, with whom even St. Nicholas could not compete. As an outstanding educational center, however, Fleury could—and I believe did—recognize and perform plays in honor of St. Nicholas, the popular patron saint of scholars, in celebration of his prime feast day, December 6, without either slighting St. Benedict, who has three feast days there, or requiring an active St. Nicholas cult on Corbin's terms.

Neither the existing church at Blois nor the sequence to St. Laumer has a more than coincidental relationship to the *Playbook* section of the conglomerate MS. 201, as we have seen. One might with equal pertinence, or impertinence, claim that the medieval presence of a small church, St. Lazare, in the surrounding village only a stone's throw from the St. Benoît abbey,[11] accounts for the creation of the music-drama *Resuscitatio Lazari* in the *Playbook,* and so enables us to extrapolate a claim to the entire *Playbook* for Fleury! At least such a tenuous, and probably specious, argument would have a merit that Corbin's does not, that the geography and chronology are right. The *Playbook* version of the *Lazarus* play and the St. Lazarus church may have co-existed in the same village, while the St. Laumer sequence is not clearly associated with the *Playbook* until four centuries after the period of the plays, and then only in a bindery in distant Orléans.

4. Corbin states that the dramas of the *Playbook,* which she regards as also a compilation, are nowhere mentioned in the two more or less contemporary service books from Fleury, and therefore cannot have been performed in that monastery in the twelfth century.

It is true that the Ordinary-Customary of Orléans MS. 129, recently authoritatively edited by Dom Anselme Davril,[12] does not mention the performance of the dramas on any of the feast days, but for the good reason that only feast days unique to Fleury are mentioned. And it is true that none of these relates to a *Playbook* drama. Even the three St. Benedict feast days are ignored, because they and those of St. Nicholas and even of St. Aignan of the regional diocese of Orléans are already to be found in the usual calendar and thus need no attention from the author of this particular Ordinary-Customary. The other service book, a Missal, would not be likely to mention a liturgical drama in any case.

This is of course a negative kind of argument, and only serves to neutralize Corbin's otherwise damaging evidence. One should, however, add that we have no documentary evidence for the attachment of the plays to St. Laumer or to any other monastery. Corbin herself finds no service books whatsoever from St. Laumer, a circumstance which she somehow brings to the assistance of her hypothesis. But on the other hand she asserts that the lack of mention by Fleury service books indicates that the plays are not to be associated with Fleury. A closer examination of the contents of Orléans MS. 129, as I remarked above, reveals that its purpose precludes the mention of the *Playbook* dramas.

5. In order to qualify her hypothesis that St. Laumer is a better choice for the home of the *Playbook,* and to dismiss its attribution to Fleury, Corbin brings up a variety of more or less cogent concerns, each of which I feel bound to comment upon in order not to seem to disregard them.

The cultural significance of the school at St. Laumer and the court of Blois as a plausible environment for the creation and performance of liturgical music-drama is presented by Corbin at some length, and is crucial to her proposition that the *Playbook* dramas could have come from that society. Elsewhere relying on Lesne's *Histoire de la propriété ecclésiastique en France* (1938) for her information about a collegiate school at Blois, she abruptly decides that Lesne's identification of that school with the collegiate church of Notre-Dame de Bourgmoyen in Blois is not convincing, and that it might just as well belong to Saint-Solenne de Blois or St. Laumer. Her case for the church of St. Laumer being collegiate and its abbey therefore being something of a cultural center rests entirely on this arbitrary assignment of the Blois school to St. Laumer. As for the court of Blois, she presents the names of four secular authors whose presence testifies to a certain amount of creative activity at that court. Lacking a secular court, where authorship was of some importance, Fleury has records of only two authors, Raoul de Tortaire and Hugues de Sainte-Marie. One can imagine, however, what gross distortions would result from the evaluation of medieval cultural centers by the quantity of names of authors whose documents have survived. The lack of abbatial interest in claims to authorship is well-known; in the field of liturgical music-drama we have not the name of a single playwright of any of the surviving *music*-dramas.[13]

Well-attested is the prime importance of Fleury as a major cultural center. It served as one of the great proto-universities before Paris and Oxford took shape. This fact helps to justify the attribution of the plays to Fleury. One may doubt that a lesser center could have produced and nurtured composer-poet-dramatists capable of the sophisticated art of the *Playbook* compositions. It probably took a great abbey—e.g., St. Martial de Limoges, Beauvais, Rouen, Fleury—to grow a great play.

More specifically, the companion arts of architecture and sculpture were also highly developed at Fleury. The church itself is one of the great achievements of Romanesque architecture, and within that building the 309 column capitals are acknowledged as among the finest of the Middle Ages.[14] Of these capitals, forty are narrational, not animal or vegetable, and many of the scenes are biblical. In a recent spot-check of five central French abbeys of the twelfth century, all especially noted for their sculptured capitals and all as likely or unlikely to be good environments for the development and production of liturgical music-dramas, I found that at Plaimpied only two of about thirty capitals have narrative subjects; at Fontevrault only four of 104; and at Vézelay and St. Laumer de Blois about the same small proportions. At Fleury, in contrast, thirteen percent of the capitals are historiated. One concludes that in that abbey was a more than usual attention to narrative. Such an intense interest is not likely to have ignored the dramatic and theatrical. A drama is an enactment of a story, a *repre-sentatio,* as the liturgical rubrics so often entitle a play.

Another example of Fleury's outstanding interest in narrative is the major contribution made there to historical studies. Professor Bautier concludes that "Fleury est alors le centre évident des études historiques. . . . La monastère a produit, rappelons-le, l'oeuvre hagiographique la plus volumineuse et la meilleure de ce temps."[15]

Corbin attempts to sidestep the implications of this obvious contrast in the cultural potentials of the two abbeys by presuming that because St. Laumer is not listed as a priory, a dependency of Fleury, as many churches in the region were, it must have had a special importance. She thus finds significance in the fact that the Fleury historian, Hugues de Sainte-Marie—also known as Hugues de Fleury—in 1109 dedicated the first part of his *Historia ecclesiae* to Adèle, the widowed Countess of Blois and Chartres, daughter of William the Conqueror and sister of Henry I of England. The practical significance seems to be that a scholar from the Fleury center was in touch with the Countess Adèle for patronage reasons since the great benefactor of the Fleury abbey, Philip I, had died the year before.

There is a triforium capital at Fleury in which Hugues himself is the identified subject, kneeling before the Virgin and Child and shepherd-like offering a gift of one of his books (probably the *Historia*) to the Christ Child. St. Benedict stands behind Hugues with his crook-crozier, another shepherd at the manger.[16] Here again Fleury's interest in story—and perhaps even in a fantasy of the "Pastores" scene of the Fleury *Play of Herod*—is demonstrated.[17]

If one may now be ready to grant that the evidence for Fleury is heavily circumstantial, one may also be prepared to agree that no other medieval abbey in central France is as good a candidate. If there had been no challenge to the attribution, we might not have discovered how superior Fleury's qualifications are.

Once the attribution to place is reasonably settled, other questions arise about the nature of the *Playbook*. Is that section of MS. 201 itself a compilation, a commonplace book, a memory-book like the *chansonniers* of the secular songwriters of the period? Is it the work of a single playwright? Are these plays the work of a group of Fleury playwrights, composing in something comparable to the workshop conditions of artists in other medieval media? Were the plays collected by a "moine de passage" from several abbeys through which he passed? Did some or all of the plays originate elsewhere, to be brought to Fleury and there revised to local standards? These and other such questions are beyond the scope of this article, but they deserve critical speculation and earnest search for answers.

NOTES

1 "Le Manuscrit 201 d'Orléans: Drames liturgiques dits de Fleury," *Romania*, 74 (1953), 1-43.

2 A section of Bibliothèque Municipale, Orléans, MS. 201, pp. 176-243, containing ten medieval church music-dramas.

3 The Medieval Latin is usually "Launemare," which would more likely have become "Laumer." Corbin and a number of other scholars prefer "Lomer."

4 Grace Frank, *Medieval French Drama* (1954), p. 44, n.1; Jean LaPorte, *Dictionnaire d'histoire et de géographie ecclésiastiques,* XVII (1969), 474; and Richard B. Donovan, "Two Celebrated Centers of Medieval Liturgical Drama: Fleury and Ripoll," in E. Catherine Dunn, Tatiana Fotitch, and Bernard M. Peebles, eds., *The Medieval Drama and Its Claudelian Revival* (1970), pp. 41-47. Donovan's best point in his effort, less comprehensive than mine, to refute Corbin is the unique combination of textual identities in the Winchester *Regularis Concordia* and the Orléans MS. 201 versions of the *Visitatio,* in conjunction with the fact of large Fleury influence on the compilation of the Winchester rule.

5 Fletcher Collins, Jr., *The Production of Medieval Church Music-Drama* (1972), p. 34, n.44.

6 Corbin's scholarship in this article is also "négligée." She has trouble with names. She refers to W. L. Smoldon as "J. Smoldon," p. 8, and "W. J. B. Smoldon," p. 8, n.4; Karl Young appears on p. 9 as "Carl Young"; Edith Armstrong Wright becomes "Edight Armstrong Wright," p. 6, n.2, while Mrs. Wright's dissertation is located at "Brynn Maur, Pens.," p. 6, n.2, and p. 8, n.1; and Wooldridge is deformed to "Wooldrige." More seriously, she describes the text of the Fleury *Play of Herod* as "en prose." Moreover, she attaches the *Copiosae karitatis* at the end of the *Filius Getronis* to Vespers when the hour of this play is pretty clearly Lauds and could not have been Vespers because the *O Christe pietas* at the end of *Tres Filiae* is (with Corbin d'accord) regularly attached to Vespers of the same St. Nicholas feast day. She also describes Romanesque actors as led "à la grille du choeur pour que le publique les voie" (p. 27), while architectural historians have long agreed that the "grille du choeur," or rood-screen, or "jubé" fortunately did not enclose existing French choir

and sanctuary areas until sometime in the thirteenth century at the earliest (see R. deLaysterie, *L'Architecture réligieuse en France à l'époque Gothique*, II [1927], 486-87). At Fleury they were not installed until the fifteenth century.

7 See Père Lin Donnat, "Recherches sur l'influence de Fleury au xe siècle," *Études Ligériennes d'histoire Médiévale* (1975), p. 165.

8 Corbin, pp. 3 and 38.

9 Ibid., p. 15, n.l.

10 *Drames liturgiques*, facing p. 83; *Drama of the Medieval Church*, II, facing p. 220; and *Four Plays of St. Nicholas*, p. 90.

11 Dom Anselme Davril, *La Vie à l'Abbaye de Fleury-Saint-Benoît au XIIIe siècle*, Bulletin de la Société Archéologique et Historique de l'Orléanais, No. 45 bis (1976) p. 22.

12 *Un Coutumier de Fleury, Corpus Consuetudinum Monasticarum*, ed. Kassius Hallinger, VII, 1978.

13 Hilarius' versions have no music, and may not have been performed.

14 Joan Evans, *Art in Medieval France* (1948), p. 32, and George Zarnecki, *Romanesque Art* (1971), p. 57.

15 R.-H. Bautier, "La place de l'Abbaye de Fleury-sur-Loire dans l'historiographie française du IXe au XIIe siècle," *Études Ligériennes d'histoire Médiévale* (1975), p. 32. See also LaPorte, col. 474.

16 See Plate 1.

17 Dom Jean-Marie Berland, an authority on the Fleury capitals and the source of my statistical data on them, tells me that he does not see the scene as a deliberate parody of the traditional, non-biblical episode of the shepherds offering gifts to the Christ Child, but rather as an offering of feudal homage.

Modal and Motivic Coherence in the Music of the Music-Dramas in the Fleury *Playbook*

Clyde W. Brockett

The Music of the Medieval Church Dramas by the late William L. Smoldon, published in 1980 six years after the author's death, brought to light scores of melodies from liturgical dramas, including many from the so-called Fleury *Playbook*, Orléans, Bibliothèque Municipale, MS. 201.[1] Although Smoldon in this publication has transcribed certain melodies, his purpose was not to become too involved with melodic analysis; hence our understanding of this repertory's musical excellence still requires additional scholarly attention. However, when we direct our energy toward what Walther Lipphardt called "modal unity"[2] we can, through modal and motivic analysis, expose these slimly explored facets of the plays' music, and we can also provide bases for comparing musical effects of other manuscripts. Indeed, Lipphardt's understanding of *tonale Einheit* is reasonable, since entire series of antiphons maintaining a single mode are to be found in chant repertories.[3] John Stevens pertinently remarks that in the Fleury *Visitatio* the mode is retained up to scene changes, while the *Tres Filiae* maintains a single melody throughout.[4] How many other modal and motivic continua are to be found in the remaining St. Nicholas and *Temporale* tetralogies and biblical miracles associated with St. Paul and Lazarus in the Fleury *Playbook?*

To launch this investigation, some preliminaries relative to the technical and terminological frameworks of medieval music may prove useful. For the transcriptions in the examples which I present, I adopt the system of notation used by F. A. Gevaert in his study of modal melodies in the tenth-century chant catalog, or tonary, of Regino of Prüm.[5] This system names pitches, as they were known and named in tenth- and eleventh-century theoretical treatises, by the same letters of the alphabet still applied today, as seen in Diagram 1. The starting pitch lies an eleventh below middle C.

DIAGRAM 1

$\underline{\text{G}}$ A B C D E F G A ♭ (B-flat) ♮ (B-natural) c d e f g $\overset{\text{a}}{\text{a}}$

Wherever there occur two or more notes (neumes) per syllable instead of one, I overscore the affected pitches. If a pitch is repeated, I place a long dash after that pitch, and if a motive is repeated, I indicate the repeat with the symbol ·/. . Pitches within parentheses are variants found in the same passage. Superscript pitches within parentheses are variants found in a parallel passage within the same or a different play. Only variants tangent to the discussion are registered. By modal coherence I mean the application of mode, which I shall shortly explain, either as a music continuum or as a link between one and another melody. By motivic coherence I refer likewise to the application of a theme or melody, or melodic fragment, for continuity or linkage.

Mode, or modality, melodic essence of Gregorian chant, is a twofold proposition. One of its strains is the psalm-tone system, a system of eight short formulas consisting of a rising intonation, a steady reciting or tenor tone, and a falling termination or cadence. Although the middle element, the tenor tone, suggests minimal melodic interest, the initial and terminal elements subsist on some variation of pitch. Actually, none of this systematized singing, called psalmody, can be termed actively "melodic." According to the tenth-century treatise *Commemoratio brevis,* a standard "modulatio psalmi" may be applied to each of the eight established modes.[6] Diagram 2 furnishes the psalmody with the prescribed verse endings per mode from this *Commemoratio.* Alternative pitches found in the compilation of Catholic church chants, the *Liber Usualis (LU),* are entered parenthetically. The only major discrepancy occurs in the fourth mode's tenor, only before and not after the mediant, where the *Commemoratio,* probably due to the notator's error, gives G instead of a. The error is not reflected in the diagram. In each of the examples to follow I identify the mode, as in Diagram 2, by Roman numbers next to the example number.

DIAGRAM 2

Mode	*intonation*		*reciting tone*	*mediant*	*reciting tone*	*possible terminations*
I	F	G	a ———	(♭)aG(a)	a ——	(a),G(F,D)
II	C	D	F ———	GF	F ——	D
III	G	a	♮ (c) ———	(d)c ♮a♮(c)	(c) ♮—	(♮,a),G
IV	E	G	a ———	Ga♮(a)	a ——	(G),E
V	F	a	c ———	dc♮	c ——	a
VI	F	G	a ———	♭aGF(a)	a ——	F
VII	c	♮c	d ———	(f)ede	d ——	(d,c,♮),a
VIII	G	a	c ———	dc	c ——	(c),G

In medieval melodies, one notices the psalm-tone paradigm whenever a pitch is consistently repeated at least three times and returned to with regularity. One of many examples associated with liturgical plays is the *Te Deum laudamus,* the traditional hymn of Matins, which is customarily found at the critical moment where often the drama at its conclusion is rejoined to its liturgical matrix. The *Te Deum* is sung with *two* reciting tones. These repetitions occur on middle a and the F just below shown in Example 1, which excerpts (from *LU,* pp. 1832, 1834) the incipit, verse 3 and verse 22.

Example 1 Mode IV

Incipit E Ga a aG aa♮c ♮a

recitation on a G♮ a c ♮ a♮ aG a E Ga a——G a♮ ♮aG G
v 3

recitation on F C DF———D F EDC C DF—FE D F Ga GFE
v 22

Modality's other constituency is its pre-established or "theoretical" melodic ranges and final pitches. There, limits and "keynotes" constitute the essence of melody, for mode in this sense approximates the bipolarity of musical scale and key. We might thus refer to this face as mode's melody, whereas psalmody constitutes mode's more formulaic face. In Diagram 3 I fix these melodic limits and finals for the eight regular medieval modes. Note that the high, odd-numbered modes do not descend below the subfinal pitch; consequently, any melody which makes any lower descents beneath its final would be assigned to the lower mode.

DIAGRAM 3

Mode	*Range*	*Final*
I	C - e	D
II	(G)A - ♮	D
III	C - f	E
IV	A - c	E
V	D - g	F
VI	C - d	F
VII	F - a a	G
VIII	C - e	G

To accommodate and define these limits and finals, certain antiphon stereotypes were invented. Not of traditional "Gregorian" origin, these formulas nevertheless predate the Fleury Playbook if not also the earliest extant liturgical drama.[7] An example of this melodically influential antiphon-type is found in the Fleury Playbook to provide us with a parallel for the psalmodic type which we quoted in the *Te Deum*, and here the melody of the stereotype of the third mode is committed to the final and range in Diagram 3. Drawn from *Luke* 24.21, the text—"Today is the *third* day since these things were done [my italics]"—is particularly well suited to the *Peregrinus* (Emmaus) play where it is quoted. Accordingly, the melody is adopted for the opening speech by four of the nine extant complete versions of the play and as the third speech in the Fleury Playbook.[8] Its original form, found in tonaries, appears in Example 2. Compare this with the version of the Fleury Playbook, paralleling its pitches on the second line of letter-notation of Example 2. The text and melody vary significantly only when the Orléans manuscript appends a single *Alleluia*. In this instance and in ensuing examples, vertical alignments accentuate the quality of coherence found. Here the high E mode—the third—in its very stereotype requires alteration or adaptation, and cannot settle

Example 2 Mode III/VIII

				(♮)				(c)				
Tonary/*Peregrinus* excluding Fleury Playbook	c	(♮)a	G	ac	a	G	G	a	G	(G)F	E	III
Peregrinus of Fleury Playbook	d c	a	G	a	a	G	G	c	G	aG	E	III
	Ter-	ti-	a	di-	es	est	quod	haec	fac-	ta	sunt.	

FGa a G G VIII

Al - le - lu - ia

for mere adoption at this point.

I have previously suggested ("Easter Monday Antiphons," p. 40) that the immediately preceding portion of the drama, "et super omnia," paraphrased from the head of the same verse of St. Luke's Gospel, was actually planned by the Fleury Playbook's dramatist to lead into "Tertia dies" musically. This is because the music drafted to set "et super omnia" acts as a transition into the then quite familiar mode-antiphon quoted in Example 2. But I have not suggested why this modal model's cadence according to the Fleury Playbook should turn back upward to G and the non-discursive "alleluia" should be added, when all other *Peregrinus* versions that start with *Tertia dies* leave its melody unaltered. Could this tampering with both mode and melody be because either the previous or the ensuing motives or both are in G rather than E? Could it be that this is the only way the Fleury Playbook dramatist, desiring not to structure out of order and context, could satisfactorily sandwich this mode-bearing text into music in a different mode?

Preceding *Tertia dies* is the highly discursive antiphon *Qui sunt hi sermones*; its two question-answer pairs, comprising the entire first episode of *Peregrinus,* are in VIII. Furthermore, this lengthy antiphon originally was punctuated by those undramatic "Alleluias" at the close of each question and response. Musical discrepancies between this *Magnificat* antiphon and the dramatic version of the Fleury Playbook are too few and idiomatic to be specified in an example;[9] therefore in Example 3 I transcribe only what immediately follows *Tertia dies* in the manuscript. The material, I have noted, derives from a second Easter Monday

Magnificat antiphon, *Jesus junxit,* also in VIII.[10] In Example 3, I indicate on the top line the antiphon and beneath it the play's melody, which, although quite discrepant, does maintain VIII.

Example 3 — Mode VIII

antiphon: DFGa FG G a c ♮ c a a Ga F F GD FG
his

Fleury Playbook: a FG G Ga F ac c♮ a cdc aG FG G a FGa G G
O stulti et tardi corde ad cre-dendum in om - nibus

G G Ga G G a FE D F Ga G G
G FE DFE DC C CD EF G aG FG G G
quae lo - cu - ti sunt prophe - tae. Al - le - lu - ia.

Although the mode continues, no appreciable motive is recalled in "O stulti" from "Qui sunt"; modal coherence is immanent up to the end of "O stulti," while the passage that follows "O stulti" is in VII. Mode accordingly appears to be critical in achieving coherence. In the conflation of the antiphons *Qui sunt* and *Tertia dies,* the following conclusions emerge: (1) this playwright depended upon pre-existing motivic material drawn from a traditional antiphon, (2) these motives occur as repeated musical phrases, (3) mode may be adjusted and exercise control over the melody to preserve motivic coherence (as here, the eighth mode is coupled to the third, which in turn rejoins the eighth).

The musical themes of the first group of plays, the St. Nicholas cycle, have largely been already identified by Smoldon. In *Tres filiae* Smoldon (pp. 261-62) has uncovered two principal themes, the first of which is transcribed into alphabetical notation in Example 4 (Arabic numbers refer to verses represented by the following rows of pitches). The opening interval, a leap up a fifth from D, is a hallmark of the first mode. Also, the high a about which this theme revolves is the dominant of I. But a is also the dominant of IV which terminates on E, and with E the termination here, IV proves to be the correct mode.

The remaining motivic material takes up with the third speech and proceeds to the concluding sixth-mode antiphon. A telltale ♭ occurs in the manuscript as a regular signature which,

Example 4 — Mode IV

1		D	a	$\overline{\text{a}♮}$	a	$\overline{\text{a}♮}$	c	♮	a	G								
2				♮	a		c	♮	a	G	a							
3	a		a	$\overline{♮\text{c}}$	a										G	F	FE	
4									a	G		F		D	G		$\overline{\text{FEDC}}$	DE
5									$\overline{\text{a}}$	$\overline{\text{G}}$		$\overline{\text{F}}$	$\overline{\text{E}}$	$\overline{\text{D}}$				
									$\overline{\text{a}}$	G		$\overline{\text{F}}$	$\overline{\text{E}}$	D	G		$\overline{\text{F DC}}$	$\overline{\text{DE}}$
6									a	G		F	E		G		FED	
7									a	G		F		D	G		$\overline{\text{F DC}}$	$\overline{\text{DE}}$

according to Diagram 2, identifies this motive, ending on D, as I (see Example 5). Except for the superposed pitches, this melody is identical to the St. Nicholas theme of the third miracle and the *Puer* or *Filius* themes of the last miracle, which we shall review in their turn. Notice the identity of verses 1 and 3, 2 and 4, offset by the tetrasyllabic verse 5 with its truncated musical phrase. Here and in the ensuing examples wherever the verse is decasyllabic as it so often is, syllabification is discernible in the count of single pitches and neumes themselves.

Example 5 — Mode I

					$(\overline{\text{cd}}$	$\overline{\text{c a}}$	$\overline{\text{F}})$	
1	F	$\overline{\text{EDC}}$ D (E)$\overline{\text{D}}$ F G		a	♭	a	a $\overline{\text{G F E}}$	$\overline{\text{D}}$
2	F	$\overline{\text{EDC}}$ D (E)$\overline{\text{D}}$ F G	$\overline{\text{FE F}}$		$\overline{\text{DE}}$ F		$\overline{\text{E}}$	$\overline{\text{D C}}$
					($\overline{\text{cd}}$	$\overline{\text{caF}}$	$\overline{\text{G F E}}$ $\overline{\text{F D}}$)	
3	$\overline{\text{FG}}$	$\overline{\text{(F)EDC}}$ D (E)D F G		a	♭	a	a $\overline{\text{G F E}}$	$\overline{\text{D}}$
4	F	$\overline{\text{EDC}}$ D (E)D F G	$\overline{\text{FE(F)}}$		$\overline{\text{DE}}$ F		$\overline{\text{E E}}$	$\overline{\text{D C}}$
5	$\overline{\text{FG}}$	$\overline{\text{(F)EDC}}$ D					$\overline{\text{E}}$	$\overline{\text{D}}$

Interesting is the adherence to this ♭ signature in all three plays wherever this motive is sung. Could this be an idiosyncrasy of the playwright or a particular singer's mannerism?

The sequel in the manuscript, *Tres clerici,* contains the same kind of repetitious music as *Tres filiae.* There are nineteen stanzas, and eighteen of them have a steady melodic pattern which is reproduced in Example 6.

Example 6 — Mode I

1				E	G	G	EDEDC		F E	DEC		D E D
2				E	G	G	EDEDC		F E	DEC		D E D
3	G	a	c♮a		Ga	GF	EDE		F E	DE	G	
4	C	D		E		F	EDE	C D		EC		D E D

There is no doubt of the modality of the "finale" of *Tres clerici:* its nineteenth and final stanza, called *Oratio Sancti Nicolai,* clearly is in I. The modal series of I, d-D is prescribed like a descending scale encompassing *all* pitches and interestingly is found first over the words "sunt omnia." Perhaps the change of melody which sets the same decasyllabic rhythm before this ultimate number was to afford a musical climax to the play. The music of the *Oratio* is shown in Example 7.

Example 7 — Mode I

1, 2		D a	(a)♮G	a ♮ c		dc	♮a		GF	ED		·/.
3	♮ c d d					dc	♮a		GF	ED		
									GF	ED	G a	
4		D a			cd	dc	♮a	F	GF	ED		
		D	F				a		GFE	FD		

This item, modally considered, does not connect well to the ensuing fourth-mode *Te Deum laudamus,* which destines the play for Matins.

Iconia, or as it is introduced in the Fleury Playbook, *Imago,* the third play of the St. Nicholas cycle, has the most varied music. Indeed its motives vary modally. The Jew's opening soliloquy proceeds octasyllabically and heptasyllabically in regular phrases of music set in a G modality, as we see in Example 8. The first two structures range high, clearly in seventh mode; the third in a median range, seventh or eighth; and the fourth low, ascribable only to the eighth. Notice the internal repetition in the first half of verses 12-18. Notice also the overall form, with its recapitulation at verses 10 and 11 of the opening phrase

Example 8 — Mode VII to VIII

1-3, 10, 11		G d c $\overline{\text{de}}$ c f $\overline{\text{ed}}$ $\overline{\text{d♮}}$ $\overline{\text{dec}}$ c ♮ $\overline{\text{aG}}$
	c $\overline{\text{aF}}$	G
4-9		G d c $\overline{\text{de}}$ c f $\overline{\text{ed}}$ $\overline{\text{d♮}}$ $\overline{\text{dec}}$ c ♮ $\overline{\text{aG}}$
	♮ c	d[11]
12-18	c(♮) $\overline{\text{aF}}$ GG	⁒. ♮ a
	♮ c	♮ a G
19, 20	G E $\overline{\text{FE}}$ D E G $\overline{\text{aF}}$ G	♮ a
	♮ c ♮ $\overline{\text{aF}}$	(a) G

ending on G after several intervening verses with a cadence on high d. Both repetition and recapitulation I consider steps toward coherence on the playwright's part. Smoldon comments (p. 268) on the composer's option to "use the cadence motive as a springboard" from verse 11 to the head motive of verse 12. Assuming this continuation of the cadence fragment (c)♮ $\overline{\text{AF}}$ G to be intentional, we have still another good example of motivic coherence.

The next speech, accommodating a metric change from octasyllable plus heptasyllable to octasyllabic couplets, has the "head motive" of Example 7, slightly modified and repeated D a $\overline{\text{♮G}}$ a ⁒., and features the sequence ca, ♮G, aF. In its internal repetition it follows the technique of Example 8, verses 12-18. The continuation of this motive and the next motive, which always dips to low D, mark this entire section as eighth mode. Example 9 exhibits both its themes, the first of which sets trochaic verse and the second dactylic verse.

Example 9 — Mode VIII

trochaic:	D a $\overline{\text{♮G}}$ a ⁒. c a♮ G	a F G G
dactylic:	G a E F G G ♮ $\overline{\text{a♮}}$ c $\overline{\text{♮a(G)}}$	$\overline{\text{a F}}$ G
	$\overline{\text{G(a)E}}$ $\overline{\text{F(E)}}$ $\overline{\text{D(E)}}$	$\overline{\text{(FE)}}$ F G G

In this example we observe another "springboard" motive G a (E) F G G, which here marries the trochaic "cadence" to the dactylic "intonation." Perhaps for rhetorical vantage the new head or "springboard" motive is reiterated at the beginning of each new speech rather than during the course of speeches. The final motives in the G modality return to the high range of mode VII, as seen in Example 10.

Example 10 Mode VII

octasyllabic	G a♮ c	♮a	G ♮a cd |	G a♮	c aGF	a F		G
	d G a♮ c	♮a	G ♮ d |	G a♮	c aGF	a	G	G
decasyllabic	G ♮ c	a	♮	G		a F	G	G ·/.
octasyllabic	d (a)♮ cdc	♮a	♮c d	♮	c♮a			G ·/.
	G a♮ cd	e	c d |	G a♮	c aGF	a	G	G

As though to reflect the change in mood describing the Jew's infuriation at the theft of his image of St. Nicholas, the motive changes at his oath "Vah! Perii!" called by Smoldon (p. 268) "the first yell to be set to Gregorian music." This new mode is maintained up to the return of the stolen treasure. Despite its opening scale-descent c♮aGFED, the mode is deceptive. Although the range belongs to I, the melody, which occasionally is colored by ♭, does not finish on D but rather on G. With ♭, this would circumscribe a transposed mode, the so-called G-Dorian or D mode relocated (transposed) a fourth higher, a common modality of the sixteenth century. The limits of this transposed mode are actually those of II, not I. Yet in none of the scalar passages (descending from higher than ♭) during the first five phrases, nor anywhere at all in the remainder of this entire section is ♭ employed. Although modally ambiguous at the beginning, the overall modal residue is the low-ranged G system in force at the ending: VIII.

There are at least three, probably more, motives in the Jew's long passage *Vah! Perii!* The turgidity of pitches, as opposed to syllables, and the nuances interlaced among otherwise similar phrases, impair melodic analysis. Concerning this lengthy diatribe, Smoldon wrote:

> There is not the order and balance that is to be found in the setting of *Judaeus*' first item. A few half-achieved attempts at repeated sentences are found, and there are a number of effec-

tive instances of . . . downward sweeps of rapid notes, but on the whole the music just drifts. (p. 269)

In these "effective downward sweeps" we find our only tangible effects of coherence, because, as Example 11 shows, the melisma may extend for any length downwards for more than two notes. It thus establishes at least three common pitches. The difference will be the starting pitch. Because the low descents will be enveloped by the high ones when extended, I omit the numerous starts on G, a and ♮ (♭?) in *Judaeus*' soliloquy.

Example 11 — Mode VIII(?)

	phrase/sentence	*scalar formula*	*text particle*
from e:	9, 10	edc♮a	[mi]ser, [la]tet
	17	edca	cre[do]
	21	(d)edc♮aGF	fla[gella], cre[mabo]
from d:	17	dc♮aG	nec
	17, 18, 19,	dcaG(F)	do[lebo], [tonde]re,
	20		[tempo]ra, [credi]ta
from c:	1	c♮aGFED	Vah
	10, 21	c♮aG	quod, Pri[mo]
	15(2), 16,	c♮a	et [vi]ge[ret], tri[standi]
	20(2), 21		ni[si], [re]pa[res], post

St. Nicholas' succeeding speech, by contrast, receives totally periodic musical treatment. Smoldon (pp. 262, 269, 272) has noted its motivic connection to the *Tres filiae* theme of Example 5 above as well as music from *Filius Getronis,* but it also is partly recalled in the Jew's triumphant finale. The eight identical cadential melismas of St. Nicholas and the three of the Jew are excerpted in Example 12 in which we note similarity to termination patterns in Example 5.

Example 12 — Mode I

St. Nicholas:	aaGFEDC	FDC	GFEDC	D	(E)D
Jew:	aaGFEDC	GFE	GFEDC	FD	

The principal distinction in Example 12 seems to lie in syllabification: for St. Nicholas (except for the first instance), a pentasyllable, for the Jew, a tetrasyllable.

What the *Imago* may lack in motivic concordance it compensates for by applying mode as dramatic indicator and adhesive. Diagram 4 outlines the drama by episode translated into mode.

DIAGRAM 4

Episode	*Mode*
Jew with image	VII/VIII
Ransacking thieves	VIII with change of motive
Jew bereft	VIII(?) ♭ intermittently indicated
St. Nicholas	I, ♭ indicated
Repentant thieves	VIII with third change of motive
Jew with returned image	I, ♭ indicated and St. Nicholas' cadential melismas quoted (Example 12)
Return to the liturgy	
Chorus:	I, ♭ indicated

The return to the liturgy is signalled by the incipit of the introit *Statuit ei Dominus*. Not only is the mode (I) preserved, but also the first four notes of the Jew's "finale" are modelled upon and carried over into the ensuing chant.[12] This typical "motto" of I—at the head of half of the score of introit texts set in the *Liber Usualis*—heads each of the Jew's four short strophes. The effect of the introit's entrance as a fifth stanza, but for chorus, is captured here. Nevertheless, the continuation of the play's melody diverges markedly from the higher-ranged introit's continuation.

The most "leitmotivic" among all the plays of Orléans MS. 201 is the last of the St. Nicholas tetralogy, *Filius Getronis*. In attempting to identify the separate motives of this drama, Smoldon (pp. 270-73) isolated four: those associated with King Marmorinus' adherents *(ministri)*, King Marmorinus himself *(Rex)*, Adeodatus, Son of Getron and Euphrosina *(Puer)*, and Euphrosina. Unfortunately, Smoldon never identified Getron's music as a special leitmotif. But this is Getron's personal theme even though only four unbroken stanzas are devoted to it. Nor did Smoldon recognize that the citizen's distinct motive with its ♭ in II is associated with the miracle: the son returned home.

The first character, portrayed by the chorus or one of their number, is the minister(s) of King Marmorinus. Example 13 renders this decasyllabic opening chorus. In it VII is indicated.

Example 13 — Mode VII

1, 2	Gd	$\overline{\text{de}}$	$\overline{\text{dc}}$	$\overline{\text{de}}$	fe	$\overline{\text{de}}$	$\overline{\text{dc}}$	d	·/.										
3						$\overline{\text{de}}$	$\overline{\text{dc}}$			♮c	$\overline{\text{aG}}$	F	G	a	c	♮	a		
4	cd				$\overline{\text{fef}}$		$\overline{\text{dc}}$			$\overline{\text{♮c}}$	$\overline{\text{aG}}$	$\overline{\text{F}}$					a	G	G

The motive of King Marmorinus, the next character, is seen in Example 14, also in VII.

Example 14 — Mode VII

1									$\overline{\text{c♮a}}$	c	c	$\overline{\text{♮a}}$	$\overline{\text{♮aG}}$	G		a	c	c
2												$\overline{\text{♮a}}$	$\overline{\text{♮aG}}$	G	G	a	c	c
												$\overline{\text{♮a}}$					c	c
3	e	f	g	g	$\overline{\text{gf}}$	$\overline{\text{fe}}$	$\overline{\text{ed}}$	$\overline{\text{dc}}$	$\overline{\text{c♮a}}$	$\overline{}$	$\overline{}$	$\overline{\text{♮}}$						c
4												$\overline{\text{♮a}}$	$\overline{\text{♮aG}}$	G	G	a		c
												$\overline{\text{♮a}}$	$\overline{\text{♮}}$ G	G	G			

We have already compared the motive of Adeodatus in Example 5 as it occurred in *Tres Filiae*. In *Filius Getronis* again, the ♭ signature identifies it. In Euphrosina's motive we encounter our first serious attempt at psalmody. Actually indicated here are both the psalmody and antiphon of VI transposed up a fifth: dominant a to e. Its first half is psalmodic, its second half in the likeness of an antiphon. Modal homogeneity between quasi-psalm and quasi-antiphon is not at once plain, however. The psalm-tone specimen might be in VI, dominant on a, transposed up a fifth, IV/a. The antiphon type might be in V or VI (F), transposed up a fifth, or VII or VIII, transposed up a fourth. Transposition of VI into high c is a Gregorian chant mechanism.[13] Because of this and the availability of an eleventh-century antiphon in transposed VI with an occurrence of ♭,[14] we may regard such modal homogeneity through transposition as a dynamic reflection of contemporary liturgical drama set to music.

In Example 15 the top rows of pitches extract from the

aforementioned psalm tone (also cf. Diagram 2) and aforementioned antiphon specimen, all in VI, and the bottom rows transcribe Euphrosina's motive. There may have been liturgical-musical reasons for such treatment in the fact that Euphrosina's role is that of a suppliant, always represented praying inside the "Church of St. Nicholas"; hence the appropriate music would involve psalmody (more elaborate than prayer tones, however), a singer with high voice range, and therefore transposition.

Example 15 — Mode VI, transposed

```
psalmody    F G a————Ga ♭aG a a   a———F Ga      G F
  1, 2      c d e e e(e) de fed e e | c d e e(e) de fe e d c
antiphony   c e g g          fed      c d e                dccc ♭c
                        . . .         c d e   c            ddc   c
  3, 4      c e  ga g e ga f fed e e | c d e de fef        d  c ♭
                                                           d c   c
```

Getron sings a motive in VII, shown in Example 16.

Example 16 — Mode VII

```
1, 2             d♮  cdc ♮a♮  c d♮  c ♮a G   ⁄.
3                        ♮a♮        c ♮a G  ♮a♮ d dc♮ d
4       G a              ♮a♮        c♮c a G F
                                        a G G
```

The last person to make an appearance, as usual, is St. Nicholas. In the ensuing motive, in which his miracle is published by Puer and a citizen of Excoranda, we recognize a certain dramatic coherence. For Puer, literally transported home by St. Nicholas, transfers to it from his own earlier leitmotif. This "Puer restored," shown in Example 17, while new to the

Example 17 — Mode II, ♭ indicated

```
1                   D a aGF ED C G F G G a
2       a c d c♭ a c           G F G G a   (⁄.)
3       a                        F G        D E C A C D D
```

play, does indicate a modicum of internal rhyme in its motivic treatment as well as ♭ throughout.

Euphrosina's final solo, in II but transposed to a level a fifth higher to end on a (probably to accommodate, as it does, a high voice), introduces into this play the type of song sung by the Jew in the *Imago.* This is identified by downward sweeps which here, as in the Jew's diatribe, are emotionally charged, with Euphrosina, in turn, overcome with joy. As in the Jew's solo, Euphrosina's melismas overlap; the longest makes a brilliant final cadence to *Filius Getronis,* occurring on the last word, "negotio" ♮ c eedc♮G Ga. (I take Smoldon's word that this final a and not G, solely visible in the very blurred facsimile published, is accurate.)

By way of an excursus, we should note that pre-existing chants to St. Nicholas, all but *Te Deum* proper to him, are specified at the end of each drama, uncovering a possible liturgical bond for all four dramas. The three antiphons are identifiable in the monastic antiphonal of Worcester at precise junctures of the December 6 liturgical *cursus.*[15] The Fleury Playbook order and my rearrangement to befit the liturgy appear in Diagram 5.

DIAGRAM 5

	Drama	*Liturgical Reference*	*Cue*
Fleury Playbook:	*Tres Filiae*	*Magnificat* antiphon	*O Christi pietas*[16]
	Tres Clerici		*Te Deum*
	Imago Sancti Nicholai	introit	*Statuit ei Dominus*
	Filius Getronis	*Benedictus* antiphon	*Copiosae caritatis*
Liturgical dispersion on Dec. 6:	*Tres Clerici*	Matins	(*Te Deum*)
	Filius Getronis	Lauds	(*Ad Benedictus*)
	Imago Sancti Nicholai	Mass	(*Ad introitum*)
	Tres Filiae	Vespers	(*Ad magnificat*)

If we seriously credit the reference in *Filius Getronis,* "Tomorrow will be the feast of St. Nicholas," then this last play might indeed have been performed before daylight or the Day Mass.

Like *Peregrinus,* the Play of *Herod* appears to rely more than the previous cycle upon purely liturgical music. But unlike *Peregrinus,* this liturgical music contributes little to musical continuity during the Magi's adorations and during transitions between several scenes of this longest of the ten plays to use borrowed material.[17] The first two scenes—the shepherds and Magi with the star—set the stage of constant modal change. For the first dozen speeches one mode shifts to another in the following order: IV, VIII, VII, VIII, VI, IV, VIII, II, V(?), VI. The strings of questions, answers, commands, acknowledgements, and hails in the lengthy scene at Herod's court occur in frequently shifting modes: I, II, VIII, VI, and IV. Yet during Herod's questioning we find some coherence in this scene which continues in I with a couple of allusions to II in drops to low A. Short questions in VIII and part of the scribes' speech in IV make exception to the insistence of I.

There is a well-wrought welding of the scribe's response, which begins in II, to their quotation from scriptural prophecy, actually a borrowed antiphon, *Bethlehem non es minima,* in IV.[18] Here as in the adaptation of *Tertia dies* to *Qui sunt* in the *Peregrinus* play, the playwright forges the connection of the scribes' introduction of the prophecy to their ensuing quotation from it. Example 18 overlays the musical setting to the last introductory word "vaticinante" on the first word of the prophecy "Bethlehem."

Example 18 — Mode II to IV

$\overline{\text{DC}}$ E $\overline{\text{FE}}$ D D (II)

$\overline{\text{C DF E FE}}$ D D . . . .E (IV)

Just as this modally and motivically diffuse play begins on a note of discontinuity, so also does its ending disperse modes liberally. The modes of the last four numbers of *Herod,* in order, progress as follows: IV, I, V (a chant borrowing), and IV.

Although motivic coherence is minimal, the few moments where the mode remains stable allow repetitions. Noticeably coherent are the following motives of King Herod repeated note for note by the Magi and the refrain of the first phrase of the Herod-Archelaus interchange shown in Example 19, a and b.

The *Interfectio Puerorum,* like *Herod,* incorporates copious pre-existent liturgical music; with a dozen such borrowings it emerges ahead of the other plays in its liturgical dependence.[19] However, unlike *Herod,* these borrowings do not disrupt the play's coherence. From a conflation of a *Communio* and two Office antiphons, all in VII, we notice undeniable similarities

Example 19 Mode II

a. HEROD/MAGI: D a $\overline{a\ G\ F\ G}$ a $\overline{FG}$ $\overline{CA}$ $\overline{CD}$ D . . ·/.

b. HEROD/ARCHILAEUS: ($\overline{D}$)a $\overline{a\ G}$

a $\overline{G\ F}$ G G a ·/.

in the Angel's two revelations to Joseph: the first advising flight to Egypt, and the second, penultimate number of this play encouraging return. The conflation excerpts the antiphon *Joseph fili David,* which is grafted to the Communion antiphon *Tolle puerum* and, later, to the antiphon *Revertere in terram Judam.* In Example 20 I align the matching phrases of music.

Example 20 Mode VII

Warning: G G c♮c d . . G $\overline{c\natural c}$ . . $\overline{ede}$ c d $\overline{eed}$ $\overline{c\natural}$ c
$\overline{cefed}$ $\overline{ed}$ . . . d c $\overline{\natural ac}$ . . . $\overline{Ga}$ G G

Return: G G c♮c d . . G $\overline{c\natural c}$ . . $\overline{ede}$ $\overline{ed}$ $\overline{c\natural}$ c
$\overline{cefed}$ $\overline{ed}$ d c $\overline{\natural ac}$ $\overline{Ga}$ G G

Actually, the borrowed antiphons themselves had this melody in common. Owing to the unfinished notation of the final number, *Gaude Maria Virgo,* whose incipit in the manuscript appears to be in VIII, we cannot tell how cleverly this liturgical antiphon for which we have no concordance is connected to the *Te Deum.*

The degree of internal rhyme in the Holy Innocents' song, *Agno sacrato,* betrays the kind of composition found in the St. Nicholas group. The tune bears study beyond Smoldon's (p. 216) for its repeated phrases, and it appears in Example 21. Music for Verse 4 has nothing but its final, E, in common with

Example 21 Mode IV

1 $\overline{EFG}$ $\overline{FE}$ D F D C $\overline{DE}$ E $\overline{GF}$ DC $\overline{DE}$ E

2 C D E $\overline{FE}$ D F $\overline{aG}$ $\overline{ED}$ $\overline{FE}$ DC DE E

3 a F E C D F E $\overline{FGGF}$ $\overline{ED}$ F DC DE E

5 $\overline{EFG}$ $\overline{FE}$ D F D $\overline{aa\ GF}$ $\overline{ED}$ F DC DE E

the other four verses and so is omitted in the example. But we encounter it later in this drama.

The well known Lament of Rachel[20] affords other clear-cut cases of motivic coherence. Example 22 gives in pitch-letters the repeated motives which connect verses of the initial portion, in VIII. Notice the variance of initial pitch—on D, G, a c d—compared to termination, always on G.

Example 22 — Mode VIII

Verses											
1, 2, 8, 14	G	c		a	(G)		E	F		G	G
3, 4, 13, 17	G	(D)	C	a			E	F		G	G
5, 6	d			a	(G)	FD		F		G	G
7, 10, 11 (14 similar)	a			a			E	F		G	G
9	G					D		F	a		G
12.	d			a			E	F		G	G
15	D					FD		F			G
16	c			a			E	F		G	G

Notice also the cadential repetitions. This is not to analyze the incidences of internal rhyme—musical repetition in one or the other hemistich which are legion (see Smoldon, pp. 217-19).

It is from the consolers' formula, ending on E, that verse 4 of the Innocents' *Agno sacrato* appears to have been drafted, or vice versa. The simple formula, sung three times with considerable elaboration in the second and third utterances, appears in Example 23.

Example 23 — Mode IV

CONSOLERS: FE DE E E E $\overline{\text{Ga}}$ $\overline{\text{ac}}$ a $\overline{\text{a GF}}$
G a E E

INNOCENTS (v 4): E G $\overline{\text{Ga}}$ a $\overline{\text{ac}}$ a $\overline{\text{Ga}}$ G G F
G a E E

The textual basis here is the sequence *Quid tu virgo* by Notker Balbulus, but not a shred of Notker's music is borrowed.[21]

The germ and what was to become the heart of liturgical drama, the *Visitatio Sepulchri*, receives in the Fleury Playbook what Smoldon (p. 168) assessed as unique treatment in its opening "entrance" scene. His documentation was his perusal of the literally scores of *Visitatio* texts and music spanning several stages of development. Smoldon (pp. 155-56) analyzed the melodies of this first scene as actually three separate tunes. His excerpts indeed indicate little that could be classified as musical rhyme such as we saw in the previous two examples. Yet there is one repeated pattern at one of the places we have come to expect it: a phrase end. This is linked to a similar cadence in the court scene of *Herod* and to another at the opening of *Conversio Beati Pauli,* both quoted, incidentally, by Smoldon (pp. 166, 207, 277). In Example 24 I quote the Magi's cadence and the Marys' cadence from the *Visitatio* concordant

Example 24 Mode I

MAGI:	D	$\overline{C}$			$\overline{GFE}$	$\overline{(F)D}$
MARYS:	D	C	(D	E)	$\overline{GFE}$	$\overline{(F)D}$

to it. Importantly, the Marys have nine speeches ending with this formula. Even after the "Quem quaeritis" interchange, it is twice recalled (on "Sustulit e tumulo"). The *Visitatio* and *Conversio Beati Pauli* contain basically four or, in a few cases, five syllables to these pitches (*Herod* sets two or more, hence the broken lines indicating the neumes in the example). Whatever lack of mutual bond the three plays' words may have had, their melodic tie, with whatever associative force it marshalled, is irrefutable.

The *Visitatio* item's stanzas are separated by the intervention of St. Peter's and St. John's speeches, thus providing the platform for recapitulation, a contrivance to make the scene cohere whenever Mary Magdalene resumes her lament. But what follows bears even closer relation to other dramas of this repertory: the mode shifts from D to E.[22] The angels' question, soon afterward Christ's question "Mulier quid ploras?" and, still later, Christ's salutation "Maria" may have been extracted from the original *Peregrinus.* That late eleventh-century play assigns this E mode and motive to Christ as he reappears to the disciples assembled in Jerusalem and greets them with "Pax vobis," and the motive is reiterated in the Fleury Playbook version. But it is also the motive of Rachel's consolers quoted in Example 23: $\overline{FE}$ $\overline{DE}$ E. In fact, the continuation of "Pax vobis" in Christ's statements "Ego sum" and "Nolite timere" may be found in the appendage sung by the consolers and Innocents, also quoted in Example 23. These three phrases appear in Example 25.

Example 25 Mode IV

FE DE E | E G Ga | a GF G Ga GFE E

This motive is also found on the words "Nolite vos" and "jam mutate" of the speech *Venite et videte* in the Orléans *Visitatio,* on "scripta sunt" of the Archangel's concluding speech, and on the Magi's response "Deo gratias!" from *Herod.* This kind of monothematic treatment prompted Smoldon to comment (p. 170) on the playwright's motivic economy in this scene of the Fleury Playbook's *Visitatio,* not fully realizing nonetheless this passage's adaptability to different contexts of representation. Much of the rest of the Orléans *Visitatio* is in E, IV, as is its sole liturgical member, the antiphon *Surrexit Dominus* which originated in the Messine *Visitatio.*[23] In fact, it is not specious to assume that *Surrexit Dominus* was seminal to this entire large scene, quoting as it does the repeated motives of this same antiphon: F E D E E.

Peregrinus, in the same Easter cycle, shares some of the *Visitatio's* music in the Fleury Playbook. We have analyzed most of the first of its four scenes already, because it is a paragon of continuity in the borrowed antiphon *Qui sunt* conflated with the antiphon *Tertia dies.* There we observed modality acting as the agent of coherence. The Orléans manuscript's scene nevertheless departs from the more conservative *Peregrinus* versions because of its shifts out of VIII and into a rare transposition of VII a fifth down, ending on low c with a ♭ and from thence to VII. The latter shift exercises the combined range of the G modes—C-g—and departs from possible objectives of modal coherence at least in the traditional sense of modality. Yet, such elasticity is a commonplace in the post-tenth-century stratum of ecclesiastical music.

Although the second scene bears hardly a trace of continuity, the third contains plenty of motivic cement, with the aforementioned "Pax vobis" motto and both words and music repeated at relevant junctures, presumably for emphasis as much as coherence. The music which is continually recalled in this scene is the remainder of the "Pax vobis" announcement to the words "Ego sum. Nolite timere" already examined in Example 25. The fourth-mode *Surrexit Dominus,* moreover, is carried over from the Orléans *Visitatio* into *Peregrinus*' third scene. A dramatically abstruse Thomas scene concludes the Fleury Playbook's *Peregrinus*, punctuated as it is by the aforementioned "Pax vobis." Related neither modally nor motivically to its immediate surroundings, this scene employs motto as interruption. Nor can we tell, because of the inexactitude of the notation, if the play's music connects smoothly with Fortunatus' fourth-mode refrain hymn *Salve festa dies,* which, I have shown, concluded the original *Peregrinus* of Le Mans as it does this version.[24]

The *Conversio Sancti Pauli* music was analyzed in a 1970 dissertation by Colonius Davis,[25] who notices two general phenomena in the play. The first (pp. 153-54) is that the ending, like that of *Herod, Visitatio,* and *Resurrectio Lazari,* is in the D mode, while the *Te Deum* following the drama is in the low E or fourth mode. As in the plays studied above, so also here modal coherence is not enhanced by this rough connection. A second phenomenon noticed by Davis (p. 154) is the persistence of a short and probably rhythmic motive sung by three of the protagonists, Saul, the High Priest of Damascus, and Barnabas, in the final three speeches. But Saul's setting (die[tatem]), in VII, lies a fifth higher than the others (Custo[dite], Te e[legit]) in I. Could these intervals' first utterance have been somehow preparatory to the others while preserving a kind of modal neutrality? The motive is rendered in Example 26.

	Example 26	Mode VII/I
SAUL	d $\overline{\text{c♮ca}}$ c $\overline{\text{ed}}$	
PRINCEPS SYNAGOGE MINISTRI	D $\overline{\text{FEFD}}$ $\overline{\text{FG}}$ a	

The shape of the scribe's original neume, identical in each of the three instances, promotes the similarity.[26]

I detect two additional motivic concordances, one already illustrated in the discussion of the *Visitatio* by Example 24, there keyed to the *Conversio*. The other occurs as the play's motto or "head motive," a rapid ascent of four pitches: D-G-a-c. Also found often in the middle of a speech, this motive may overlap phrases of text. The latter feature is indicated with a vertical stroke in this motive, shown in Example 27. I count fifteen recurrences discounting the several abbreviations to solely the first three pitches.

Example 27 Modes I and VIII

D | G a(♮ G) c(♮) a

The three modes employed in *Conversio* are I, VII, and VIII. Here, the musicologist's review is again required to discern these modes' interplay (or retention as the case may be, owing to Davis' misjudgment of modal properties and Smoldon's penchant for modern transposition).[27] Such a review reveals that the entire play adheres to the eighth mode except for Saul's introduction and the Damascus High Priest's and Barnabas' motives, both in I, and Saul's credence motive, in VII. Accordingly, motivic unity may outweigh modal considerations. But it is the order of the fourteen speeches which convinces us that modal unity is this play's essence. The outline of the *Conversio's* components indicates this order, as follows:

Speech	*Mode*
1 (Saul)	I
2-10	VIII
11 (Saul)	VII
12, 13	I

Modal continuity for its part outstrips dramatic (but not religious) coherence, as appears to be the case in the last two episodes. There the convert is separated from Jewry and associated with the Christians by Barnabas to the same mode. The melody, however, carries over into speech 13 only the opening dozen pitches of speech 12. Motivic relationships are, on the other hand, not a foregone conclusion of modal relationships, as proven here by the almost total disagreement between the motives of the last two speeches and of the first, their modal counterpart in I. Furthermore, the motive analyzed in Example 27 does not appear in numbers 11 through 13 even though it recurs on an average of one and a half times in each of the foregoing speeches in both I and VIII. Motive in this play, therefore, correlates mode, a function it not infrequently had been performing for Gregorian chant, occasionally incurring dilemmas for tonary compilers as to ambiguous modal assignments.

The last drama of the set, *Resuscitatio Lazari,* suggests a head-end connection to the liturgy in references to *In sapientia disponens omnia* and *Mane prima sabbati.* Neither text, unfortunately, survives in an authentic chant,[28] and therefore the degree of cohesion of the initial phrase of this raising of Lazarus to its liturgical antecedent cannot be ascertained. *Resuscitatio Lazari* enables our analysis to recapitulate handsomely, however, as the musical content recalls earlier examples which showed the symbiosis of psalm and antiphon-type. Not only is the play in its entirety hymnic because it repeats one tune for its homologous stanzas, but also much of this motive itself is quasi psalmodic. Certain motivic phrases fashion such an interlock with mode that one recognizes the latter in the melody proper, as we have seen before in Example 15. Now, the mode both as melody and "psalmody" is I. From its six-versed structure, 10 10(4+6) 4, I quote the setting for the first, fourth, and initiation of the fifth verses in Example 28 and enter the psalmody directly underneath. Compare this to Diagram 2, and also to Example 15, where a motive in VI, transposed, dichotomizes psalm and antiphon but admits their interdependence. Here, however, "psalmody" predominates even to the attainment of overlap of melody and text between the pitches a and ♭.

Example 28 — Mode I

	Verse					
SIMON/JESUS, etc.	1	D F G a a a	a G F	G F		
	4	a F G a	(G)FED			
		F G F G a			5^1	♭ a G a
Psalmody (*LU*, p. 113)		F G a ———				♭ a G a
F termination		———	G F	Ga G F		
D termination		———	G F	Ga		
			G FED			

Needless to say, this specimen's words as apart from music invite the attention of analysts of medieval lyrics, a field of study beyond the scope of this paper.

Looking back over this study of the effects of modes and melodic fragments in the dramas of the Fleury Playbook, several phenomena are observable. Reviewing the modes first, we verify all eight from the discussion, all but V and VI from the twenty-eight examples; additionally, the transposition of II, VI, and VII has been undertaken by the ingenious dramaturge who created the Playbook. Clearly, however, the lion's share of the melodies belongs to I with a strong preference for VII and VIII also. This choice of mode relates the playbook's repertory to liturgical chants, especially antiphons, whose principal modes, seen in tonaries, are I and VIII. Another observation is that mode acts like a fiber, stitching together sections where it may be retained, as in the *Conversio* and *Peregrinus,* to form a kind of tone complex or tone background. Otherwise, mode may become a copulative agent through change, as happens in the brief *Tertia dies* of *Peregrinus* or in the incorporation of *Bethlehem* in its original mode into *Herod.*

In this musical corpus we have also observed motivic involvement in the process of linking, often through repetition, in hymn-like series of verses or stanzas. Four other motivic coherences emerge from the foregoing analysis. We observe (1) leitmotifs of characters, usually enlisting the support of mode, (2) the synthesis of psalmody and antiphon-like melody in the same musical passage, (3) the non-recurrence of mode under the aegis of an unchanged motive, e.g. in *Conversio,* motive over-riding mode as it were, and (4) the migration of motive from one drama to another as the fragments "Pax Vobis" *(Peregrinus),* "Nolite timere" *(Visitatio),* and "scripta sunt" and "Deo gratias" *(Herod)* succeed in doing. Of course the music analyzed here is more complex and demanding of study than the examples have made it appear. Still, these examples more than sample this music; they present, I believe, a fair assessment of formulaic ingredients as a whole, particularly if one considers the galaxy of variants with which any student of plainsong is normally confronted. Of persons, Christ said, "By their fruits ye shall know them" (*Mt.* 7.20); of the dramas in the Fleury Playbook, may I rephrase, however prosaically: By their modes and musical motives may we know them.

NOTES

[1] William L. Smoldon, *The Music of the Medieval Church Dramas,* ed. Cynthia Bourgeault (London: Oxford Univ. Press, 1980). Hereafter this work will be abbre-

viated *Music* in the footnotes, while references will appear parenthetically by page number in the text. Those portions devoted to the Fleury Playbook are pp. 165-72, 191-98 (considered with other manuscripts of *Peregrinus*), 204-10, 214-20, and 259-82. The entire manuscript in facsimile has been published in G. Tintori and Raffaele Monterosso, eds., *Sacre rappresentazioni nel manoscritto 201 della Biblioteca municipale di Orleans,* Instituta et Monumenta, Serie I: Monumenta, No. 2 (Cremona, 1958). I have checked every example of this article against these facsimiles. An outdated version in "Gregorian" notation, neume-for-neume, of the manuscript appears in C. E. H. de Coussemaker, *Drames liturgiques du Moyen Age* (1860; rpt. New York, 1964), pp. 83-222. Rhythmic transcripts appear in Tintori and Monterosso, eds., *Sacre rappresentazioni,* and Fletcher Collins, Jr., ed. *Medieval Church Music Dramas* (Charlottesville: Univ. Press of Virginia, 1976), pp. 111-64, 195-258, and 285-395. Here Collins transcribes and edits the *Visitatio Sepulchri* and *Peregrinus* from other manuscripts, not the Fleury Playbook, but he recently has edited a companion to a filmed production of the Fleury Playbook *Visitatio* at St. Benoît de Fleury: *The Visit to the Sepulcher—Visitatio Sepulchri—Commentary and Score* (1979). A new facsimile appears in the plates in the present volume.

[2] Walther Lipphardt, "Liturgische Dramen," *Die Musik in Geschichte und Gegenwart,* VIII, cols. 1014-18.

[3] E.g., in series of rituals and processional antiphons. See my "Antiphons and Antiphon Series Found in the Gradual of Saint-Yrieix," *Musica Disciplina,* 26 (1972), 7. Four successive processional antiphons in first mode occur in the Lenten series and seven in seventh mode in the Maundy Thursday Foot-Washing *ordo.* Transcribed on p. 19 are three antiphons in fourth mode associated with the Unction of the Sick.

[4] John Stevens, "Medieval Drama," *The New Grove,* ed. Stanley Sadie (London, 1980), XII, 32.

[5] François August Gevaert, *La Mélopée antique* (1885, rpt. Osnabrück, 1967).

[6] See Martin Gerbert, *Scriptores ecclesiastici de musica* (St. Blasien, 1784), I, 216-17, and *Liber Usualis* (Tournai, 1947), pp. 113-17. Hereafter, the latter will be abbreviated *LU.*

[7] On the estimate of date of origin of the Latin-texted stereotypes, see Michel Huglo, *Les Tonaires: Inventaire, Analyse, Comparaison* (Paris, 1971), pp. 387-88.

[8] "Easter Monday Antiphons and the *Peregrinus* Play," *Kirchenmusikalisches Jahrbuch* 61/62 (1977), 33. Smoldon never located the tune's source; he regarded the piece as anomalous. See "Liturgical Music Drama," *Grove's Dictionary of Music and Musicians,* 5th ed. (London, 1954), V, 328 ("apparently a setting peculiar to Saintes" [i.e., B.N. lat. 16309, fols. 604-05]); also *Music,* p. 189 ("a phrase from Luke's verse 22 . . . set to a short tune that I cannot identify").

[9] The antiphon *Qui sunt* is found in at least two medieval manuscripts published in facsimile: The Sarum Antiphoner (*Antiphonale Sarisburiense,* ed. W. H. Frere [1901-26; rpt. Farnborough, 1966], p. 241) and the twelfth-century Lucca Cathedral codex 601 (*Paléographie Musicale,* IX [Solesmes, 1906-09], 218). See "Easter Monday Antiphons," p. 34.

[10] "Easter Monday Antiphons," p. 40. This speech with its music of the antiphonal version is compared to all *Peregrinus* versions on pp. 40-41. *Tertia dies* is similarly compared on p. 39.

[11] Erroneously reported by Smoldon (*Music,* p. 267) as s[ol] l[a] t[i] equivalent of G a ♮, whereas he should have reported ti-do-re equivalent of ♮ c d.

[12] I express thanks to Michael Norton of Ohio State University for this notice.

[13] For the termination c $\overline{\text{de}}$ d c to psalmody from c, see *LU,* p. 908. Cf. the F-base psalmody, *LU,* p. 116 (first of the two formulas). Euphrosina's psalmodic melody is thus fairly ruined by recent rhythmic transcriptions such as Smoldon's (*Music,* p. 272).

14 This antiphony is ascertainable in the Marian antiphon *Ave Regina coelorum* in VI (*LU*, pp. 274-75) setting the words "Gaude Virgo gloriosa, Super omnes . . . exora." The psalmody seen in simple form in Diagram 2 is found complete in *LU*, p. 116.

15 Worcester, Cathedral Codex F.160 (thirteenth century), folio 121r. See *Paléographie musicale,* XII (Solesmes, 1922-25), 242. The twelfth-century identical use of these texts is corroborated by antiphonals from St.-Denis and St. Maur-les-Fossés, whose order is published in *Corpus Antiphonalium Officii,* ed. René-Jean Hesbert (*Rerum Ecclesiasticarum Documenta, Series Major: Fontes,* VIII [Rome, 1963]), II, Rites 120 and 150.

16 At least one other St. Nicholas legend involving one Girardus of Cluny, considered to be the provenance of the thirteenth century, cites this antiphon. See Charles H. Beeson, *A Primer of Medieval Latin* (Chicago, 1925), pp. 306-09.

17 Smoldon's accounts (*The Play of Herod* [New York, 1965], pp. 98-99; *Music,* pp. 204-11) of the adaptation of Gregorian chant to *Herod* are incomplete. To be added are the following pieces easily found in the Worcester Antiphonal: invitatory antiphon (Epiphany) *Venite adoremus eum,* antiphon (variously in Advent, Christmas) *Bethlehem non es minima,* responsory (Christmas) *O regem coeli* (called an obsolete antiphon by Smoldon), responsory (Christmas) *Quem vidistis pastores,* and its verse (in certain sources) *Secundum quod dictum est.*

18 For the complete text and melody, see Gevaert, *La Mélopée antique,* p. 342, also *Paléographie Musicale,* XII, p. 9 of the facsimile.

19 Here again, Smoldon (*The Play of Herod,* p. 99; *Music*, pp. 211-21) failed to recognize several borrowings, as follows: responsory (All Saints) *Emitte agnum, Domine* (called a Lauds antiphon by Smoldon), antiphon excerpt (variously in Advent, Christmas) *Joseph, fili David;* Communion antiphon excerpt (Christmas Octave) *Tolle puerum et matrem*; antiphon (Christmas) *Ecce [Salve] Agnus Dei*, verse (Christmas Eve) *Vos qui in pulvere estis* to responsory *Constantes estote;* and antiphon (Purification) *Revertere in terram Judam.*

20 In addition to the already noted transcriptions, others have recently been published: Richard H. Hoppin, *Anthology of Medieval Music* (New York, 1978), pp. 38-40 (No. 28), and Stevens "Medieval Drama," *The New Grove,* XII, 34-35.

21 See Richard L. Crocker, *The Early Medieval Sequence* (Berkeley: Univ. of California Press, 1977), p. 132.

22 Perhaps partly due to the influence of an antiphon for Lauds of the Thursday of Easter Week, *Ardens est cor,* which is interjected at this juncture. This antiphon is published in the *Antiphonale Romanum* (Paris, 1949), p. 466.

23 This melody in IV, which sets text *Surrexit Dominus de sepulchro, qui pro nobis pependit in ligno,* followed by a threefold alleluia, all in IV, is a liturgical chant as is the setting ending with one alleluia, all in VIII, as I prove in "The Role of the Office Antiphon in Tenth-Century Liturgical Drama," *Musica Disciplina*, 34 (1980), 17, 28. Also from Easter dramas I document two settings of the text *Surrexit enim sicut dixit,* one a Vesperal antiphon, the other a processional antiphon sung at the Easter Mass (pp. 18-19). This information improves upon Smoldon's which reported (*Music*, p. 290) one of these liturgical chants "apparently specially composed" and "not that of the (Hartker) liturgical antiphon, but what appears to be an independent composition, which seems to have arisen first in the eleventh century" (p. 363).

24 "Easter Monday Antiphons," p. 32. As for the ambiguity of musical notation, it is possible to read the final pitch of this item, from its height on the staff, as E or (following Coussemaker) D. See Tintori and Monterosso, eds., *Sacre Rappresentazioni*, p. 99 (MS. in facsimile, p. 230), system 3. E is more logical, because of the median alleluias of the piece, all on G, a cadence much more harmonious with the E than the D modes.

25 Colonius S. Davis, "The Fleury Conversio Beati Pauli—A Study of the Liturgical Drama and Its Setting," Ph.D. diss., Ohio University, 1970.

26 See Tintori and Monterosso, eds., *Sacre Rappresentazioni*, p. 100 (MS. in facsimile, p. 238); cf. systems 2 and 4 of the MS. page.

27 Although Davis' transcriptions remain faithful to pp. 230-33 of Orléans 201, he fails to recognize (p. 194) as being in a G modality the guard motive, Paul's second and third speeches, and the High Priest of Jerusalem; also he analyzes as in VII melodies actually in VIII. Smoldon, on the other hand, transposes Saul's opening motive up a fourth (p. 277) and produces only the first half of his conversion speech (p. 279) with an ending on c while its second half does end on G. Other unwarranted transpositions by Smoldon alienate musical examples from any true modal contextuality; a few of Smoldon's numerous misquotations are illustrated correctly, untransposed, in the present article (e.g., Examples 21, 24, 27, and 28).

28 I have checked explicits as well as incipits of the St. Nicholas repertory in the Worcester Antiphonal hoping to find these words ending some chant, but to no avail.

The Staging of Twelfth-Century Liturgical Drama in the Fleury *Playbook*

David Bevington

In what sense do the ten plays of the so-called Fleury *Playbook* employ a common theatrical tradition of staging and presentation? Do they share, among themselves and with other twelfth-century church dramas at Beauvais and elsewhere, certain assumptions about the architectural church interior as stage space, or is their approach to staging the haphazard result of varying sources and redactions?[1] Did the Benedictine brethren who mounted these plays have in mind a common method of dramaturgy for their productions? What conventions of presentation can be adduced from regarding the Fleury play texts collectively as scripts indicative of theatrical performance? Through what sort of figurative language do gesture and stage movement convey meaning? These are the questions I should like to pursue here, much as Bernard Beckerman, John Styan, Ann Slater, and others have recently looked at Shakespeare's play texts as primary indications of how the plays were performed.[2] The method of analysis is a fairly recent one, even for Elizabethan and Jacobean drama,[3] and has been applied only seldom to medieval church drama.[4] The clear advantage of doing so is that play texts and their stage directions or rubrics in any age both explicitly and implicitly contain vital information about staging not always reliably available through iconographical or other external sources.

To move from the now-familiar terrain of stage-oriented analysis of Shakespeare's plays into twelfth-century church drama, on the other hand, is to encounter immense differences in the very concept of stage "action" and the symbolic meaning of gesture. Medieval religious drama began with no clearly recognized view of itself as dramatic spectacle. The earliest tropes and dramatic ceremonials celebrated as part of the order of worship for Easter, in various monastic communities of the tenth and eleventh centuries, derived their language from the liturgy and their visual images from ritual practice. From a theatrical point of view, the language is repetitive, characterization is often inadequately motivated, and gesture is ceremonial. Even though some rubrics encourage the participants to use affective gesture, as in the *Regularis Concordia* at Winchester where three brethren dressed as the three Marys are to move haltingly to the sepulcher "in the manner of seeking for something" as though in imitation (*ad similitudinem*) of the women coming to anoint the body of Jesus,[5] the event remains liturgical rather than theatrically mimetic.

In such a liturgical milieu, we need to be cautious about assuming that "performance" could aim at expressive use of gesture or arrangement of theatrical space in any consciously theatrical sense. The concept of an "audience" was essentially foreign to the conditions under which the early ceremonials were performed: monastic brethren chanted an office among themselves, even when tropes of a dramatic character were added. In the choir where they assembled, they had little occasion to worry about "sight lines." The structures and properties they employed were by and large liturgically determined. Because the story being presented was so well known and the occasion it celebrated so close at hand, their very texts need not concern themselves with consistency of characterization or motivation.[6] The lines of sung dialogue in Easter dramatic ceremonials were to be found in the liturgy, and were ultimately based on scriptural account. Bearing such sanction, they did not require further elucidation.

Nonetheless, as liturgical drama began to achieve self-awareness of its potential for theatrical performance, it inevitably needed to deal with such considerations of dramaturgy as audience, stage movement, employment of properties and structures, and the like. This essay proposes that the Fleury *Playbook* gives evidence of such increased theatrical awareness. The Fleury *Playbook* holds a key position among collections of twelfth-century church drama, and is hence especially well suited for such an investigation. As in other twelfth-century collections, such as that of Benediktbeuern, we begin to find religious dramatic texts that are truly regarded by their authors and scribes as plays. They are set down not as tropes or brief ceremonials inserted into service books intended for Matins or Mass, but in collections of plays, sometimes along with nonliturgical material such as goliardic songs. These plays are artifacts unto themselves, however much inspired by the liturgy and still composed in most cases with a specific liturgical celebration in mind. Even among such collections, Fleury is unusual for the inclusion of the congregation as audience; according to William Tydeman, only at Beauvais do we find a comparable staging of action in the nave with the people as spectators.[7] The Fleury collection of plays is also large and varied.

Fleury thus provides us a single and fairly extensive corpus of plays associated with one monastic community. Here we can compare staging methods in different sorts of plays seemingly gathered together at one location, even if we cannot be sure that all these plays were performed in their collected form at one location. We can see in any case what staging problems are commonly shared, rather than conflating versions of a single play or dramatic ceremonial (such as the Visit to the Sepulcher) from separate locations in Europe.[8] Fleury offers itself as a particular workshop where dramatic innovation seems to have been judiciously weighed and applied to different sorts of church drama.

The ten plays of the Fleury *Playbook* deal with a challenging variety of subjects. In manuscript order, we find four St. Nicholas plays, an *Officium Stellae* (that is, a play of Herod, the Magi, and the shepherds), an *Ordo Rachelis* play of the Slaughter of the Innocents with the lament of mother Rachel, a *Visitatio Sepulchri* or Visit to the Sepulcher, a *Peregrinus* play about Christ's appearance to his disciples after his Resurrection, a Conversion of St. Paul, and a Raising of Lazarus. We cannot be sure that, even if they were in fact performed in a single church, the church in question was at the Benedictine monastery at St.-Benoît-sur Loire. The link between plays and Fleury itself cannot with certainty be traced back earlier than 1522. Even though in recent years the building has been largely restored to its twelfth-century condition, we cannot rely too heavily on its architectural details in speculating about stage arrangement for these particular plans. We are on safer grounds if we posit an interior space common to monastic churches of the period, with a long nave, side aisles, north and south transepts, no screen between the choir and the nave, a west door, and a monastic cloister to one side providing access to the nave (see fig. 1).[9] At the same time, the play texts themselves call for extensive use of such a space, and do so in ways that seem responsive to the presence of a congregation or audience in the nave. The devisers of these plays were aware that they were producing dramatic spectacle, even though they also remained closely in touch with the liturgical occasions that brought worshipers together.

The Fleury Visit to the Sepulcher, intended seemingly for the end of Easter Matins and ending with the singing of the *Te Deum*, is distinguishable from many Easter tropes and ceremonials of the tenth and eleventh centuries first of all in its attentiveness to an audience. On at least four occasions, the performers address themselves to the people who are present. The terms *populus* and *plebs* appear directed at those persons in the nave—lay brethren, others connected with the monastery, conceivably persons from outside the monastic confines—who are in attendance at Easter matins. The inclusion of the congregation is emphatic, and stresses the idea of a community of belief achieved through faith in Christ's Resurrection.[10] When the three Marys have spoken with the angel before Christ's tomb, and have heard the good news of his Resurrection, they turn to "the people" *(ad populum)*, singing "We came mourning to the tomb of the Lord; we have seen an angel of God sitting and saying that he has risen from death." Later, after Mary Magdalene's encounter with Christ as gardener, she turns toward "the people" *(ad populum)* singing "Congratulate me, all you who love the Lord," and so on. Shortly afterward, the three Marys depart from the sepulcher saying to "the people" *(ad plebem)*, "The Lord has risen from the sepulchre, who for us hung on the cross, alleluia." And then they spread out the shroud in which Christ was buried for all the congregation to see, saying "to the people" *(ad plebem)*, "Behold, you companions, here is the shroud of the blessed body, Who lay abandoned in the empty tomb." The congregation present (including lay members) is thus not only addressed repeatedly and directly, but is given a symbolic role as the "companions" *(socii)* of those who first witnessed to the truth of Christ's Resurrection.

The presence of the congregation as *socii* has dramaturgic as well as thematic consequences. Even though the play's action

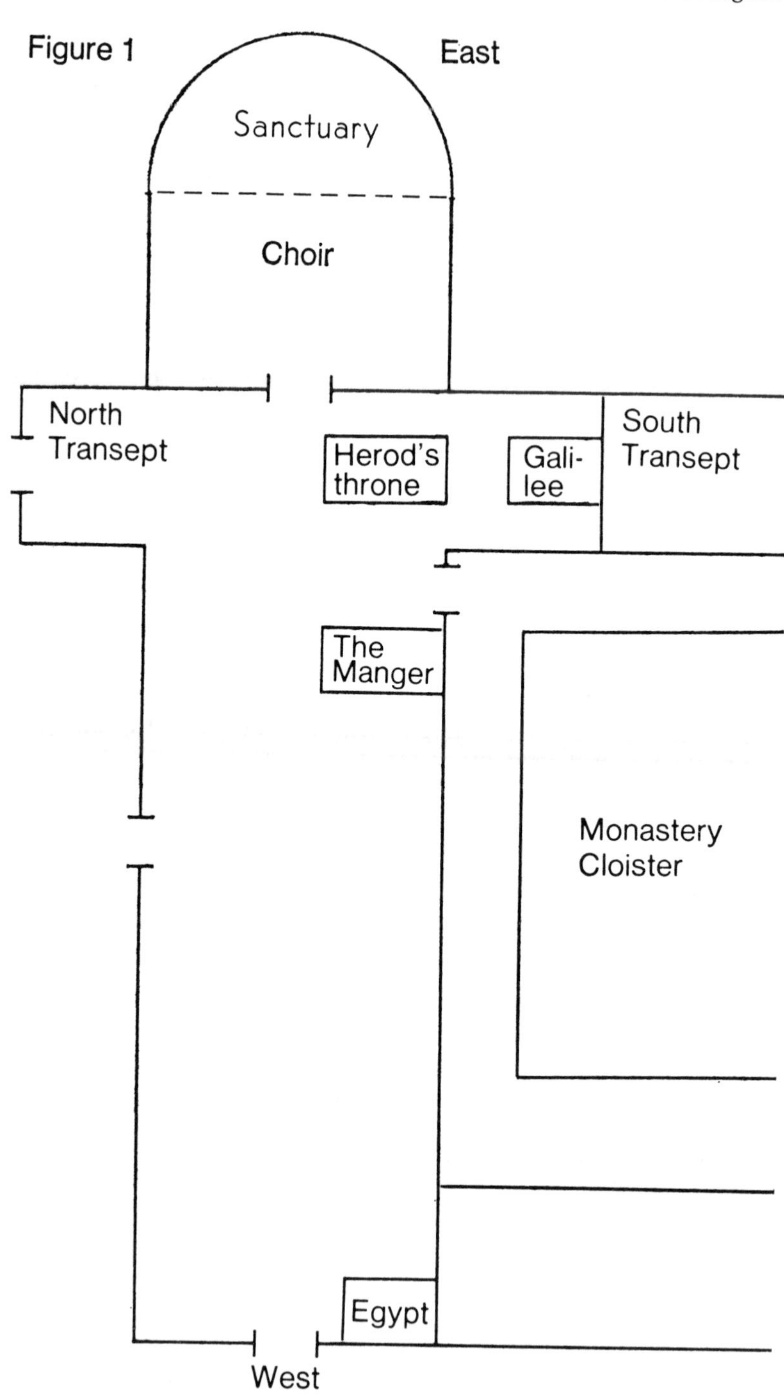
Figure 1
East
Sanctuary
Choir
North Transept
Herod's throne
Galilee
South Transept
The Manger
Monastery Cloister
Egypt
West

passes among the congregation of "people" in the nave as the play begins, the action soon shifts to the sepulcher and choir where most of the significant action of this play is located. How much of the central mysteries of this play can the congregation see and hear? Earlier *quem quaeritis* ceremonials, devised for monastic brethren alone, take place comfortably and naturally in the choir area of the church; now that a congregation is present, what are we to suppose about sight lines and the like? We are dealing with an early church, lacking the elaborate choir screen of later Gothic churches, and yet, as we shall see, these Fleury plays repeatedly refer to the entrance way from the nave into the choir, suggesting a marked sense of separation between the two areas. Architectural evidence too indicates that sanctuary and choir were invariably separated by some means from the nave, though sometimes by a low screen or railing that allowed the choir to be seen.[11] Accordingly, we find evidence in the Fleury plays strongly suggesting that the witnessing of dramatic action in the choir from the nave did indeed present some difficulties but was not impossible if staging arrangements took this problem into account. We shall see repeated indications that those who mounted plays at Fleury were not unaware of the problem, and sought with some success for a solution. They did not give up the choir as a playing area, but instead struck a meaningful balance between highly visible action in the nave and more concealed action in the choir and sanctuary.

In the Visit to the Sepulcher which we are currently examining, the devisers of the play begin by making visible to the congregation the part of the action most directly pertinent to lay persons: the procession of the three Marys to the sepulcher. This portion of the *Visitatio* takes place in the nave and is considerably expanded, in comparison with earlier and more cloistered *quem quaeritis* ceremonials, by the fervent and elaborate laments of the three women. The relevance of their laments for worshipers in the nave is evident in the Marys' role as vicarious mourners and seekers after comfort. The three singers process through the congregation, "vested in imitation of the three Marys," going forward "haltingly and as though sorrowful," presumably carrying thuribles representing the spices with which they intend to anoint Christ's body. Their journey from west to east is one of symbolic meaning for the congregation, who thereby participate with the Marys in a journey of faith and eschew the example of the faithless Jewish congregation deplored in the Marys' chant. The communal opening of the play teaches the congregation the way to Christ's Resurrection.

Once the Marys have entered into the choir *(in chorum)*, on the other hand, the rest of this traditional dramatic ceremonial takes place exclusively in the choir and sanctuary, even if the performers remain aware at times of the need for ocular demonstration of mysteries *ad populum* and *ad plebem*. Some of the action cannot have been very visible from the nave, just as congregations at Mass were accustomed to being unable to see much of the relevant action. The sepulcher, near the altar, must evidently be large enough for the disciples Peter and John to enter it: "*Let them . . . go quickly to the sepulchre as if running, but . . . let the elder, that is to say Peter . . . enter at once; and afterwards let John enter.*" This unambiguous rubric indicates the use of a large *sepulchrum Domini*, like those at Aquilèa Cathedral in the eleventh century and Augsburg in the twelfth,[12] or perhaps a wooden-framed temporary structure hung with rich fabrics and providing ample space for entry, rather than the smaller niches in the north wall of the chancel common in England from the thirteenth century.[13] Even though the disciples do not sing until they have "come forth from within" *(inde exierint)*, wondering aloud at the marvels they have seen, their discovery is a significant action more easily witnessed by the choir than the congregation. Even more strikingly, Mary Magdalene is soon addressed by two angels seated "within the sepulchre" *(infra sepulchrum)*. Sung dialogue from within the *sepulchrum Domini* may have been audible throughout the church, but as stage action it remains secret. The subsequent encounter between Mary and Christ as gardener takes place at the mouth of the sepulcher, as does Christ's final appearance splendidly "vested in a white dalmatic, adorned with a white infula, a costly phylacterium on his head, having a cross with a standard in his right hand, a garment woven of gold in the left hand." The central experience, the *anagnorisis*, of this play, as in earlier ceremonials, is shared primarily by the choir. Lay witnesses are appealed to at times as *socii*, but their involvement remains intermittent and partly obscured.

In the dual staging impulse of this play, toward inclusive demonstration in the nave and secret monastic celebration in the choir, one senses an imperfectly resolved conflict of aims. The issues of the conflict are well defined, and help elucidate a growing sense of what a lay audience might do at dramatic presentations in a monastic church. The laity were included as witnesses of the good news of Christ's Resurrection, but were excluded from close inspection of the sacred event itself. In many continental churches at this time (although England was more permissive in this regard), the laity were not permitted to see the *Elevatio*, the ceremonial reenactment of the Resurrection itself; their participation came afterwards, as those to whom the meaning and reality of Christ's Resurrection needed to be explained.[14] Especially in monastic churches on pilgrimage routes, where laity were often in the church building, barriers became necessary to guard the choir against intrusion during the singing of daily services by the monastic community alone.[15] The Fleury *Visitatio* nicely reflects an interest in instructing the laity as congregation while at the same time limiting their participation in the most sacred mysteries associated with the altar and the sanctuary. The play reaches out in fellowship of witnessing, yet holds back at the very center.

The Fleury Service for Representing Herod, evidently designed for performance at the end of Matins on Epiphany, January 6, in commemoration of the coming of the Magi and the revelation of Christ to the Gentiles, appropriately makes still more ambitious use of the entire church space, since Christmas is a feast of incarnation aimed at the whole Christian community. The laity have always enjoyed a sense of participation in the quintessentially human event of the birth of a child who is also God, and the favorite stories of Christmas are those of witnessing by ordinary shepherds and by kings from diverse lands. Accordingly, the play makes use of all parts of the nave as well as the sanctuary, and exploits vertical dimensions as well. Angels appear from on high, perhaps from a gallery or simply from the slightly elevated area of the sanctuary,[16] at critical points to direct the action below on earth. They appear at the start of the play to sing *Gloria in excelsis Deo* to the shepherds who, thoroughly frightened (*perterriti*), cower on the ground and then, arising, proceed to the manger. Evidently, for reasons to appear soon, this action of the cowering shepherds must occur in the nave in the midst of the congregation. Later, at the very end of the play in fact, an angel appears "from above" to warn the Magi in their sleep to return to their native lands unespied of Herod. Their lying asleep, evidently on the floor of the nave in front of the manger *(ante praesepe)*, must also take place among the congregation. We might suppose that falling or lying prostrate among the spectators in one portion of the nave would create sight line problems, and indeed may well have done so, but we can scarcely doubt that such actions on the floor took place. We will find similar prostrations, often at a crucial dramatic moment, in the Slaughter of the Innocents and in the Conversion of St. Paul. A small congregation, able to move from place to place, would make such dramatic techniques more feasible.

The extensive use of the nave in this play provides the congregation a significant role, for the journeys of the Magi and of the shepherds are once again journeys of faith by means of which those present affirm their commitment to the newborn Christ. Some journeys take place in the midst of the witnessing congregation. The shepherds, who are seemingly in the nave when they hear the angelic announcement at the commencement of the play, proceed through the nave to the manger which, according to a rubric or stage direction, "will have been readied at [one of] the doors of the church." (I follow Karl Young here in taking *quod ad januas monasterii paratum erit* to mean not at the outer doors of the monastery itself, but at a door connecting the monastery with the church.[17]) When the shepherds arrive at the manger, seemingly never having left the nave, they "invite the people standing around" them *(populum circumstantem)* to adore the Christ child. The spatial closeness of the congregation to this acting station emphasizes the role of the ordinary people, at the time of Christ's historical birth and at the present moment, in witnessing Christ's Resurrection.

The Magi, meanwhile, who first meet one another in the eastern part of the church, "before the altar" (*ante altare*), soon proceed on a journey from east to west, following the star to the entrance of the choir *(ad ostium chori)*. Whether the star moves overhead by means of wires from east to west, as at Limoges,[18] or is borne as a symbol before the Magi, it provides both theatrical splendor and a symbolic journey of incarnation; the star proceeds from altar and choir, in the most sacred area of the church, to the nave, where Christ's humble manger is to be found among the people who dwell in this world. As they arrive at the entrance to the choir, where they are now presumably visible to the congregation, the Magi address passers-by as citizens of Jerusalem. These citizens, who do not answer, may well be members of the congregation; if so, we have another instance in which the members of the congregation not only see and hear but are given symbolic roles in the drama itself. The Magi's encounters with Herod evidently occur in full view of the congregation. At the very end of the play, after their visit to Herod and to the manger, the Magi return into the choir to signify their journey homeward, having evaded Herod as they come up the nave "by another way" *(per aliam viam)* than that by which they first traveled to the manger.

Thus, although the Magi assemble and eventually disappear into the choir where their movements may seem, from the congregation's point of view, mysterious, the central part of this elaborate play has taken place in full view of the congregation, and indeed in its very midst. The continued presence of two scaffolds or *sedes* makes possible a dramaturgic technique of visual juxtaposition, through which the congregation is invited to see a meaningful contrast between worldly insolence and spiritual innocence. Herod's platform and the manger, both visible throughout the play and both manned by the performers prior to the commencement of the action, are perceived to be very different from one another because the staging arrangement insists on a visual comparison. In each acting station a king is worshiped and deferred to; each king receives the visitation of the Magi. Herod's platform is, however, fraught with symbols of power and arrogance. It must be a large acting platform, since it needs to accommodate not only Herod but his son, his man at arms, his companions dressed as gallants *(in habitu juvenili)*, the scribes who are summoned from a separate room where they have been gotten ready, and of course the Magi. That Herod's acting station is a platform cannot be flatly asserted as fact, but it can be strongly inferred by the elaborateness of the processions to and from this acting station, by the likelihood that the manger is a platformed station constructed in the guise of a crèche, and perhaps most tellingly by the parallel we find in other Fleury plays, such as the Conversion of St. Paul and the Son of Getron, for the location of raised acting platforms in the nave near the entrance to the choir.

The emphatic use of procession in this Christmas drama of Herod, as in the more or less contemporary Play of Daniel from Beauvais and in the Christmas and Passion Plays from Benediktbeuern, bespeaks an interest of twelfth-century church drama (at least at certain centers of learning) in colorful symbolic stage movement aimed at wider inclusion of a congregation. The Fleury *Playbook* is notable for including such movement in several plays. In the Herod play, when the shepherds have heard the good news of Christ's birth, they "proceed" *(procedant)* to the manger, singing "Let us go now even unto Bethlehem," etc. Evidently they pass along through the nave and among the congregation as they sing, like the three Marys in the Fleury Visit to the Sepulcher. The Magi, appearing in procession "each from his own corner as if from his own land"—that is, from various parts of the church—gather in front of the altar and then proceed following the star to the choir entrance and thence into the nave, singing "Let us go therefore and seek him," etc. The parallel between this procession and that of the shepherds is unmistakable, and in both the congregation is invited to see the procession as expressive of its own search for the newborn Christ. Once Herod has espied the Magi from his station, a regular flurry of processions ensues as the King dispatches his ambassadors to escort the Magi to him. The ambassadors sing in procession as they return to the Magi, "They are kings of the Arabs," etc. And so the processions continue, through the nave and among the spectators, as the Magi go to Bethlehem, encounter the shepherds, and return another way to their homes. The play is almost a continuous journey in which processional movement takes on the symbolic significance of discovery or revelation. Appropriately, movement is almost invariably accompanied by processional singing.

Another prominent feature of staging in this play, one that again gives evidence of a growing sense of theatrical consciousness at Fleury, is simultaneity of action. A constantly recurring word in the rubrics is "meanwhile," *interim*. "Then," *tunc*, is also a common first word of rubrics in these plays, but *interim* occurs with notable frequency. For example, while the shepherds visit the manger and invite the people standing around to worship Christ, meanwhile, *interim*, the Magi are to begin their separate journeys toward a common meeting place at the altar. These simultaneous actions occur in widely separated portions of the church. Later, while Herod is dismissing the Magi and sending them on their way to Bethlehem, meanwhile, *interim*, the shepherds return from the manger, singing and rejoicing as they go. This "meanwhile" indeed prompts us to ask an important staging question: what have the shepherds been doing while the Magi have been detained and questioned by Herod? Perhaps they can remain at the manger for a while, worshiping silently while the center of dramatic interest shifts to Herod's scaffold; but the "meanwhile" also suggests some significant overlap. It is important to remember that Herod and his party, the shepherds, and the Magi are all simultaneously visible throughout most of this play, and are at times simultaneously in motion. Imagine, if you will, Herod and his son threatening the departing Magi with angry gestures while the Magi go on their way and the shepherds make their way back from the manger—three centers of attention at once, meaningfully juxtaposed by their simultaneous presence in the church space.

One other striking feature of staging in this Herod play tends to the opposite extreme but is no less effective as a means of directing the congregation's attention to the cosmic events taking place in its midst: periods of silence accompany an action that is mimed at some considerable length. When Herod's scribes are brought forth to see him, for example, they "turn over the leaves of the book for a long while [*diu*], and at length [*tandem*], as if having found the prophecy," they tell Herod of the newborn Christ. Again, when the Magi go to sleep in front of the manger after having worshiped Christ, they remain asleep "until [*donec*] an angel, appearing from above, warns them in their sleep to return into their country by another way." Such moments focus on the crucial process of revelation of divine truth, and may be part of a more inclusive pattern of contemplation and silent worship that is to continue at the manger even when the action is centered elsewhere.

The Fleury Slaughter of the Innocents, designed for Innocents Day on December 28, continues a number of staging practices of the Herod play in its pronounced use of processional movement, juxtaposition, and simultaneous action, most of which is designed as impressive spectacle in the nave to be witnessed by a congregation. The play begins with a procession of the Innocents themselves, "rejoicing through the monastery church" *(per monasterium).* I follow Young and Arnold Williams in supposing that the Innocents enter from the monastery cloister into the nave of the church proper. They are led by the lamb bearing the cross. Meanwhile, *interim*, a man at arms greets Herod on his throne, located presumably in the nave as in the Herod play. *Meanwhile* an angel appears to Joseph, presumably at the manger, warning him to flee into Egypt. Joseph and Mary go in procession through the nave to Egypt, located possibly near the west door, singing "Egypt, weep not." *Meanwhile* on Herod's throne the man at arms gives Herod notice that the

Magi have fooled him by returning to their homes via another road. The technique of juxtaposition repeatedly opposes vengeful anger to beleaguered innocence, stressing the paradoxical spiritual triumph of the meek over their oppressors. Clearly Herod's throne and the procession of Joseph and Mary with the Christ child are of simultaneous visual and auditory interest. Yet what of the Innocents all this while? Well, meanwhile, *interim*, the Innocents, "walking hitherto in procession behind the lamb, sing repeatedly 'To the hallowed lamb slain for us, To Christ, we consecrate, under this banner of light, The splendor of the Father,' " and so on. The phrase *sing repeatedly (decantent)* leaves open the possibility at least that the Innocents sing this hymn again and again while Herod is reacting so violently to the news of the Magi's eluding him, and then decides to kill all innocent children as an act of vengeance and as a way of possibly slaying Christ as well. (Liturgical practice generally allows for the extending of hymns, sequences, conductus, and other strophic, "extra-liturgical" music to fit whatever activity is going on; hymns and sequences always accompany such activity.) Similarly, the processional singing of the Innocents may also continue while the journey of the Holy Family to Egypt is being completed. The nave of the church is busy indeed with movement.

Once the Innocents have been slaughtered by Herod's soldiers, however, the pace suddenly slows. The children's mothers, having appeared from some unspecified place, fall down weeping on their children's bodies. Rachel, accompanied by two comforters, stands over the children and falls at times to earth. Instead of colorful processions and bustling action performed on raised platforms, we encounter, in the second half of this play, stasis and the kind of problems with sight lines presumably encountered when performers fall to the floor of a church surrounded by a standing congregation. Despite what seem to us practical difficulties, the contrast between movement and stasis must have been dramatically effective, adding great poignancy to Rachel's sorrowing. In any case, no further movement occurs at all until the final moments of the play, when the children rise and go in procession into the choir, while simultaneously (*dum haec fiunt*, while these things are done), and in pantomime, King Herod dies and is replaced by his son Archelaus. Choir area and sanctuary, associated as always with heavenly mystery, receive the souls of the slaughtered children while in the nave the worldly demise of Herod occupies a focus of attention. His death is not the only stage action in the nave during the concluding moments of the play, however. Meanwhile, *interim*, Joseph and Mary receive angelic assurances of their safety and return with Christ from Egypt into Galilee. Once again, the three centers of dramatic interest in the play are simultaneously in use, either through procession or through action on Herod's scaffold. The acting style of the play thus returns at the end to where it began, in processional movement and simultaneously juxtaposed images of worldliness and innocence.

Both the Herod play and the Slaughter of the Innocents present relatively less action or song in the choir area than does the Visitatio Sepulchri, even though the choir area retains its critical symbolic spatial significance. The Magi gather in the east, before the altar, and for a few moments they must be heard and seen from within the choir, before they begin their journey westward. When they emerge into the nave, they find simultaneously juxtaposed the worldly kingdom of Herod and the otherworldly kingdom of Christ (the manger). The Magi's departure into the choir at the end signifies their return homeward. In the Slaughter of the Innocents, the choir area is used only at the very end, as the Innocents depart in joy to their heavenly reward, having been summoned by Christ's comforting words, "Suffer the little ones to come unto me." They leave behind them the edifying spectacle of Herod's demise and the safe return of the Holy Family out of Egypt. In both plays as well, an elevated acting space (such as a gallery or pulpit) is reserved for angelic messengers. The nave in these plays, occupied by the congregation, takes on symbolic meaning as the arena of the world, into which innocents are born and from which they depart into heaven. The world is depicted as a place of varied human activity, of bustle and pride but also of grief and sacrifice. It is above all a place of journey and discovery.

Two plays of the Fleury *Playbook* intended for other occasions in the church calendar, the St. Nicholas play representing how the saint freed the son of Getron from his imprisonment by King Marmorinus and the Conversion of St. Paul, occupy the nave of the church with processions and simultaneously beheld actions in a way that supports the idea of a growing theatrical consciousness. Again the congregation is included so that it may be a witness of divine revelation. Each play features a contrasting vision of two cities, as Thomas Campbell notes, one heavenly and one worldly.[19] In each play, the two cities are simultaneously visible throughout, evidently in the front part of the nave at the crossing of the transepts. The two cities are somewhat distant from one another in each play, just as Herod's throne and the manger are separated by considerable space in the Christmas plays just examined.

In the St. Paul play we see Jerusalem and Damascus. Each scaffold is further subdivided to provide five seats or *sedes* in all and fairly elaborate action, including the lowering of St. Paul and his disciples to the ground in a hamper from some high place, as if from a wall *(Saulus cum discipulis suis in sporta ab aliquo alto loco, quasi a muro, ad terram demittatur).* It is on the journey from one city to another, presumably on the floor of the nave, that St. Paul falls to the ground and experiences his blinding conversion. The difficulty with sight lines, worrisome to us as we try to imagine such action on the church floor among standing spectators, is evidently of less concern to those who produced this play; just as with the sleeping Magi or the cowering shepherds in the Herod play, or the fallen babes and their mothers in the Slaughter of the Innocents, action on the church floor is encouraged seemingly because of the immediacy of contact between the actors and those who are nearby. Even if not everyone can see or hear well, the action takes place in the midst of the congregation in a way that emphasizes the witnessing of divine revelation.

The stage arrangement of the St. Nicholas play about the son of Getron calls for a similar juxtaposition of *sedes* and similar use of the space in between for processional movement. The opening rubric tells us that on one side is to be readied in a suitable place *(in competenti loco)* the kingdom of King Marmorinus, with the King himself sitting in a high seat and attended by armed followers as though in his kingdom. In another place *(in alio loco)* is Excoranda, the city of Getron, and in it Getron, his wife Euphrosina, his comforters, and his son Adeodatus. In Excoranda too, in the eastern part of the city *(ab orientali parte civitatis Excorandae)*—that is, nearest the choir with its symbolic value of divine presence—is the Church of St. Nicholas, in which the boy Adeodatus is to be seized by King Marmorinus' soldiers. As in other twelfth-century liturgical dramas, all this is simultaneously visible and fully ready before the play begins. Simultaneous action abounds: at the start, for example, the King dispatches his soldiers to conquer any who resist his worldly authority while at the same time *(interim)* a throng of clerics *(multitudine clericorum)* gather at the Church of St. Nicholas for a festival. The staging of the raid on Excoranda, then, and the seizing of the boy Adeotatus involve movement from one scaffold to another and a good deal of violent, colorful action.

One effective theatrical device growing out of the simultaneous presentation of two contrastive acting stations—a device that turns up later, for example, in the fifteenth-century *Mary Magdalene*—is the staging of two banquets, at once parallel and yet very unlike one another. When Adeodatus' mother Euphrosina discovers that her son is missing, she goes out from the church and proceeds homeward to prepare a table with bread and wine from which the clerics and poor may refresh themselves. Before this repast has been completed—specifically, when the clerics and the poor have been served and have begun to eat—Marmorinus is heard on his scaffold expressing a desire to eat and drink and be waited on by his new captive. The contrast is edifying; a cosmic battle is underway between the pagan Apollo and the true Christian God, and St. Nicholas' rewarding of those who feed the hungry is a demonstration of God's caring for good men and women. Wine is symbolic of gluttony as well as of the sacrament. Although King Marmorinus is not destroyed as is Herod—indeed, one wonders what happens to King Marmorinus at the end of this play, when the boy suddenly disappears from his side—the triumph of the heavenly city over the worldly city has once more taken on dramatic form.

Other Fleury St. Nicholas plays, though generally simple in staging requirements, are consistent in their use of symbolic spatial effects with those already examined. The play of the Three *Clerici* or Scholars requires the open space of the *platea* or church floor to represent the highway outside an inn, while a scaffold presumably presents the inn itself containing a public room and perhaps the bedroom as well.[20] The motifs of journey and banqueting reinforce a visual contrast between worldly danger and divine protection; the saint is dressed as a traveler, like the scholars who are murdered in their beds, and he refuses to partake of tainted hospitality at the table *(ad mensam)* of the murderers. As in the play about the son of Getron, the table betokens charity in its true and false guise. For the play of the Image of St. Nicholas, two *sedes* are needed, one for the Jew's house with its treasure-laden chest and the other for the robbers' retreat where they are confronted by the saint as they are dividing the spoils. The staging plan once again affords visual contrast between two stations, one of them containing the image of the saint. Simultaneity of action *(Interim veniant Fures)* and travel between the two locations reinforce visual and thematic contrast. The play of the Three Daughters provides few staging indications other than the throwing of gold, presumably as though from some outside location into the *sedes* occupied by the father and his three daughters.

In all the Fleury plays we have been examining, the dramatic conflict of world and spirit takes place in the nave. The sanctuary, always close at hand, is a place of divine mystery: it is in the east, and is the place of Christ's Resurrection or of the Innocents' being gathered to their heavenly reward. St. Nicholas' church is located there. Movement from west to east takes the play toward its central event of *anagnorisis* in several cases, even if at the expense of visibility for the congregation in the nave. We see this movement once again in the Fleury Raising of Lazarus. One scaffold or *sedes* is needed to represent both the house of Simon the Leper and the house of Lazarus and his sisters in Bethany *(Domus vero ipsius Simonis, ipso remoto, efficiatur quasi Betthania)*, furnished with tables and benches to suggest a dwelling.[21] This structure seems intended for the nave, for much of the action occurs here and Jesus and his disciples approach the house of Simon across the *platea* or open space in the church *(Post haec veniat Jhesus in plateam cum Discipulis)*. Jesus must be led into this dwelling and placed at the table where Mary Magdalene is to fall at his feet. Galilee and Jerusalem are also represented in the staging of the action, and movement is visually important as messengers are sent to conduct Jesus from Galilee to Bethany. The last focus of action is the tomb where Lazarus is brought back to life. It is referred to as *sepulchrum* and *monumentum*, and seems identified with the Easter sepulcher. Once again, then, dramatic action seemingly moves away from the congregation toward the relative seclusion of the sanctuary. However unfamiliar the practice may seem to us, it is common in the Fleury plays, and it does signify a movement from human witnessing to the ultimate mystery of incarnation and miraculous return to life.

Even in their sacred finalities, however, the Fleury plays seemingly do not forget the need of the congregation to know something of the event and to be a partaker even at the kind of distance the laity could expect to find in a monastic church. The Fleury *Peregrinus* play once again locates its initial dramatic conflict in the nave, at Emmaus, evidently in accord with long-established tradition associating Emmaus with the west door of the church or center of the nave.[22] The opening rubric says only that the two disciples to whom Jesus reveals himself are to proceed to a suitable spot *(procedant duo a competenti loco)*, but the language points clearly enough to the nave, for only after Christ's vanishing from them are the disciples to enter into the choir *(Venientibus illis in chorum)*. Certainly the climactic action of Christ's appearance to all the disciples takes place in the choir; members of the choir serve as the disciples, and repeatedly the rubrics specify that Christ leaves them by means of a door of the choir and later reenters into the same space *(dum chorum intraverit)*. Yet for all this insistent focus on performance in a part of the church traditionally reserved from secular gaze, the rubrics do specify that the disciples are to lead Christ *per chorum ut videatur a populo*, through the choir in order that he may be seen by the whole congregation. This action occurs after Christ has bidden his disciples teach the Gospel in foreign lands; in other words, the emphasis is once again on witnessing, on reaching out to those who must be told of Christ's Resurrection. The rubric suggests that, though seeing from the nave into the choir was designedly not easy, the devisers of the dramatization foresaw the necessity of "blocking" their action in such a way as to share the announcement of the church's ministry with all those who are present. This sharing takes on major significance when we consider the broader question of the complex relation between ritual and drama; since rites in traditional societies are usually performed by a specifically defined group and are not witnessed by a more general public,[23] the movement in the drama we are studying toward inclusion of a congregation can be interpreted as an essential condition of dramatic performance rather than of ritual celebration.

A case can be made, then, for a common staging tradition in the Fleury plays, one not peculiar to it as distinguished from other centers of twelfth-century drama but instead attuned to a new movement in church drama generally toward meaningful spectacle for a congregation. To an extent we find remarkable, this drama makes use of simultaneously visible scaffolds, processional movement from one scaffold to another amidst the spectators, and bustling simultaneous action interspersed with long moments of quiet dramatic focus on one spot and a small group of characters who frequently throw themselves to the floor despite whatever difficulties in sight lines these movements may have created for some spectators. These techniques of twelfth-century drama are all the more momentous because of their significance for the religious drama of the following three hundred years, certainly not excluding the cycle plays, saints' plays, and large-scale moralities of the fourteenth and fifteenth centuries.

NOTES

1 Cf. Thomas P. Campbell, "Augustine's Concept of the Two Cities in the Fleury *Playbook*," below, pp. 82-99, who argues for a thematic continuity among the Fleury plays, based on St. Augustine's *The City of God*. Scholars disagree as to whether Fleury was the actual site of performance. Fletcher Collins, Jr., "The Home of the Fleury Playbook," above, pp. 26-34, believes that it is, while Julia Bolton Holloway, "Monks and Plays," *Studies in Medieval and Renaissance Teaching*, 10, No. 1 (1983), 10-12, believes that the manuscript came to Fleury from elsewhere, possibly even from England; citing Solange Corbin, "Le Manuscrit 201 d'Orléans: Drames liturgiques dits de Fleury," *Romania*, 74 (1953), 1-43, and Diane Marie Dolan, "The Notation of Orléans Bibliothèque Municipale, MS. 201," *Studia Anselmiana*, 85 (1982) 279-88, who notes that the neumes are not of Fleury.

2 Bernard Beckerman, *Shakespeare at the Globe, 1599-1609* (New York: Macmillan, 1962); John Styan, *Shakespeare's Stagecraft* (Cambridge: Cambridge Univ. Press, 1967); and Ann Pasternak Slater, *Shakespeare the Director* (Totowa, N. J.: Barnes and Noble, 1982). See also Alan C. Dessen, *Elizabethan Drama and the Viewers' Eye* (Chapel Hill: Univ. of North Carolina Press, 1977), and my forthcoming *Action Is Eloquence: Shakespeare's Language of Gesture* (Cambridge, Mass.: Harvard Univ. Press, 1984).

3 Among the pioneers of the method are R. A. Foakes, "Suggestions for a New Approach to Shakespeare's Imagery," *Shakespeare Survey*, 5 (1952), 81-92; Alan Downer, "The Life of Our Design: The Function of Imagery in the Poetic Drama," *Hudson Review*, 2 (1949), 242-63; and Maurice Charney, *Shakespeare's Roman Plays: The Function of Imagery in the Drama* (Cambridge, Mass.: Harvard Univ. Press, 1961).

4 Recent staging approaches to medieval church drama include William Tydeman, *The Theatre in the Middle Ages* (Cambridge: Cambridge Univ. Press, 1978), and Fletcher Collins, Jr., *The Production of Medieval Church Music-Drama* (Charlottesville: The University Press of Virginia, 1972). Karl Young, *The Drama of the Medieval Church* (Oxford: Clarendon Press, 1933), 2 vols., discusses matters of staging in the various Fleury plays, though he does not consider the matter of stage gesture as figurative language.

5 Citations are from David Bevington, ed., *Medieval Drama* (Boston: Houghton Mifflin, 1975), for plays included in that collection, and from Young, ed., *The Drama of the Medieval Church*, for other church dramas. On the question of ritualized gesture as conceptual rather than a naturalistic imitation of nature, see E. H. Gombrich, "Ritualized Gesture and Expression in Art," *Philosophical Transactions of the Royal Society of London*, Ser. B, Biological Sciences, 251 (1966), 393-401.

6 Mary Magdalene, for example, not infrequently is seen first as one of the three Marys at the tomb, assured by the angels of Christ's Resurrection, and then almost immediately afterwards as the grieving Mary who encounters Christ as a "gardener" whom she asks for information concerning the whereabouts of Christ's body. Despite her earlier having been told of Christ's victory over death, she now fears that his body has been taken by unknown persons. There is no explanation as to her renewed doubt concerning the Resurrection, nor does the compiler of the text appear to feel that any explanation is necessary.

7 Tydeman, *The Theatre in the Middle Ages*, pp. 55-56.

8 See Fletcher Collins, *Medieval Church Music-Dramas: A Repertory of Complete Plays* (Charlottesville: Univ. Press of Virginia, 1976) and my review of Collins' *The Production of Medieval Church Music Drama*, in *Modern Philology*, 72 (1975), 287-90. The extent of Collins' conflation in the *Visitatio* is in fact small, nor is conflation employed in other play texts in the volume; my report in an earlier version of this present chapter, in *Comparative Drama*, 18 (1984), 97-117, gives an erroneous and misleading impression for which I wish to apologize.

9 See Dunbar H. Ogden, "The Use of Architectural Space in Medieval Music-Drama," *Comparative Drama*, 8 (1974), 63-76.

10 Campbell, "The Two Cities in the Fleury Playbook," links this idea of community of belief to the sermons of St. Augustine.

11 Tydeman, *The Theatre in the Middle Ages*, p. 52, and Ogden, "The Use of Architectural Space," pp. 63-76.

12 Tydeman, *The Theatre in the Middle Ages*, p. 54.

13 Pamela Sheingorn, "The *Sepulchrum Domini*: A Study in Art and Liturgy," *Studies in Iconography*, 4 (1978), 37-60.

14 Ibid., pp. 50-51.

15 Tydeman, *The Theatre in the Middle Ages*, p. 53.

16 Ibid., p. 56.

17 Young, *Drama of the Medieval Church*, II, 89.

18 Ogden, "The Use of Architectural Space," pp. 63-76, and Tydeman, *The Theatre in the Middle Ages*, pp. 167-68, who also cites Rouen in the thirteenth century and presents the theories of Gustave Cohen and Fletcher Collins as to how the star may have been moved.

19 Campbell, "Augustine's Concept of the Two Cities and the Fleury Playbook" pp. 82-99, above.

20 Tydeman, *The Theatre in the Middle Ages*, p. 59, and Young, *Drama of the Medieval Church*, II, 334.

21 Tydeman, *The Theatre in the Middle Ages*, p. 58.

22 Young, *Drama of the Medieval Church*, I, 475, and Tydeman, *The Theatre in the Middle Ages*, p. 55.

23 Richard F. Hardin, "'Ritual' in Recent Criticism: The Elusive Sense of Community," *PMLA*, 98 (1983), 846-62, citing Anthony Graham-White, "'Ritual' in Contemporary Theatre Criticism," *Educational Theater Journal*, 28 (1976), 318-24.

Augustine's Concept of the Two Cities and the Fleury *Playbook*

Thomas P. Campbell

The collection of plays found in MS. Orléans 201 is one of the great achievements of medieval literature. Individual dramas—the *Play of Herod,* the *Son of Getron, Lazarus*—have become familiar to students of medieval drama partially because of their successful production in modern times. Yet, little critical attention has been paid to the collection as a whole. In fact, we are very far from knowing why it was brought together, or even where it was originally written. The purpose of this essay is to present an assessment of its literary value and to suggest some principles of coherence that apply to the group of plays collected in the manuscript.

Despite its uniqueness, the Fleury Playbook has been seen by most scholars as basically a compilation of liturgical plays available from other sources. According to such thinking, a redactor, or redactors, simply copied versions of the plays, perhaps with slight modification, and bound them into the book. But why would so many plays—more than exist in any other manuscript of Latin drama—have been collected? And why from so many diverse traditions? I would like to suggest that, contrary to the prevailing view, the Fleury plays form a coherent and distinct group, and that a clear purpose guided their selection and presentation. I propose that the playwright who was responsible for the Fleury plays was strongly influenced by the Augustinian doctrine of the Two Cities, and that he modified, adapted, or created dramas which illustrate this concern.

Augustine articulated the theme of these two communities in *The City of God* thus:

> What we see, then, is that two societies have issued from two kinds of love. Worldly society has flowered from a selfish love which dared to despise even God, whereas the communion of saints is rooted in a love of God that is ready to trample on self. The city of man seeks the praise of men, whereas the height of glory for the other is to hear God in the witness of conscience.[1]

And, although man was created capable of achieving the City of God through his own merits, he has fallen because of sin into bodily corruption:

> It was surely enough that on that day [i.e., the day on which Adam and Eve ate the fruit] their nature became defective and was changed for the worse, and that, by being justly deprived of the tree of life, they became subject to that necessity of bodily death, which is now for us innate.[2]

It is not until Christ established a "model" through his Resurrection that man was delivered from the worldly death he had created for himself.[3]

This philosophical interpretation of history established by Augustine became the predominant form of Christian historiography during the Middle Ages. In fact, the Universal History, tracing the conflicting fates of good and evil men beginning with Adam and continuing to the date of composition, is found in every era from Fulgentius in the early sixth century to the end of the Middle Ages.[4] Nor was the primary importance of Augustine's work forgotten. Charlemagne, according to his biographer Einhardt, read the *City of God* daily; and by the mid twelfth century, the work became the very basis of the most highly regarded medieval history, the *Chronica* of Otto, Bishop of Freising. As Otto acknowledges in his Prologue:

> Sequor autem in hoc opere preclara potissimum Augustinum et Orosium ecclesiae lumina eorumque de fontibus ea, quae ad rem propositumve pertinent, haurire cogitavi. Quorum alter de gloriosae civitatis Dei exortu sive progressu debitisque finibus, quomodo inter mundi cives semper profecerit, quique eius cives vel principes quibus principum seu civium seculi temporibus extiterint, acutissime disertissimeque disputavit.

> (In this work I follow most of all those illustrious lights of the Church, Augustine and Orosius, and have planned to draw from those fountains what is pertinent to my theme and my purpose. The one of these has discoursed most keenly and eloquently on the origin and progress of the glorious City of God and its ordained limits, setting forth how it has ever spread among the citizens of the world, and showing which of its citizens or princes

> stood forth preeminent in the various epochs of the princes or citizens of the world.)[5]

Nor should the influence of the *City of God* be restricted only to its specific citation in medieval histories. Whatever the exact origins of the *Quem queritis* dialogue, it seems quite clear that the earliest medieval plays imply an Augustinian interpretation of the Resurrection. O. B. Hardison, Jr., in his influential *Christian Rite and Christian Drama in the Middle Ages,* has pointed out a number of phrases in Augustine's sermons which emphasize the creation of a "community of belief" through the Resurrection which leads to Salvation.[6] Moreover, Augustine dwells upon the idea at some length in the last book of the *City of God.*[7] In fact, the very phrasing of the *Quem queritis,* in which the angelic messenger is referred to as *celicola* (heaven dweller) and the Marys as *Christicolae* (followers of Christ), reinforces a communal identity. That the altar was treated allegorically and dramatically as the tomb of Christ is further proof that the contemporary believer and the actor portraying the historical figure were seen as part of a single community who together celebrated the Savior's victory over death. Later amplifications of the Easter *Quem queritis,* the more complex *Visitatio* plays, contain many specific examples of a close interrelationship between the historical figures and the viewing congregation. In several plays, the Marys turn toward the choir to announce *Surrexit Dominus,* or to display to them the empty grave clothes as ocular proof of the Resurrection.[8]

In light of these observations, it might seem as if the Fleury plays represent simply a logical development of the Two Cities theme. However, the manifestations of this theme in the examples above are merely implicit in the dialogue and action; but such is not the case in the Fleury plays. The Fleury *Visitatio* differs significantly from other versions; every unique addition to the text has some explicit bearing on the theme of the Two Cities. The rubrics of the Fleury *Ad faciendam similitudinem Dominici Sepulcri* instruct the actors to address their comments specifically to the people *("ad plebem," "ad populum")* instead of to the choir, at the same time requiring the showing of the empty gravecloths. The dialogue itself contains several specific references to the Two Cities. The opening procession features several strophic laments sung by each of the three Marys in which they condemn the Jewish nation for putting Christ to death; yet, at the end of the play, they offer reconciliation to these same people:

> Resurrexit hodie Deus Deorum!
> Frustra signas lapidem, plebs Iudeorum.
> Iungere iam populo Christianorum.
> Resurrexit hodie rex angelorum.
> Ducitur de tenebris turba piorum.
> Reseratur aditus regni celorum! (Young, I, 396)
>
> (Today the God of Gods has risen!
> In vain do you seal the stone, Jewish people.
> Join now with the Christian people.
> The king of angels has risen today.
> The throng of the just is led from darkness.
> The entrance to the kingdom of heaven is opened.)[9]

Mary Magdalene sadly laments the disappearance of her Lord; and, even after the apostles have displayed the grave cloths as sufficient proof of Christ's resurrection, she again laments his disappearance; only after discovering that the gardener is Christ does she turn joyfully to announce her realization to the people. To announce Christ's resurrection is to emphasize its communal significance. Hence, until all the visible and verbal proofs of Christ's victory have been assembled—the repeated assurances of the angel, the demonstrations of the empty grave cloths, the specific invitations to the congregation, and the revelation of Christ in the persona of the Gardener—the full celebration of the Resurrection is withheld. The final verses of the Fleury play, with their specific reference to the new community now established by Christ's victory, emphasize the meaning of his Resurrection both historically and liturgically. Their meaning is reinforced by the appearance of the risen Christ, robed in priestly vestments at the very end of the play, calling upon the women to announce his victory to the disciples.[10]

The other Fleury Easter play, the *Peregrinus,* is constructed similarly—a series of three repetitive scenes which emphasize the meaning of the Resurrection. In contrast to other versions of this play, however the Fleury version does not focus upon the obvious symbolism of the pilgrim as a testimony of belief in Christ's Resurrection and to his role as a priest.[11] Rather, the play uniquely personifies his gift of peace in the symbolic breaking of bread, in his appearance to the entire band of disciples, and in his invitation to the doubting Thomas to feel his wounds.[12] To emphasize the extent of his mercy now extended to all mankind as well as the participation of all men in his kingdom, Christ reminds the disciples that his power extends over heaven and earth, and admonishes them to preach the Gospel to all men since *"Qui crediderit et baptizatus fuerit, saluus erit"* (Young, I, 475) ("Whoever believes and is baptized, will be saved"). As if to underline the availability of Christ's saving grace to all men, the play ends with the disciples leading the Savior through the choir, *"ut uideatur a populo"* (Young, I, 475) ("so that he might be seen by the people"), while the Easter hymn *Salve, festa dies* is intoned.

Achieving a dramatic emphasis upon Christ's gift of grace, rather than merely presenting the symbols of his victory, is a typical technique of both Fleury Easter plays which contrasts with all other versions of the *Visitatio* and *Peregrinus*. Both plays repeatedly demonstrate through action and dialogue a literal "community of belief," now actualized by the Savior's victory over death. The community is all-inclusive: the entire congregation and (at least in the *Visitatio*) even the unbelievers are invited to share kinship in the City of God, now made available to all men.

The Fleury Christmas plays—the *Ordo ad representandum Herodem* and *Ad interfectionem puerorum*—add yet another dimension to the community of belief: a visual, scenic portrayal of the City of God and, in contrast, a realistic depiction of the City of Man. As a result, the Fleury Christmas plays even more graphically embody the theme of the Two Cities. In both, representatives of the City of Man—only alluded to in the Easter plays—are depicted. Herod, as a symbol of the earthly tyrant, is given a dominant role; the Epiphany Magi play is even named after him. Herod's throne is represented by a separate scene of rather large proportions, since it must contain a realistic cross-section of worldly society—attendants, advisors, ambassadors, and even young gallants. Although specific directions are vague, the dialogue and action seem to locate Herod's throne at the entrance to the chancel, literally blocking access to the altar. The manger, on the other hand, is clearly placed among the congregation, at one of the church doors.[13] These plays establish more than a physical contrast between the City of God and the City of Man. Both shepherds and Magi, as members of the Heavenly City, address the congregation, inviting them to worship Christ or inquiring where he might be found; the adoration scenes therefore become a locus for all humble believers, both actors and audience, worshipping together.[14]

An important aspect of this contrast between the Two Cities, of course, is the victory of the City of God. In the *Ordo ad representandum Herodem,* Herod's power is represented as impotent rage. Hearing the prophecy testifying to Christ's divinity, the tyrant flings the book to the ground; catching sight of the star guiding the Magi, he can only wave his sword at it; and his attempt to recall the Magi is thwarted by a heavenly angel who warns them to return by another route. The Magi, on the other hand, are guided to the manger and, like the shepherds before them, worship the child. In *Ad interfectionem puerorum,* also known as the *Ordo Rachelis,* Herod orders the slaughter of the children. Already celebrating their participation in the kingdom which they will earn by their deaths, the Innocents are set upon and killed by Herod's soldiers in front of the tyrant's throne. Crying out for vengeance, the children are assured of victory by an angel *"ab excelso"* (Young, II, 112). Rachel, as a symbol not only of the grieving mothers but also of the Virgin who will lament her fallen son, falls, prostrate over their bodies. Her comforters lift her up—a symbolic action repeated in a more specific context later in the play—and testify to the Innocents' victory:

> Si que tristaris, exulta que lacrimaris.
> Namque tui nati uiuunt super astra beati. (Young, II, 112)
>
> (Although you grieve, rejoice that you weep.
> For truly, your sons live blessed above the stars.)

Moreover, they remind her,

> Numquid flendus est iste, qui regnum possidet celeste,
> Quique prece frequenti miseris fratribus apud Deum auxilietur?
>
> (Is it fitting that he be wept over, he who occupies the heavenly kingdom,
> And who by frequent prayer may succor his wretched brothers before God?)

In a series of concrete actions which illustrate these words, the fallen children are literally resurrected by the comforting words of the angel and called into the choir to sing Christ's praises for drawing their souls through his mercy. Yet, the triumph of the Heavenly City, so effectively illustrated here, also necessitates the defeat of the Earthly City. Consequently,

Herod is removed from his throne, while Joseph and Mary are recalled from Egypt by the angel who has led the Innocents into the choir. As the Holy Family process to the front of the Church, they repeatedly sing the antiphon *Gaude Maria;* and their triumph is celebrated by the whole church, as all present join in on the *Te Deum laudamus* at the play's finale.

This skillful use of symbolic and literal contrast sets the Fleury plays quite apart from other dramatizations of the Christmas story in the medieval church. The use of church space is particularly innovative: the City of Man seeks to block the believers' access to the City of God—represented by both the manger and the altar. Moreover, the innovative elements in these two plays are uniformly concerned with articulating the theme of the Two Cities. The location of the manger among the congregation, the symbolic raising of both Rachel and the Innocents, and the deposition of Herod are found in no other versions; yet we have seen that they are used in these plays to symbolize concretely the reactions of characters to the City of God or the City of Man. Finally, both Fleury Christmas plays emphasize through their dialogue the futility of clinging to the City of Man contrasted with the universal availability of the City of God. Like the Easter plays, then, the Christmas plays in this collection embody the theme of the Two Cities in an unusually consistent manner.

The remaining plays in the Fleury Playbook are quite diverse—so diverse, in fact, that one is tempted to explain their inclusion by considering the interests of a compiler (or of his abbey) rather than seeing them as part of a unified collection. It is true that the striking textual interconnections we have found among the strictly liturgical plays cannot be demonstrated with any certainty among these six compositions; there are, however, strong thematic ties among them. Indeed, comparison of four of these plays to their extant analogues offers compelling evidence that, diverse as they are, they very likely came from the same hand.

Perhaps the best transition between the wholly liturgical plays and the remaining productions in the playbook is the Fleury *Raising of Lazarus (de Resuscitacione Lazari)*. Like the seasonal liturgical dramas, this play seems firmly bound to a church service through the use of a prefacing sequence and a concluding *Te Deum;* unlike these plays, however there is no clear indication of a seasonal attachment—in fact, two separate prefaces, one appropriate for Easter and the other for Advent, are called for in the manuscript. Moreover, the Fleury *Lazarus* depends upon scriptural narrative, and hence abandons the primarily symbolic mode of representation found in the liturgically bound plays, choosing instead a focus on verisimilitude and narrative coherence. Furthermore, the play employs only one basic melody—repeated fifty times—which severely restricts the variety of characterization and dialogue.[15] Given only the Fleury version of the *Lazarus,* we might be tempted to hypothesize that liturgical and scriptural dramas are in fact quite different in the playbook, and hence must be derived from quite different sources reflecting different intentions. Fortunately, an analogue, the *Suscitacio Lazari* by Hilarius, can be compared to the Fleury version.[16] Such a comparison reveals that the Fleury play is far more like its companion plays than like its analogue.

The version of the Lazarus story is dramatized by Hilarius in a severely limited, carefully structured, and formally static composition, whereas the Fleury version is quite broad in scope (encompassing three events to the single one in Hilarius), less carefully structured (even apparently interrupting the stanzaic form with scriptural citation or prose recitation[17]), and strikingly dynamic, particularly through the use of thematic reinforcement. Whereas Hilarius focuses solely upon the resurrection of the dead Lazarus, the Fleury play draws upon three separate events: Christ's forgiveness of the whore (*Luke* 7.39ff); the sickness and death of Lazarus; and Christ's resurrection of the dead man. Like the Fleury Easter plays, where three separate incidents are bound into a coherent whole by the repetition of a dominant theme, the *Lazarus* similarly emphasizes the real presence of the Redeemer to those who request his aid: in each scene, a community of believers is granted comfort by the expected Savior—a motif echoed in the sequences with which the play begins.[18] Equally important, communal participation is strongly emphasized. In contrast to Hilarius' *Lazarus,* where the Jews can offer little consolation to the sorrowing Mary, the Jews in the Fleury play not only aid her understanding, but even seem to be converted to belief in Christ at the end. Moreover, when Christ finally raises Lazarus from the tomb, he, not Lazarus (as in Hilarius), delivers the last speech, a testimony to the very ministers[19] at the altar about God's redemptive grace:

> Quid stupetis?
> Omne Deo esse possibile
> per hoc patet satis credibile
> quod uidetis. (Young, II, 208)
>
> (Why do you wonder?
> Everything is possible to God:
> Through this is made credible
> What you witness.)

The four St. Nicholas plays of the Fleury playbook seem at first unrelated to the others in both theme and content, and as a result are rarely treated in conjunction with the rest of the playbook. All four are devoted to illustrating the distinctive feature of the Nicholas legends: "He is the good bishop, the doer of good deeds for his patrons, whether they are wandering scholars, dutiful daughters, distressed parents, unconverted pagans or Jews."[20] Yet, a comparison of these plays with their contemporary dramatic analogues illustrates that again the Fleury playwright has altered their shape and scope to accord with the theme of the Two Cities. Because the plays are not directly linked to a liturgical feast, however, different techniques are employed to achieve this end. Three of the St. Nicholas plays, in fact, achieve accordance to the theme of the Two Cities in quite different ways.

The play of the dowry, or the *Tres Filiae,* has one other analogue (see Young II, 311-16) in the Hildesheim Manuscript, dating from the early twelfth century. In Hildesheim, the father laments his destitute state and is consoled by his daughters, who first propose becoming prostitutes and then, abhorring the degradation, resolve to comfort their father. Nicholas arrives in the nick of time to save them and their father's money. In Fleury, on the other hand, three suitors come, one after another, to sue for the daughters' hands and, coincidentally, to take the father's dowry money. Scholars have found this repetitiousness distressing; however, the Fleury play seems less concerned with the concrete action of the monetary reward than with the symbolic growth of the father's faith. As the play opens, the father laments the lack of joy, which for him is identified with money. His first daughter offers to become a prostitute to secure cash; just then, however, a bag of gold mysteriously appears; but soon after, a young man enters and abruptly departs with the girl and the gold. The father, again destitute, laments. A second bag of gold appears, and soon after another suitor. And again the father is left destitute. His third daughter, instead of trying to find a means of alleviating his poverty, reminds him that through fear of God all will be rewarded. Immediately appears not simply a third bag of gold, but also the saint himself. The father prostrates himself at St. Nicholas' feet—and at that point, of course, the third suitor arrives to relieve him of his last daughter and his last hope of wealth. The father is left destitute, as before. But he has changed. No longer content to reckon his fortune in terms of monetary recompense, he is ready to accept God's grace. To underline this, St. Nicholas closes the play by admonishing the father (and presumably the audience):

> Lauda Deum ex dato munere;
> hanc ne michi uelis ascribere
> largitatis laudem dominice,
> queso, frater. (Young, II, 320)
>
> (Praise God from whom this is given.
> Do not try to ascribe to me
> Praise for his great bounty,
> I beg you, brother.)

The Fleury *Image of Nicholas (de Sancto Nicholao et de quodam Iudeo)* concerns the miraculous restoration of money—this time not to a faithful father but to an unrepentant Jew. In contrast to the more famous version by Hilarius[21] in which an unbelieving pagan is literally converted to Christianity by St. Nicholas after the miraculous return of his stolen property, the Jew in the Fleury play seems to remain stubbornly unrepentant despite the return of his money. Like other Fleury plays, however, thematic structure determines a more sophisticated treatment of the dramatic situation. Instead of one barbarian, the Fleury play provides two types of unbelievers: the Jew who entrusts his money to the statue without locking it up, and three clumsy robbers who steal it because the chest is unlocked.

Consequently, the single conversion of the barbarian in Hilarius becomes separated into two separate "conversions" in the Fleury play. The robbers, surprised by St. Nicholas as they greedily divide the loot, are convinced to return it by the threat of physical violence. As representatives of the City of Man, they can understand only the punishments of this world. The Jew, on the other hand, is not brazenly converted to Christianity like Hilarius' *barbarus;* rather, upon discovering that this treasure has been returned, he turns directly to the audience and—in phrases which recall those of the joyful Mary Magdalene in the *Visitatio*—he testifies to the power of Nicholas. Realizing that the blind trust which he has placed in the idol—and in the things of this earth, his treasure—are useless, he vows to abjure idols, inviting the assembled audience of Christians to share with him in celebrating Nicholas' grace:

Congaudete michi, karissimi,
restitutis cunctis que perdidi.
 Gaudeamus!
Que mea dispersit incuria,
Nicholai resumpsi gracia.
 Gaudeamus!
Conlaudemus hunc Dei famulum;
abiuremus obcecans idolum.
 Gaudeamus!
Vt, errore sublato mencium,
Nicholai mereamur consorcium.
 Gaudeamus! (Young, II, 348)

(Rejoice with me dear friends,
For everything lost is restored.
 Rejoice!
What was lost through my carelessness
The grace of Nicholas has restored.
 Rejoice!
Let us praise this servant of God;
Let us abjure false idols.
 Rejoice!
That, error having left our thoughts,
We may be deserving of Nicholas' patronage.
 Rejoice!)[22]

The Fleury *Tres Clerici,* for which a full analogue in the Hildesheim manuscript exists, dramatizes one of the most popular of the St. Nicholas legends. As the patron saint of scholars, Nicholas' resurrection of the three clerks from the stew pot was a well-known iconographical and literary motif. Again, a contrast of the Fleury play with other versions reveals that the playwright has made a significant change. In Hildesheim, the three scholars appear at an inn, ask for shelter, and fall asleep. The host then suggests to his wife that they kill the boys. She at first finds it offensive to God, but finally relents. In the Fleury version, the host is entirely subservient to his wife's wishes. In fact, the wife is entirely dominant; the murder is her idea. This striking reversal of order is reminiscent of Adam's fall according to Augustine's *City of God*. Adam's subservience to Eve is, to Augustine, indicative of obedience to social compulsion rather than divine law.[23] In Fleury, the host's wife totally dominates the action and, one would assume, should receive the punishment for her sin. In contrast to Augustine, however, where Eve is condemned for her sin, in the Fleury play Nicholas raises the clerks from death and forgives both the wife and the host, stressing that they have been saved because of their willingness to repent. This spiritual resurrection, coupled with the physical resurrection of the clerks, seems reminiscent of the treatment of the Innocents in the Fleury *Ad interfectionem puerorum*.[24]

I have saved the two original compositions in the Fleury playbook for final consideration. They are particularly important in my discussion, for they are closely related thematically and structured similarly. The *Filius Getronis* is the most elaborate of the extant St. Nicholas plays. As students of the liturgical drama know, it establishes an elaborate contrast between Excoranda—the home of Getron, his wife Euphrosina, and his son, Adeotatus—and Agareni—the seat of king Marmorinus—set up in simultaneously visible locations. King Marmorinus is the very personification of the earthly tyrant; Getron is the paradigmatic Christian. While the inhabitants of Excoranda attend the church of St. Nicholas, Marmorinus' soldiers attack the town and seize Adeodatus. Realizing that her child is taken, Euphrosina laments—a striking parallel to Rachel in the Innocents' play—and is reminded by her comforters not to despair of God's grace. She and her husband vow to pray for God's help, asking for St. Nicholas' intercession. Returning home, they prepare a table from which bread and wine are distributed to the clerics and the poor. Simultaneously, a contrasting riotous feast is taking place at Marmorinus' palace. Suddenly, Nicholas appears and takes Adeodatus home, still clutching a cup of wine from Marmorinus' feast. The sorrow of his parents turns to joy, and they praise God and St. Nicholas for their mercy. The theme of the Two Cities is the very essence of this play. Drawing upon the theme as it is manifested in the Christmas drama through a contrast between Herod's court and Bethlehem, the Fleury playwright here establishes a visual contrast between Excoranda and Agareni. The inhabitants of Excoranda lament the loss of their child, but turn to God for their salvation; the tyrant in Agareni trusts in Apollo and his own might, both of which fail him in the end. The contrasting feats are particularly significant, for here the playwright artistically pits the unselfish sacrifice of the Mass against the gluttonous feast of the court, even in such a small detail as the cup of wine which causes drunkenness in the latter, salvation in the former.[25]

The *Conversio Beati Pauli Apostoli,* which many scholars have considered a totally impossible play to stage, is constructed even more elaborately upon the principle of the Two Cities.[26] As in *Getron,* two contrasting scenes are established: Jerusalem, in which Paul, like the tyrant Marmorinus, is seated upon a throne; and Damascus, where the high priest of the Jews is similarly enthroned. On the road to Damascus to deliver a message to the high priest, Paul is stricken blind, and delivered to the house of Judas where he is informed by Ananias that

> Ad te, Saule, me misit Dominus
> Ihesus, Patris excelsi Filius,
> qui in uia tibi apparuit;
> ut uenirem ad te me monuit.
> Predicabis coram principibus
> nomen eius, et coram gentibus;
> ut sis ciuis celestis patrie,
> multa feres pro Christi nomine. (Young II, 221)
> (To you, Saul, The Lord
> Jesus, son of the most high Father,
> Who appeared to you on the road, has sent me;
> He admonished me to come to you.
> You are to preach his name
> Before the princes and the nations.
> In order that you may be a citizen of the heavenly kingdom,
> You will suffer many things in Christ's name.)[27]

Now, hunted by armed attendants of the high priest, he flees to Jerusalem—but it is not, so the structure of the play indicates, the same Jerusalem he left. As a nonbeliever, he knew only the earthly Jerusalem, but now, as a believer who will suffer for Christ, he becomes immediately accepted among the apostles in the heavenly Jerusalem as together they sing the Church's song of praise to God, the *Te Deum.*[28]

The plays in the Fleury collection differ from others not only in their skillful and energetic use of music, dialogue, and setting, but also they reveal an unusual philosophical coherence which indicates the direction of a single learned playwright.

We are accustomed to thinking of dramas in this tradition as primarily derivative; and, no doubt, one could argue that there are pre-existent sources for the two original compositions in the Fleury playbook. But that is not the point. Comparison of these plays with available analogues reveals that alterations have been wrought in each play along strikingly similar thematic lines. It is moreover compelling that a large collection of plays should consistently repeat the same basic message—and that its concrete manifestation in two opposing, and often literal, "cities" should be the very basis of several works in the collection. While arguments based upon orthography or subject matter might provide grounds for discovering the actual home of the Fleury playbook, an approach based upon thematic issues enables us at least to see the influence of a single, dominant personality in their construction. While this is not evidence for the monastery of St.-Benoît-sur-Loire, it certainly does not argue against such a possibility—especially given the creative and experimental nature of several plays.[29] Moreover, one must consider the possible influence of Otto of Freising's *Chronica,* which had gained currency at just about the same time as the composition of these plays. Could there in fact be some relationship between the monasteries of Fleury and Freising at this time? More importantly, there seems to be convincing thematic evidence that the playwright had examined Otto's history, for many of its basic ideas may be found at the heart of the Fleury plays, distinguishing them from a wholly Augustinian approach.[30]

What this study finally suggests, I believe, is that the "Drama of the Medieval Church" was not a unified genre whose plays were merely passed from hand to hand without alteration, but that during the twelfth century in particular the drama of the liturgical tradition was seen as a distinct art form within which a remarkable amount of experimentation and variation was possible. The evidence for such experiments during this century—the Hildesheim manuscript, the works of Hilarius, the Benediktbeuern plays, the elaborate Freising and Rouen compositions, the Beauvais *Daniel* and *Peregrinus*—is overwhelming proof that the plays in this tradition have become dramas in their own right, and are susceptible to significant change and alteration by creative dramatists. But unlike any other great dramas of the twelfth century, the Fleury plays demonstrate a clear, central concern with the salvation of man, as seen in their consistent emphasis upon the Augustinian theme of the Two Cities. This philosophical coherence is remarkable and surprising; but more than that it is pleasing and humane.

NOTES

1 St. Augustine, *The City of God,* trans. Gerald G. Walsh and Grace Monahan (New York: Fathers of the Church, 1952), Book XIV, 28; see also XIV, 9, 33-34. For the Latin text, see the edition edited by Philip Levine (Cambridge: Harvard Univ. Press, 1966).

2 *City of God,* XIII, 23.

3 See ibid., X, 32; XVIII, 47.

4 "[T]he medieval historian treats [his] material from a universalistic point of view. . . . His business was not to praise England or France but to narrate the *gesta Dei*. . . . The great task of medieval historiography was the task of discovering and expanding this objective or divine plan" (R. G. Collingwood, *The Idea of History* [New York: Oxford Univ. Press, 1956], p. 53). See also James T. Shotwell, *The History of History,* I (New York: Columbia Univ. Press, 1939), 364-77; Page Smith, *The Historian and History* (New York: Knopf, 1964), pp. 15-22; *The Development of Historiography,* ed. Matthew A. Fitzsimmons and Alfred G. Pundt (Port Washington, N. Y.: Kennikat, 1967), pp. 15-50.

5 *Chronica sive historia de duabus civitatibus,* ed. Adolf Schmidt (Darmstadt: Wissenschaftliche Buchgesellschaft, 1961), p. 14; English translation from Charles C. Mierow's version, *The Two Cities: A Chronicle of Universal History to the Year 1146 A.D.* (New York: Columbia Univ. Press, 1928).

6 O. B. Hardison, Jr., *Christian Rite and Christian Drama in the Middle Ages* (Baltimore: Johns Hopkins Press, 1965), p. 228.

7 See *City of God,* XXII, 3-6, 9-10, 30.

8 These actions may be found earliest in the rubrics accompanying the famous *Visitatio* in the *Regularis Concordia,* dated approximately 975 A.D. See Karl Young, *The Drama of the Medieval Church* (Oxford: Clarendon Press, 1933), I, 249-50. Many other examples of these actions—particularly the display of the gravecloths—occur in plays of the eleventh and twelfth centuries; two especially interesting ones are plays from Aquilia (ibid., I, 628) and Zwiefalten (ibid., I, 266-67).

9 The text of the Fleury *Visitatio* has been re-edited by David Bevington in his *Medieval Drama* (Boston: Houghton Mifflin, 1975), pp. 39-44. Translations from this play and from other Fleury plays included in Bevington's anthology are utilized in this paper.

10 It is quite possible that the vestments specified in the rubrics—the dalmatic, the infula or stole, i.e., a white set appropriate for Easter (Young, I, 396-97)—also testify to the playwright's overt interest in depicting a literal community of belief.

11 The usual emphasis in the *Peregrinus,* the fraction of the bread among the Pilgrims, followed by Christ's disappearance, is not emphasized in Fleury. Yet, as F. C. Gardiner has pointed out in *The Pilgrimage of Desire* (Leiden: E. J. Brill, 1971), p. 126, it is a brief but very important action. For instance, in the Beauvais

Peregrinus, which parallels the Fleury version until this point, the breaking of the bread becomes literally a priestly act:

> *Tunc accipiat panem et dicat:*
> Accepit panem, benedixit (faciat+), ac fregit (frangat), et porrigebat eis.
> (Young, I, 468)

12 So important is this emphasis upon Christ's gift of peace that the Fleury play repeatedly directs that he should sing *Pax vobis*—either antiphonally with the choir, or to the band of disciples gathered around him. This musical repetition contrasts most strikingly with other versions, in which the *Pax vobis* is treated merely as part of the necessary scriptural dialogue.

13 See the diagram in Bevington, p. 54, based upon a similar concept in Karl Young, "Ordo Rachelis," *University of Wisconsin Studies in Language and Literature,* No. 4 (Madison, 1919), pp. 37-41. Interesting support for my contention is provided by William Tydeman, *The Theatre in the Middle Ages* (Cambridge: Cambridge Univ. Press, 1978), pp. 55-59. Since the Magi meet *"ad hostium chori"* (Young, II, 85), one assumes that this is also the location of Herod's throne, for they are immediately confronted by the tyrant's man-at-arms, who turns back from them to greet the king.

14 Inclusion of the congregation as audience is unusual enough among liturgical plays; actually to stage the action of the play among them is more unusual still. Tydeman (p. 56) suggests that such use of the nave seems to be prevalent only in Fleury and Beauvais. At no other point in the liturgical drama do the world of the congregation and the world of the play come into so intimate a contact—with the possible exception of the Fleury *Filius Getronis,* where it would seem that bread and wine are distributed among the poor of the congregation, and in *Herod,* where the adoration of the shepherds specifically includes the congregation since the rubrics direct that the shepherds *"inuitent populum circumstantem adorandum Infantem"* (Young, II, 85) ("invite the people standing by to adore the Child").

15 See William L. Smoldon, *The Music of the Medieval Church Dramas,* ed. Cynthia Bourgeault (London: Oxford Univ. Press, 1980), pp. 280-81.

16 For a discussion of Hilarius' work and bibliography, see Young, II, 211. For his *Suscitacio Lazari,* see ibid., II, 212-19.

A recent version of the Fleury play with music and English translation may be found in Fletcher Collins, Jr., *Medieval Church Music-Dramas* (Charlottesville: Univ. Press of Virginia, 1976), pp. 189-241.

17 See Fletcher Collins, Jr., *The Production of Medieval Church Music-Drama* (Charlottesville: Univ. Press of Virginia, 1972), pp. 157-59, for the argument that the lines in question—Simon's "Sic hic homo esset a Deo" and Martha's "Magister te uocat"—fit neither the incipit of another musical piece nor the present musical scheme. The reasons for this lapse in musical setting remain obscure, though I tend to believe they serve as points of emphasis: Simon's speech is angry *("indignans")* and he will soon be put in his place; Mary's speech will convince Christ to recall Lazarus from the dead. Thus, the thematic connection between Christ's forgiveness of the whore and his raising of the dead man is explicitly underlined by these interruptions in the otherwise regular melody of the play.

18 The opening sequences of the Fleury *Lazarus* have been a problem to many scholars. Young, for instance, remarks that "Neither composition is very appropriate" (II, 471). On the other hand, both sequences perform a thematic function: the Advent sequence emphasizes Christ's kingship, the Easter sequence his resurrection. It is moreover compelling that each sequence contains references to elements of specific occurrences in the play: the Advent sequence enumerates Christ's miracles (Young, II, 471, stanzas 21-23) as do the Jews when they realize the Savior's power to resurrect Lazarus (cf. Young, II, 207; 11. 275-80); and the Easter sequence refers to Mary Magdalene (Young, I, 235, stanza 14) and Christ's powers of forgiveness (stanza 15).

19 Anticipating objections to my interpretation of *ministris,* let me simply present my reasoning. The complete rubric reads, *"Iam Lazaro sedente, dicat Ministris"*

(Young, II, 208). Young renders this term as "bystanders" (II, 209) and Collins as "Disciples" (*Music-Dramas,* p. 238). However, the latter term is always rendered "*discipuli*" in the text (e.g., Young, II, 200, 1. 8; 201, 1. 51; 205, 1. 190); and the only other possible "bystanders" might be the Jews (rendered consistently as "*Iudei*" in the text) or Mary and Martha (together, *Sorores*). The usual referent of the term during this time was "deacon" or any religious officer or assistant below the office of priest; occasionally it referred (in humility) to the priest or bishop himself. See D. Du Cange, *Glossarium Medieae et Infinimae Latinitatis* (Paris: Librarie des Sciences et des Arts, 1939), and J. F. Niermeyer, *Medieae Latinitatis Lexicon Minus* (Leiden: E. J. Brill, 1976).

[20] George R. Coffman, *A New Theory Concerning the Origin of the Miracle Play* (Menasha: George Banta, 1914), p. 66. See also Otto E. Albrecht, *Four Latin Plays of St. Nicholas* (Philadelphia: Univ. of Pennsylvania Press, 1935).

[21] Hilarius' *Iconia Sancti Nicolai* is, of course, the source of Young's title (II, 337) for the play.

[22] Compare his speech with that of Mary Magdalene:

Congratulamini michi omnes qui diligitis Dominum, quia quem querebam apparuit mihi, et dum flerem ad monumentum, uidi Dominum meum, alleluia. (Young, I, 396)

(Congratulate me, all you who love the Lord, for he whom I sought has appeared to me, and, while weeping at the tomb, I saw my Lord, Alleluia.")

[23] See *City of God,* XIV, 11: "So, too, we must believe that Adam transgressed the law of God, not because he was deceived into believing that the lie was true, but because in obedience to a social compulsion he yielded to Eve, as husband to wife, as the only man in the world to the only woman." See also ibid., XIV, 14.

[24] Unlike Hildesheim, where the resurrection of the Clerks is only reported by an angel, in Fleury St. Nicholas himself prays for their restoration. While the rubrics do not specify that the Clerks are indeed bodily resurrected, such an interpretation has been made by Collins (*Music-Dramas,* pp. 332-33). Since such a resurrection does take place in the Innocents' play as well as in the Hildesheim play, this interpretation seems likely.

[25] While the use of scenic and verbal contrast is certainly characteristic of the Fleury plays, no other play in the collection so artistically employs it. The rubrics direct that bread and wine should be prepared by Euphrosina "*unde Clerici et Pauperes reficiantur*" (Young, II, 355) ("from which the clerics and the poor may refresh themselves"); as these members of the audience partake of the bread and wine, Marmorinus is directed to summon his own attendants to prepare a feast to satisfy his seemingly insatiable hunger, and to request that Adeotatus bring him the wine. Verbally, Euphrosina's unselfish prayer to St. Nicholas contrasts with Marmorinus' demand for earthly satiation:

Audi preces ad te clamancium,
qui in mundum misisti filium,
qui nos ciues celorum faceret. . . . (Young, II, 355)
(Hear our prayers as we cry unto you,
You who sent your son into the world,
That he should make us citizens of heaven.)

Marmorinus, on the other hand, demands:

Uos igitur quo uesci debeam
preparate, ne mortem subeam.
Quid tardatis? Ite velocius;
quod manducem parate cicius. (Young, II, 355)
(Prepare you therefore what I should eat,
Lest I suffer death.
Why do you delay? Go faster;
Quickly make ready something I may devour.)

When Adeodatus is returned by Nicholas, he carries the wine of the riotous feast, now transformed into the communion wine being distributed among the congregation.

Thus, verbally, scenically, and symbolically, this play establishes a most striking and most original contrast between the Two Cities.

26 On the difficulties of staging, see especially Collins, *Production,* pp. 175-80.

27 The centrality of this moment in the play is emphasized by the paucity of action which surrounds Paul's blinding on the road to Damascus. The blinding itself is not the central moment in the play's structure; this is why it is treated so perfunctorily. Rather, the emphasis is upon conversion; hence, two conversions—of Ananius and of Paul—are treated in parallel fashion.

28 The Fleury interpretation differs significantly from the scriptural version (*Acts* 9.26), in which the disciples argue heatedly about accepting Paul as one of them. Both Young (II, 223) and Collins (*Production,* p. 176) have noted this difference with distress, but have missed the reason for its elimination. The unity among the disciples as members of the Heavenly City is necessitated by the play's emphasis upon conversion; thus, Paul's immediate acceptance among the apostles emphasizes the harmony appropriate to the City of God. Moreover, this idea seems inherent in the play's manuscript title, *Ad representandum Conversionem Beati Pauli Apostoli.*

29 The most noticeably experimental are the St. Paul and Getron plays; however, nearly every play in the collection represents a significant departure from its type. The general tendency of the playwright to combine three scenes into a thematically coherent whole may be found not only in the two original plays, but also in the Easter and Christmas dramas as well as *Lazarus* and *Tres Filiae.*

30 The church at Fleury was an important cultural center during the eleventh and twelfth centuries, and was particularly noted for historical studies. It would not be unusual if a copy of Otto's *Chronica* had found its way to the Fleury library. The parallels between the Fleury treatment of the Two Cities theme and Otto's version of it are too complex to render in detail; however, some points to consider are the following: First, throughout the *Chronica,* the essential unity of mankind is of special importance. As Karl F. Morrison notes, in his recent study of Otto's history, "Otto of Freising's Quest for the Hermeneutic Circle," *Speculum,* 55 (1980), 214: "Alongside Otto's somber eschatological narrative of division among men and the decline of the world caused by sin, there runs a second, quite different narrative. Such was the complexity of his thinking that he was also able to teach that, in some fashion, all men were one, and that the history of the world traced the ascent of man through the developing powers of human reason." Otto often addresses this theme, particularly in his prologues (cf. especially Book V). Second, Otto distinguishes the eventual inhabitants of the heavenly city by their lack of earthly excesses. By drunkenness and the drive for power and riches, the earthly city makes itself known (cf. Book III, Prologue), but will be humiliated and its wrongs turned to good (Book VII, Prologue). Third, the City of God will be exalted on earth (Book VIII, Prologue). All three aspects of this particular view appear in the Fleury treatment of the Two Cities theme. A universal community of mankind, including even Jews and unbelievers, is offered opportunity to join the Heavenly City on earth; the ways of the Earthly City are shown to be clearly unsatisfactory and are turned aside by actions of the righteous; and, finally, the triumph of the city of God is depicted in a worldly setting.

The Fleury *Raising of Lazarus* and Twelfth-Century Currents of Thought

Kathleen M. Ashley

For the non-theologian attempting to understand the intellectual background of medieval literature, undoubtedly one of the most influential modern essays has been the last chapter in R. W. Southern's *The Making of the Middle Ages.*[1] The chapter puts the twelfth-century literary shift from epic to romance—from the *Chanson de Roland* to Chretien de Troyes—into the broader perspective of a whole society newly interested in spiritual introspection and human emotions, and delineates succinctly the parallel theological shift from the "Abuse of Power" doctrine to a theory of redemption in which Christ's humanity was the functional element.

The model Southern proposed for distinguishing early from late medieval art, literature, and piety was immediately persuasive because of its clarity and elegance, but its very applicability may have had the unfortunate result of blunting the sensibilities of those who read later medieval religious literature because their expectations were formed before they actually confronted the text. (The text had been "pre-read," so to speak.) Southern himself points out that the emphasis on Christ's humanity was not felt everywhere in Europe at the same time. It should therefore come as no surprise that there would be a period of transition during which both the older and the newer emphases might co-exist in various combinations.

In this paper I would like to propose that the *Raising of Lazarus* from the Fleury *Playbook* exhibits just such transitional features. Considerable injustice is done to this play if we attempt to restrict it exclusively to one mold when its distinctiveness lies in the fact that elements of both the newer and the older theology are combined in the character of Christ and the meaning given the action by the twelfth-century dramatist, who has enriched the biblical story by means of the intellectual emphases of his day.

In order to appreciate the twelfth-century dramatic version we must first return to the meanings which earlier commentators perceived in the biblical narrative of *John* 11.1-45. According to these exegetes, the Lazarus story provided evidence for both Christ's historical humanity and his supernatural powers. The Lazarus miracle was seen as proof of Christ's divinity, and as a prefiguration of his own resurrection; the power thus manifested was further a sign of the power which could release all sinners from their spiritual death. The Lazarus story thus provided the perfect setting for the image of *Christus Victor,* the resurrected Christ, triumphant in his divinity over the power and wiles of Satan, sin, and death.

At the same time, the biblical story says that "Jesus wept" (*John* 11.35) over the grave of Lazarus, and this was taken in all exegesis as evidence of Christ's human affections and thus as definitive proof of his humanity.[2] Some early theologians like Clement of Alexandria, much influenced by Stoic philosophy to elevate the virtue of impassibility, the imperviousness to all transient human emotions, had presented a Stoic Christ, serenely and immutably above the fray of human emotional and physical life; this is the image of the crucifixion presented in most early sculptures, illuminations, and hymns.[3] But the Lazarus story suggested an Incarnate Savior whose emotions were truly human, whose affections could be moved by love and sorrow, and it thus became a crux for theological discussions of Christ's humanity. To cite the most eminent theologian of the twelfth century, Bernard of Clairvaux, who calls on the model of a grieving Christ to justify his own expressions of grief on the death of his brother Gerard:

> Ille flevit compatiendo, et ego patiendo non audeam? Et certe ad tumulum Lazari nec flentes arguit, nec a fletu prohibuit, insuper et flevit cum flentibus: *Et lacrymatus est,* inquit, *Jesus.* Fuerunt lacrymae illae testes profecto naturae, non indices diffidentiae. Denique et prodiit mox ad vocem ejus qui erat mortuus, ne continuo putes fidei praejudicium dolentis affectum. Sic nec fletus utique noster infidelitatis est signum, sed conditionis indicium. (*PL* 183.911)

> He wept over the sorrows of others, and shall I not dare to weep over my own? Assuredly He did not at the sepulchre of Lazarus either rebuke those who were weeping, or forbid them to weep; and even more than this, He wept with them, for it is said *Jesus*

> *wept.* Those tears were, it is certain, the evidences of His Humanity, not the signs of His disapproval. Moreover, at His Voice the dead man came forth from the tomb, so you must not imagine that a person cannot yield to grief without prejudice to his faith. It is thus with my tears also. They are not a sign of unbelief, but an indication of our human condition.[4]

We see, then, within the Lazarus story itself as it came down in its exegetical context a two-fold conception of Christ—that of Christ the Victor, who redeems through his divine attributes of power and wisdom, and Christ the Incarnate One who shares man's sufferings and redeems through his human *passio*. Southern has suggested that the two theologies implied here were sequential in the Middle Ages, that up to the eleventh century one view dominated and after the twelfth century the other. In his definition, the two theologies tend to be mutually exclusive and to imply exclusive forms and styles. Thus Southern links up the dominance of one theological type with literary and artistic manifestations of the age: the *Christus Victor* model is suited to a vision of life as a battle with evil, the epic in literature, and abstract, symbolic representation of deity in art, while the human suffering Christ model is allied to a view of life as a journey, the romance form in literature, and historical realism in artistic representations of Christ's life and Passion.

As we have seen, the Lazarus story contained within it the possibility for both Christologies, and the Fleury *Lazarus* play in particular presents both images of Christ. They not only co-exist within the play, but their synthesis dramatizes a Christ who is truly Incarnate—both man and God—who comes to redeem both as a human friend and as a Physician of divine power. There is no tension between the two theologies although both are fully exploited within the play, as I will attempt to show.

In the first place, the play clearly reflects the new "mood of emotional tenderness which runs through the literature of the twelfth century."[5] It was an age fascinated by the emotions, by love between men and women, by spiritual psychology which explains the processes by which the soul falls into sin or rises to the love of God,[6] and by God's redeeming love for man. The prominence of Mary Magdalene in the twelfth-century Lazarus plays is a reflection of this new interest in the role played by the emotions in the conversion process of the individual sinner, for whom Mary had become a patron saint.[7] As Sandro Sticca points out:

> Although certain general characteristics about Mary Magdalene were known in the early Middle Ages through homiletic and exegetic literature, the dramatization of her life seems to be traceable to the intensity of the Magdalene cult in the West, which, beginning in the eleventh, found its greatest manifestation in the twelfth century.[8]

From the eleventh century on, penitential hymns in the first person which stressed the emotion of sorrow for sin were composed and attached to the feast of Mary Magdalene in particular.[9] Thus, although Lazarus had long been seen by medieval exegetes as an archetypal sinner and his death interpreted allegorically as entrapment in the bonds of sin, it is Mary whose emotional role as the repentent sinner is chiefly dramatized here.

The Fleury *Lazarus* opens with a scene of Mary Magdalene washing Jesus' feet with her tears as he sits at supper with Simon the Jew.[10] Mary does not speak, but her tears convey her emotional state. And the parable with which Jesus chastizes Simon calls attention to the greater love which the greater debtor must feel when his debts are forgiven. The scene functions as an *exemplum* for the repentance process of all sinners, for Christ explicitly tells Mary that her sins are washed away through the confession of her mouth and the compunction of her heart. This verbal formula for inner and outer repentances is given to show the audience how the sacrament of penance functions for them, but in fact what has been dramatized is only Mary's inner emotional repentance, symbolized by her weeping, for there is no literal confession of mouth.

The play is notable for its personal, tender emotions, epitomized by the Mary Magdalene figure, but these are emotions not just of sorrow but of mutual love and affection. Fletcher Collins, Jr., has remarked that "the key to the characterization of all the persons of this play, even of the Jews . . . is the mutual friendliness of all the characters. Two sisters and a brother were never more genuinely devoted to each other than Mary Magdalene, Martha, and Lazarus. . . . Jesus apparently regards Lazarus as his dearest friend outside the circle of disciples."[11] Thus, for example, we note that when Simon invites Christ to eat with him, Jesus turns to his disciples and tells them he wants to accept the hospitality of their friends *(amici)*. Simon calls Jesus "dear Doctor" *(Doctor care).* And Lazarus also addresses his sisters with the adjective "dear" *(care soror),* and is in return called *care frater* or *delecte frater.*[12] At the tomb, the stage directions specify that Jesus with trembling and inward crying should respond to a grieving Mary Magdalene since her misery, sighs, and sorrows move him. The Fleury *Lazarus* is a play which dramatizes tender emotions and shows Christ as the exemplar of friendship. In its emphasis on friendship, the play reflects twelfth-century monastic intellectual life,[13] for Cicero's *De Amicitia (On Friendship)* was popular within a monastic setting where, combined with Gregorian language of the heart "seeking the object of its desire," it had fostered a tradition of "letters of pure friendship" during the early Middle Ages, an epistolary tradition which flourished during the twelfth century.[14]

The personal, sentimental element in friendship, so openly expressed in twelfth-century letters and in the Fleury play, is striking, but we would be remiss to see this element outside its total context, for the love between friends was always seen as an earthly manifestation of heavenly love.[15] Whereas Collins goes no further with his observation that "almost every action in the play is an act of friendship" than to use it as a guide to characterization in performance,[16] we must explore the possibility that the recurrent acts of friendship in the Fleury *Lazarus* are meant to make a doctrinal point.

The Lazarus story functions this way for Aelred of Rievaulx, a twelfth-century Cistercian abbot whose treatise *On Spiritual Friendship* epitomizes what has been called the medieval "theology of friendship."[17] The thought of Aelred is deeply imbued with Augustinian and Gregorian themes and imagery, and spiritually he was a son of Bernard of Clairvaux, the leading Cistercian of the day; however the treatise on friendship—a dialogue really—is most directly inspired by Cicero's treatise *De Amicitia* which Aelred had read as a young man. In his prologue Aelred says that "At length there came into my hands the treatise which [Marcus] Tullius [Cicero] wrote on friendship, and it immediately appealed to me as being serviceable because of the depth of his ideas, and fascination because of the charm of his eloquence."[18] Despite the indebtedness to Cicero on every page, Aelred's treatise makes explicit immediately the difference between his definition of Christian friendship and Cicero's non-Christian concept: "For it is evident that Tullius was unacquainted with the virtue of true friendship, since he was completely unaware of its beginning and end, Christ."[19] Aelred substitutes the term "friendship" for the word "charity" in *I John* 4.16, which allows him to say "he that abides in friendship, abides in God, and God in him," for "God is friendship." And Aelred explicitly links this theology of friendship to the human relationships shown in the Lazarus story in another treatise, where he engages in a meditation on the life of Christ:

> But we must leave this scene and come to Bethany, where the sacred bonds of friendship are consecrated by the authority of our Lord. For Jesus loved Martha, Mary and Lazarus. There can be no doubt that this was on account of the special friendship by which they were privileged to be more intimately attached to him. That is borne out by those sweet tears with which he associated himself with the mourners and which all the people interpreted as a sign of love: "see," they said, "how he loved him."[20]

The friendliness which all characters in the Fleury *Lazarus* show must, I think, be seen against a monastic theology of friendship like Aelred of Rievaulx's. The first image of Christ in the play is thus as one whose human emotions enable him to grieve and rejoice with his friends, and whose love leads him to forgive Mary and resurrect Lazarus. This is an image of the Savior which is familiar from the affective spirituality of late medieval art, literature, and meditation.[21]

But there is another equally prominent image in the Fleury play, one of a cosmically triumphant Savior. As Jesus goes to the sepulcher he announces that now will be manifested the power of God. As it is opened he repeats to those assembled that they will see the Glory of God the Father and the power of the Son, and he describes himself in his prayer as eternal, not temporal, power as Son of God. The final words of the play are that the resurrection makes visible God's omnipotence, that all things are possible to him.

> Videbis gloriam Dei Patris atque potenciam sui nati. Deus, cuius virtus et filius eternalis non temporaneus credor esse. . . . Omne Deo esse possible, per hoc patet satis credibile quod videtis.

All of these references to divine power are added to the Biblical text, which speaks only briefly (verses 4 and 40) of the raising as a demonstration of God's glory. The power of God over death has been thematically emphasized in the Fleury play, and this is because in the play's elaborate consolation scene (also added to the scriptural account) the chief idea is Death's power over humanity. The development of this contrast between the power of Death and the power of God can only be attributed to the twelfth-century playwright, who wished to show both a God of friendship and a God of divine power.

The Fleury *Lazarus* can be tied even more specifically to the doctrine variously called the "Ransom," the "Abuse of Power," or the "Rights of the Devil" theory which was found in the writings of Patristic theologians.[22] As summarized by Southern, the view of salvation dominant until the eleventh century was that at the Fall of Adam and Eve man had been disobedient to his rightful Lord in voluntarily submitting himself to the service of the Devil. According to the rules, which all including God must follow, God could not by sheer omnipotence take back the rights over man which the Devil had won by man's free choice of evil. Man could, of course, change his mind and return to God's service, or the redemption of mankind could be accomplished if the Devil forfeited his claim to man by abusing his power—that is, by breaking the rules of the game. According to the theory, God tricks the Devil by becoming Incarnate so that the Devil, not perceiving the divinity beneath the human flesh, claims Jesus in death. He thus abuses his power because a sinless God cannot be subjected to the rule of death.

This view of redemption was attacked most vehemently at the beginning of the twelfth century by Abelard and Anselm. Anselm's denunciation of the theory that the Devil has rights has been called by Southern "one of the most powerful pieces of argument" in the treatise *Cur Deus Homo* as well as one of the most revolutionary.[23] According to Anselm, the logic of the Incarnation was that as a sinner Man has an obligation to God, but cannot pay. God has no obligation but he does have the ability to pay. Therefore a God-Man is conceivable, having *both* obligation and power to pay the debt of sin.[24] The Devil plays no starring role in this theory of redemption as he had in the Patristic one. Redemption ceases to be a cosmic battle of power or wits between God and the Devil and becomes instead a confrontation of Man with a God who endured human suffering on the cross.

Implied references to both these theories of redemption may be found in the consolation scene of the play, which as the most notable amplification of the scriptural story deserves our close attention.[25] The scene opens with Lazarus announcing that he is dying of an incurable disease. He says that he can only be cured by the Father, who alone is authentic consolation. Mary and Martha then send a messenger to summon Christ, affirming that only by virtue of his power can their sadness be abated. When Christ receives the message he promises to go revive Lazarus and thereby cause all non-believers to admire his power:

[Lazarus:] Cara soror, hunc miserabilem
esse reor inmedicabilem
morbum fratris.
Ut germano reddatur sanitas,
est oranda summa benignitas
nostri Patris.
Ipse solus nostra protectio,
nostra solus est consolacio. . . .

. . .

[Maria:] ut virtute sue potencie
iam recedat tante tristicie
tantum onus.

. . .

[Ihesus:] Quod sit eger, propter vos gaudeo,
quos tamdiu esse condoleo
non credentes.
Iamiam vestri cordis duriciam
deponetis, Christi potenciam
admirantes. (ll. 52-59, 85-87, 106-11)

Before Christ the Consoler appears, however, Simon and other Jews visit the sisters, and by the time they come on stage we have been prepared to regard their consolations, no matter how well-intentioned, as inadequate and ultimately ineffectual. The audience has, in other words, been alerted to the potential for dramatic irony.

Whereas in the classical *consolatio* the central issues are what type of grief is permissible and what kind of comfort can be offered, the Fleury scene focuses its interest on the issue of whether one must accept the "rule of death" over the body. Curtius points out that in classical consolatory orations and treatises the major topos is "everyone dies,"[26] but here Lazarus himself not only will rise but will function as a prefiguration of Christ, who was not subject to the rule of death, so that all invocations of this general rule of mortality have an ambiguous if not clearly ironic ring. Furthermore, within the Christian consolatory tradition the most important topos of consolation is the resurrection of the dead.27 In this context, the non-Christian platitudes of the three comforters ring hollow. Martha, for example, calls attention to Lazarus' body yielding to the rule of death, and Magdalene reiterates that now the rule of death has been fully proved. This prompts Simon to say that even in the worst of circumstances some consolation may be found: Lazarus is not dead as long as he is mourned by them. The second Pharisee adds that all people are caught equally on death's hook and that this at least allows us to escape the prison of the flesh:

[Martha:] Iam fraternum corpus dissolvitur
lege mortis. . . .

. . .

[Mary:] Care frater, frater carissime,
legem mortis iam passus pessime. . . .

. . .

[Simon:] Inter tantos caus solacium
est habendum.
Hac de causa vobis congemimus,
sed defunctum non esse credimus
sic deflendum. . . .

. . .

[2 Pharisee:] omnes gentes aduncat pariter
mortis hamus. . . .

. . .

ut quandoque carnis ergastulum
exeamus.
(ll. 125-26, 130-31, 137-41, 142-43, 146-47)

His consolatory argument sounds reasonable, but the image of the hook means one thing to an exegetically trained Christian audience and another to the Jewish speaker. Within Patristic descriptions of the means by which God redeemed man, the most popular image for the divine trick which deprived the devil of his rights was the fishhook. Satan is tempted by the bait of Christ's human nature to swallow the hook of his divine nature. Believing Christ is merely human, the Devil causes his death and thus abuses his own powers. Gregory the Great writes:

> Dominus itaque noster ad humani generis redemptionem veniens, velut quemdam de se in necem diaboli hamum fecit. Assumpsit enim corpus, ut in eo Behemoth iste quasi escam suam mortem carnis appeteret. . . . In hamo ergo ejus incarnationis captus est, quia dum in illo appetit es eam corporis, transfixus est aculeo divinitatis. (*PL* 76.680)28
>
> Our Lord, therefore, when coming for the redemption of man-

> kind, made, as it were, a kind of hook of Himself for the death of the devil; for He assumed a body in order that this Behemoth might seek therein the death of the flesh, as if it were his bait. . . . He was caught, therefore, in the "hook" of His Incarnation, because while he sought in Him the bait of His Body, he was pierced with the sharp point of His Divinity.

The hook of Death the second consoler mentions will soon be ironically transformed into the hook which slays Death itself. For an analogous passage which uses the patristic doctrine and the hook metaphor within a consolation setting we can turn again to Bernard of Clairvaux's moving sermon on the Song of Songs, where he laments the death of his brother Gerard. Commenting on the verse from *I Cor.* 15.55 ("O Death, where is thy victory? O Death, where is thy sting?") Bernard introduces a series of paradoxes which lead up to the image of Death itself caught on the hook by the Resurrection:

> Jam non stimulus, sed jubilus. Jam cantando moritur homo, et moriendo cantat. Usurparis ad laetitiam, mater moeroris; usurparis ad gloriam, gloriae inimica; usurparis ad introitum regni, porta inferi: et fovea perditionis, ad inventionem salutis: idque ab homine peccatore. Juste nimirum, quia tu inique in hominem innocentem et justem potestatem te meraria usurpasti. Mortua es, o mors, et perforata hamo quem incauta glutiisti, cujus illa vox est in propheta: "O mors, ero mors tua; morsus tuus ero inferne" (Ose. xiii, 14). Illo, inquam, hamo perfonata, transeuntibus per medium tui fidelibus latum laetumque exitum pandis ad vitam. Girardus te non formidat, larvalis effigies. Girardus per medias fauces tuas transit ad patriam, non modo securus, sed et laetabundus et laudans. (*PL* 183.910)

> Thou hast no sting any longer, but a song of praise and victory. For a man dies while singing, and sings while dying. Thou who art the mother of sorrow art taken as a subject for joy; thou, the enemy of glory, as an occasion for glory; thou, who art the gate of hell and the gulf of perdition, as the portal of the kingdom of God and the entrance into salvation; and all this by a man who is a sinner. This, too, is justly done, since thou hast rashly and unjustly usurped dominion over One who is a Righteous Man and Blameless. O Death, thou art thyself dead, and pierced with the hook which thou hast incautiously swallowed, of which thus speaks the Prophet: "O Death, I will be thy death; O grave, I will be thy destruction" (Hosea xiii:14). Pierced, I say, with that hook, thou shalt open a broad and joyful passage into life for those faithful ones who pass through thee. Gerard does not fear thee, O shadowy phantom. Gerard passes through thy jaws to his heavenly fatherland, not merely with security, but with joy and thanksgiving.[29]

A similar cluster of metaphors may be found in a twelfth-century sequence written by Adam of St. Victor for Easter, which speaks of the consolation brought by the resurrection when the robber (death) is caught on the hook of Christ's divinity: "Praedo vorax, monstrum tartareum,/ Carnem videns, nec cavens laqueum,/ In latentem ruens aculeum/ Aduncatur;/ Dignitatis primae conditio/ Reformatur nobis in Filio/ cujus nova nos resurrectio/ consolatur."[30]

The consolation scene of the Fleury play therefore contains a covert reference to the earlier theory of redemption, whose Christ is the triumphant figure on the cross of Resurrection, but it also offers a veiled reference to the newer theory of redemption whose Savior is the human figure suffering on the cross of the Passion. The third Pharisee urges Mary and Martha not to mourn for Lazarus who has escaped life's sufferings, which the rest of them must endure. He uses the verb *paciendum* for enduring or suffering, a verb which has Christian doctrinal connotations hidden to him just as the hook metaphor is obscure to the second consoler. In classical, especially Stoic, philosophies of consolation, the desirable state was one of escape from the world's experiences of passion and pain. However, in Christian Incarnational theology it is precisely Christ's *passio*—his full suffering with and for man—that leads to salvation, and therefore the Christian connotations of the word *paciendum* are positive, not negative as in Stoic thought. Auerbach, discussing the mysticism of the Passion, says, "What strikes us as significant in these mystical texts is not only the *rapprochement* between suffering and passion but even more so the yearning for *passio* in both senses, *desiderium et gloria passionis*. In marked contrast to all ancient conceptions and especially to the ideas of the Stoics, *passio* is praised and desired."[31] Against this background of Christ's redemptive suffering, the reference to *paciendum* as a state to be escaped at all costs appears inadequate.

The Fleury consolation scene manages to present the three Jews as sympathetic characters comforting the sisters out of honest friendship and yet also as men whose understanding is limited by their blindness to the paradox that life arises out of death through Christ's Passion and Resurrection. Their limitations are made clear at the beginning of Scene iii, when Jesus enters to awake Lazarus from his death sleep and comfort the sisters. He says that the power of God which has been hidden from the Jews will now be manifested. Death, which was seen as an inevitably fatal hook by the non-Christian consolers, will itself be hooked by the miraculous resurrection, and resigned endurance to the world's suffering will be replaced by the image of ardently embraced suffering as means to mankind's reunion with God.

The scene, which reveals the limitations of the Jewish consolers in order to portray Christ as the sole authentic consolation for the human condition, is thus structured by the familiar contrast between the Old Law and the New. Margaret Schlauch remarked long ago that the contrast of Old and New Laws was especially elaborate and frequent during the twelfth century when disputations between Jew and Christian, Synagogue and Church, became "something of a literary mode with Latin church writers."[32] She finds evidence of this twelfth century interest in the epics, romances, debates, and tracts of the period as well as in iconographic schemes of painted glass windows and cathedral sculptural programs. Blindness is the most conspicuous trait of Synagogue in medieval iconography, and especially relevant to our play's consolers is the fact that Jewish commentators were opposed to figurative interpretations of scripture.

If my reading is correct, the Fleury playwright is making his own comment on the Christian's ability to find consolation through allegorical interpretations of scriptural words and events—a consolation to which the literal-minded Jews do not have access. That the Jews knew only the letter of the Scripture and not the spiritual meaning was a commonplace of Augustine and Bede well-known in the twelfth century. Beryl Smalley emphasizes Jerome's influence on the idea that the Jews expound scripture in the literal sense and Christians in a spiritual, and that that was accepted as the chief difference between them.[33] According to the *Glossa Ordinaria,* the stone of Christ's tomb that was rolled away at his resurrection represents the letter, the Old Law, beneath which the spirit, the New Law, was hidden.[34] Henri de Lubac notes:

> En sortant du sépulcre, le Christ écarte la pierre qui le recouvrait, cette pierre de la lettre qui jusqu'alors mettait obstacle au jaillissement de l'intelligence spirituelle, cette pierre qu'il avait déjà prophétiquement fait ôter du tombeau de Lazare.[35]

We can say with Michael Rudick that the play's didactic objective is "to demonstrate the grounds for belief in Christ's divine nature"[36] if we add that those grounds are not just the action of raising Lazarus from the dead. For the Jewish characters *within* the play the literal fact of Lazarus' resurrection might be sufficient to convince them of Christ's divine powers; but the play's appeal is primarily to a Christian audience for whom the literally enacted event has spiritual significances of even greater import. The twelfth century is generally considered one of emphasis on the letter of the text—the literal or historical level—and the meaning for the interior life of the individual—the moral or tropological level.[37] However, we need not strain in the least to see all the four levels of scriptural interpretation operating within the Fleury play as grounds for belief in Jesus' words: "I am your resurrection."

The historical level we have noted; Jesus is literally Lazarus' resurrection. Beyond that, at the so-called allegorical level in which Old and New dispensations, Synagogue and Church, are compared, the consolation offered by the Lazarus event prefigures Christ's own resurrection in which he becomes the Divine Physician of all mankind. The next level, moral or tropological, concerns the spiritual life of the individual for whom, as we have also suggested, Lazarus and Mary Magdalene are figures. As types for the sinner, they demonstrate the loving mercy and power over sin that Christ will exhibit to those who repent. In the most interior sense, therefore, Christ is man's means of resurrection from sin. Finally, there is the level we have not yet discussed, the anagogical, which refers to the end of things or the afterlife. The resurrection of Lazarus, spiritually understood, is a figure for the resurrection of the dead at the Last Judgment, to which all believers look forward. Martha calls attention to this expectation when she says, "This in my soul is fixed, that he will arrive at the New Day, that day when the last judgment is made, at which time will arise all men from their dust": "Hoc in meo fixum est animo, quod resurget die novissimo, die illa, qua supremum fiet iudicium, in qua caro resurget gencium ex favilla."

The play is filled with eschatological allusions. Martha represents Death as a thief, snatching Lazarus from them, and the description is repeated by Mary at the tomb: "mors huc accedere atque fratrem nostrum obruere fuit ausa." The image may echo the tale in *Matthew* of the unwatchful householder whose house is broken into by a thief as he sleeps (*Matt.* 24.42-44). This is a parable told by Jesus as a warning of his Second Coming at the Last Judgment, which was especially to be contemplated as an aid to penitence during Advent. The sleep of the unwary is also a motif in the eschatological parable of the wise and foolish virgins which follows the thief parable in *Matthew* (25.1-13). The necessity to rise from the sleep of spiritual sloth to greet one's salvation is a major theme of the first Sunday in Advent when *Romans* 13.11 is the epistle: "And this do, understanding the time, for it is now the hour for us to rise from sleep, because now our salvation is nearer than when we came to believe." The same emphasis on the role of sleep in an eschatological setting occurs in the twelfth century *Sponsus* play, leading Rosemary Woolf to comment that "theme and treatment suggest the first Sunday in Advent, when it is Christ's second coming that is heralded."[38]

These eschatological allusions lead me to the conjecture that the play was affiliated most closely not with the Easter season, as some critics have concluded,[39] but with Advent, when the liturgy celebrates the various comings of Christ, not only as redeemer of mankind by his Incarnation, but also as judge at the end of the world. Bernard of Clairvaux in the twelfth century popularized a third Advent—Christ's coming into the heart of the individual believer—so that Advent, as much as Lent, became the season for a call to repentance.[40] The play culminates dramatically indeed in an evocation of all three Advents, when Jesus appears finally in Bethany to the announcement of the messenger—"Ecce, vestrum adventat gaudium; ecce venit Salvator gencium expectatus!" "Look! Your joy approaches. See! Here comes the savior of mankind, the expected one!"—which is a paraphrase of various Advent antiphons, for example the seventh of the Great O Antiphons of the third Sunday in Advent: "O Emanuel rex et legifer noster expectatio gentium et salvator earum: veni ad salvandum nos domini deus noster." The other Advent antiphons are also charged with the expectation of the coming of a Savior king to bring joy to his people.

The concept of the three advents allows us to see how the Fleury playwright can synthesize the two Christologies which in Southern's model are opposed, for, as Bernard points out, in the first Advent, the Incarnation, Christ comes in flesh and weakness as our redemption. This is the Christ in the play who weeps for Lazarus and commiserates with the sisters, the Christ who in his human nature suffers the Passion on the cross. In the second Advent, Bernard continues, Christ comes in spirit and in virtue as our Repose and our Consolation; this is the Christ who forgives the individual's sins, symbolized by his treatment of Mary Magdalene and Lazarus. Finally, Bernard concludes, in the third Advent Christ will come in glory and majesty as our life; this is the image of the resurrected Christ who raises Lazarus from the dead, rises himself, and returns at the end of the world as cosmically triumphant lord.[41]

The kind of close examination of a work of religious literature I have been conducting here should help correct distortions (of the kinds that occur when a generalization is applied) by showing us deviations and subtleties in the culture that the model is designed to ignore. Thus, while Southern's analysis of the theological shift which occurred in the twelfth century carries the implication that the two theories of redemption are incompatible, and that an affective spirituality would naturally find the image of a loving and suffering human Christ more congenial than the figure of an impassible and victorious Christ locked in struggle with the Devil or Death, our play reveals a harmonious coalescence of both Christologies in the Jesus who comes to Bethany as loving friend *and* eternally powerful Lord over death. The play reveals the complexity of twelfth-century religious thought and it should come as no surprise to discover that Bernard of Clairvaux, the great mystic and theologian of the age who with his fellow Cistercians did most to foster emotional meditation upon the earthly life and sufferings of the Savior, was the most ardent and articulate defender of the Patristic theory against the new theories of the atonement offered by Abelard and Anselm. When Abelard denies the rights of the Devil to have dominion and power over man, Bernard asks, "Which shall I call the more intolerable in these words—the blasphemy or the arrogance . . . the rashness or the impiety?"[42] Furthermore, contrary to our facile assumptions, when Aelred passes from the historical level of meditation on Christ's human life to the allegorical or moral level in "Jesus at Age 12," he suggests that we now leave the historical sense to develop the spiritual sense that will "arouse your affections."[43]

Although perhaps in strictest theory the two Christologies could not be reconciled, as Anselm argued with powerful logic, in practice elements of the two were found together with no sense of their incompatibility. Southern's description of the twelfth century shift has too often been taken as an historically complete account rather than as a brilliant distillation of two basic modes which continued their viability through the whole of the Middle Ages. While the Victor model may have dominated early medieval art and thought, it by no means excluded the other model, nor did it vanish, as Southern claims, when the Victim model assumed popularity and eventually dominance. Brian P. McGuire argues in fact that St. Anselm's "liberal or humanistic" theory of Redemption "remained the minority view throughout the Middle Ages and lost all importance after the fourteenth century. The dualistic ('abuse of power') view not only totally dominated the period before 1100 but remained strong throughout the high Middle Ages (1100-1300) and finally triumphed in the fourteenth century."[44]

We must use Southern's and other models as guides to potential configurations within medieval culture and its texts, rather than as a set of blinders which prohibits us from seeing the full range of possibilities. Certainly our appreciation of the impact a play such as the Fleury *Raising of Lazarus* must have made on its monastic audience is diminished if we have focused our view of its theological possibilities too narrowly, for the play reveals a multi-leveled symbolic richness in perfect harmony with its forward narrative thrust—an achievement it owes, I would argue, to its twelfth-century intellectual context.

NOTES

1 (New Haven: Yale Univ. Press, 1953), pp. 219-57.

2 "The Christian savior was one who gave vent to his feelings, who wept over Lazarus. Some care must be taken in interpreting the Cappodocians on this point. In their case, it would be mistaken to read the statement that Jesus was subject to [*pathé*] as an incidental or grudging concession to the gospel accounts. It was an assertion to which orthodox theologians attached positive significance, for Jesus' possession of passions or emotions testified to a true humanity, and consequently made untenable the docetism which had beguiled segments of the church from its very beginning" (Robert C. Gregg, *Consolation Philosophy: Greek and Christian Paideia in Basil and the Two Gregories*, Patristic Monograph Series, 3 [Philadelphia: Patristic Foundation, 1975], pp. 172-73). See also St. Augustine, *De Civitate Dei* 14.9: "Verum ille hos motus certae dispensationis gratia, ita cum voluit suscepit animo humano, ut cum voluit factus est homo" (*PL* 41.415) ("Jesus wept when he raised Lazarus from the dead because 'as he became man, when it pleased him, he

experienced those emotions in his human soul' "). Cf. the *Glossa Ordinaria* (*PL* 114.910).

3 Adolf Katzenellenbogen, "The Image of Christ in the Early Middle Ages," in *Life and Thought in the Early Middle Ages,* ed. Robert S. Hoyt (Minneapolis: Univ. of Minnesota Press, 1967), pp. 66-84.

4 From 26th Sermon in *Cantica Canticorum: Eighty-six Sermons on the Song of Solomon,* trans. Samuel J. Eales (London: Elliot Stock, 1895), p. 165.

5 Southern, p. 221.

6 See, for example, Bernard of Clairvaux's treatise *De gradibus humilitatis et superbiae,* ed. Barton Mills (Cambridge: Cambridge Univ. Press, 1926).

7 The Benediktbeuern Passion Play contains a lengthy dramatization (ll. 36-152) of the conversion of Mary Magdalene.

8 *The Latin Passion Play: Its Origins and Development* (Albany: State Univ. of New York Press, 1970), p. 138.

9 Colin Morris, *The Discovery of the Individual 1050-1200* (London: SPCK, 1972), p. 71. See Joseph Szövérffy, " 'Peccatrix Quondam Femina': A Survey of the Mary Magdalene Hymns," *Traditio,* 19 (1963), 79-146; also his article with M. Wynne, "Typology in Medieval Latin Hymns: Notes on Some Features in the Mary Magdalene, Martha and Lazarus Hymns," *Medievalia et Humanistica,* 12 (1958), 41-51. More recently, Clifford Davidson, "The Visual Arts and Drama, with Special Emphasis on the Lazarus Plays," *Le Théâtre au moyen âge,* ed. Gari Muller (Montreal: Les Éditions Univers, 1981), pp. 44-59.

10 The text of the play may be found in Karl Young, *Drama of the Medieval Church,* II (Oxford: Clarendon Press, 1933), 199-208. Medieval tradition, authorized by Gregory the Great, identified Mary Magdalene, Jesus' follower in *Luke* 8.1-3, with Mary the sister of Lazarus and Martha, and with the penitent sinner of *Luke* 7.37ff as well; see Helen Garth, *Saint Mary Magdalene in Mediaeval Literature* (Baltimore: Johns Hopkins Press, 1950), pp. 18-20.

11 *The Production of Medieval Church Music-Drama* (Charlottesville: Univ. Press of Virginia, 1972), p. 160.

12 With regard to these terms of endearment, Jean Leclercq says, "Dans les lettres comme dans les traités du XIIe siècle sur l'amitié, les termes *dilectio, caritas, amicitia* sont souvent synonymes" ("L'amitié dans les lettres au moyen âge, "*Revue du moyen age latin,* 1 [1945], 403n).

13 While the manuscript in which the play is found, Orléans MS. 201, the so-called "Fleury Playbook," has been ascribed to the Abbey at St. Benoît-sur-Loire by some critics, others have challenged the location; see Solange Corbin, "Le Manuscrit 201 d'Orléans: drames liturgiques dits de Fleury," *Romania,* 74 (1953), 1-43. However, references to the "fratres" and "monasterium" in plays of the manuscript make it likely that the play was written and produced in a monastic setting; see Collins, pp. 33-34.

14 F. Gardiner, *The Pilgrimage of Desire: A Study of Theme and Genre in Medieval Literature* (Leiden: E. J. Brill, 1971), pp. 55-85; E. Gilson, *La theologie mystique de saint Bernard* (Paris: Librairie Philosophique, 1934), pp. 68-72; Leclercq, "L'amitié dans les lettres au moyen âge," pp. 391-410; and John C. Moore, *Love in Twelfth-Century France* (Philadelphia: Univ. of Pennsylvania Press, 1972), pp. 38-43.

15 St. Anselm, in particular, was responsible for developing a theology which linked human relationships based on an identity of wills with the unchanging joys to be experienced in heaven. Friendship alone, of all human experiences, gives us a foretaste of "that holy society where there will also be unfailing and perfect friendship" (Douglas Raby, Introduction to *Aelred of Rievaulx, Spiritual Friendship,* trans. Mary Eugenia Laker [Kalamazoo: Cistercian Publications, 1974], p. 16); Southern

thinks Anselm would have learned the classical doctrine of three types of friendship not from Cicero but from Cassian's *De Amicitia* (*St. Anselm and His Biographer: A Study in Monastic Life and Thought, 1059- c.1130* [Cambridge: Cambridge Univ. Press, 1963], pp. 67-76).

16 *Production of Medieval Church Music-Drama,* p. 161.

17 Amedee Hallier, *The Monastic Theology of Aelred of Rievaulx,* trans. Columban Heaney (Shannon: Irish Univ. Press, 1969), pp. xi-xii, 25-55.

18 Ed. Raby, pp. 45-46.

19 Raby, p. 53.

20 *The Works of Aelred of Rievaulx, I: A Rule of Life for a Recluse,* trans. Mary Paul Macpherson (Spencer, Mass.: Cistercian Publications, 1971), p. 85.

21 The image of Christ as a friend persists until the fifteenth century, as Rosemary Woolf has pointed out (*The English Religious Lyric in the Middle Ages* [Oxford: Clarendon Press, 1968], pp. 214-18). The continuity between classical formulations of the virtue of friendship and Middle English versions of the theme, especially in romances, is discussed by Rob Roy Purdy, "The Friendship Motif in Middle English Literature," *Vanderbilt Studies in the Humanities,* 1 (1951), 113-41.

22 The first clear statement of this theory of redemption is found in Irenaeus in the second century A.D. (*Contra Haereses,* V.i, III.xxxii.2). See also Hastings Rashdall, *The Idea of Atonement in Christian Theology* (London: Macmillan, 1925), pp. 247-48.

23 *St. Anselm and His Biographer,* p. 85.

24 *Cur Deus Homo,* i.22-25 and ii.6-9.

25 Young, *Drama of the Medieval Church,* II, 209. The scene developed out of the verse which tells that "many of the Jews had come to Martha and Mary to comfort them on account of their brother" (*John* 11.19).

26 *European Literature and the Latin Middle Ages,* trans. Willard R. Trask (1953; rpt. New York: Harper and Row, 1963), pp. 80-82.

27 See Mary M. Beyenka, *Consolation in Saint Augustine,* Patristic Studies, 83 (Washington: Catholic Univ. of America Press, 1950), pp. 50, 87-91. Rosemary Woolf says that the author of the Fleury Play has "ingeniously given to the comforters a very moving but non-Christian consolation" (*English Mystery Plays* [London: Routledge and Kegan Paul, 1972], p. 44).

28 From Gregory the Great's Commentary on the Book of Job (xxiii.14). For other early exegesis of Job, see Émile Mâle, *The Gothic Image: Religious Art in France of the Thirteenth Century,* trans. Dora Nussey (1913; rpt New York: Harper and Row, 1972), pp. 379-80. The metaphor of the hook remained familiar until the end of the medieval period; see the Middle English *Stanzaic Life of Christ,* ll. 6337-68, where doctrinal symbolism of hook and bait were spelled out to explain the "good sleght" by which Christ defeated the Devil (ed. Frances A. Foster, EETS, e.s. 166 [London, 1926]).

29 Ed. Eales, *Cantica Canticorum,* p. 164.

30 *The Liturgical Poetry of Adam of St. Victor,* I (London: Kegan Paul, 1881), p. 66.

31 Erich Auerbach, "Excursus Gloria Passionis," in *Literary Language and its Public in Late Latin Antiquity and in the Middle Ages,* trans. Ralph Manheim, Bollingen Series, 74 (New York: Pantheon Books, 1965), p. 78. Note also Bernard of Clairvaux's use (p. 2) of the verbs *compatiendo* and *patiendo* to describe Christ's and his own sorrows over the human condition.

32 "Allegory of Church and Synagogue," *Speculum*, 14 (1939), 450.

33 *The Study of the Bible in the Middle Ages* (Notre Dame: Univ. of Notre Dame Press, 1964), pp. 170-73.

34 In Matt. xxviii, in Marc. xvi, in Luc. xxiv, *PL* 114.177, 241, 350.

35 *Exégèse Médiévale*, Pte. I, T. 1 (Aubier: Éditions Montaigne, 1959), p. 327.

36 "Theme, Structure and Sacred Context in the Benediktbeuern 'Passion Play'," *Speculum*, 49 (1974), 279.

37 See, for example, Bernard of Clairvaux's four sermons for the Feast of the Assumption in which he uses Christ's reception into the home of Mary, Martha, and Lazarus (*Luke* 10.38-43) as an allegory first for the Virgin Mary's soul and then for the soul of any penitent. Lazarus becomes a type for those who need to "cleanse their conscience from dead works" (*Hebrews* 9.14), the sinful who are like "the wounded sleeping in the sepulchres" (*Psalms* 87.6) (*St. Bernard's Sermons for the Seasons and Principal Festivals of the Year*, III [Westminster, Md.: Newman Press, 1925], 233). The four sermons are found in Latin in *PL* 183.415-30. In Bernard's scheme, only Lazarus represents the sinner, who is called from the grave by the voice of power; for Bernard, as for many monastic exegetes, Mary is a figure of the holy contemplative.

38 *English Mystery Plays*, p. 45. Albert S. Cook, *The Christ of Cynewulf* (Boston: Ginn, 1900), pp. xxv-xliii, gives a useful summary of the Advent liturgy in the medieval church.

39 See Karl Young, *The Drama of the Medieval Church*, II, 211: "from the presence of the Easter sequence, *Mane prima sabbati*, at the beginning, several critics have inferred that the play was designed for performance during the Easter season. This inference, however, is far from secure, for the sequence was used, probably, not because of its Easter associations, but because in it is celebrated the *beata peccatrix*, Mary Magdalen, who appears in the opening scene. It is possible that the play was intended for the feast of St. Lazarus (Dec. 17), who was honored in numerous communities of Southern and Central France."

40 See, for example, the sermons for Advent in *St. Bernard's Sermons for the Seasons and Principal Festivals of the Year*, I (Westminster, Md.: Newman Press, 1921), 1-52, especially his Third Sermon on the three comings of the Lord—"His coming *to* men, His coming *into* men, and His coming *against* men" (p. 25). The sermons are found in *PL* 183.35-56. Aquinas, in a sermon for the first Sunday in Advent, adds a fourth advent—that is, the moment of an individual's death (Jean Leclercq, *L'ideé de la Royauté du Christ au Moyen Age* [Paris: Éditions du Cerf, 1959], p. 84). The *Legenda Aurea* also says that the coming of the Lord is fourfold—and he is thus celebrated for four weeks of Advent—but adds that "while the Coming is in reality fourfold, the Church is especially concerned with two of its forms, namely with the coming in the flesh and with the coming at the Last Judgment" (*The Golden Legend of Jacobus de Voragine*, trans. Granger Ryan and Helmut Ripperger [New York: Arno Press, 1969], p. 2).

41 *PL* 183.50.

42 *Epistola 190 ad Innocentium II Pontificum* (*PL* 182.1063), trans. B. Scott James, *The Letters of St. Bernard of Clairvaux* (London: Burns Oates, 1953), pp. 312-29. See also A. Victor Murray, *Abelard and St. Bernard* (New York: Barnes and Noble, 1967), pp. 117-35. Although the supposed home of the play, St. Benoît-sur-Loire, is a Benedictine Abbey, I think we are justified in identifying St. Bernard, a Cistercian, as our epitome of twelfth-century monasticism. As Jean Leclercq points out, St. Bernard at once symbolizes the "new sensitivity" of the age and the world of monasticism based on patristic literature and the Benedictine rule (*The Love of Learning and the Desire for God: A Study of Monastic Culture*, trans. Catherine Misrahi [New York: Fordham Univ. Press, 1961], p. 137). In its synthesis of old and new, Bernardine spirituality is very close to the Fleury *Raising of Lazarus*.

43 *Works of Aelred of Rievaulx, I: A Rule of Life for a Recluse,* p. 14.

44 "God-Man and the Devil in Medieval Theology and Culture," *Cahiers de l'institut du moyen-âge grec et latin,* 18 (1976), 23. See also McGuire's unpublished Oxford D. Phil. Thesis (1970), "The History of St. Anselm's Theology of Redemption in the 12th and 13th Centuries," which undermines Southern's thesis about Anselm's influence through careful documentation of Anselm's limited acceptance.

The Iconography of Herod in the Fleury *Playbook* and in the Visual Arts

Miriam Anne Skey

Twelfth-century art and drama are rich in representations of Herod the Great. The sculptural decorations and stained glass windows of the cathedrals being built in France provided excellent opportunities for artists to portray large-scale cycles of the Infancy and Passion of Christ, while in England manuscript illuminators were using similar subject material for cycles of the Life of Christ which were prefixed to the text of the Psalter. Since there also was an increasing interest at this time in the story of the Magi, their visit to Herod was often portrayed within Magi cycles as well as in series of paintings devoted to the Infancy of Christ. Twelfth-century art is notable not only for the variety of contexts in which Herod appears, but also for the dramatic changes which take place in the iconography of this king. He becomes less and less regal, and, with the introduction of devils to advise him and a sword to replace his scepter, he is now unmistakably associated with the forces of evil.

These new developments in the art of the twelfth century were reflected in the Latin liturgical drama of the same period. Although the earliest Latin drama of the church was based on liturgical elements and included the singing of antiphons, sequences, and hymns, an element of free composition soon crept in, particularly in the case of plays dealing with Herod the Great. Drama, like the visual arts, also reflected an interest in the Infancy of Christ, culminating in the development of the *Officium Stellae* plays of the Magi, "exhibiting an unusual variety in their content, a considerable breadth of action, and, in several instances, a rather remarkable literary sophistication."[1] The Fleury playbook preserves "the most polished examples of liturgical drama that survive"[2] while the Herod plays in particular have attracted the attention of scholars who have produced full transcriptions and translations as well as elaborate performances of these plays.[3]

Karl Young first commented on the successful construction and the literary sophistication of both the *Ordo ad Representandum Herodem* and the [*Ordo*] *ad Interfectionem Puerorum* from the Fleury manuscript, and at the same time he noted the increasingly complex role given to Herod in almost all of the *Officium Stellae* plays.[4] Later scholars differ in their opinions of the importance of the role of Herod in relation to the whole play bearing his name: Noah Greenberg sees the play as "a series of highly contrasting scenes, each developing its own mood,"[5] while Fletcher Collins, Jr., insists that "the play is Herod's. All of the events are organized as much around the machinations of Herod as they are around the birth of the Christ Child."[6] This view seems to confirm the earlier view of Grace Frank about the possibilities of dramatic development in the early liturgical plays when Herod was included:

> As soon as Herod himself appeared in the plays further opportunities for dramatic development became obvious and liturgical authors soon made effective use of his presence. They could now introduce not only a complicated plot, with an element of suspense, but also portray a villain whose speech and actions, costume and accessories might be used to suggest his vicious character. The Three Kings had been slightly individualized in dress, perhaps in deportment, but Herod's was the first role capable of giving us a real person and not a type.[7]

It is perhaps overly enthusiastic to see Herod in liturgical drama as a "real person," but it is true to say that he was given individualistic touches. And his role in the drama, as in the visual arts, was greatly increased. Scenes involving Herod became quite lively and displayed a great range of interpretation. The Fleury Herod plays, when compared with other music-drama of the period and with the visual arts, prove to be dynamic yet dignified. They incorporate most of the newest developments of the time, occasionally introducing unique details, but the treatment is always controlled and entirely appropriate for church performance. The playwright does not go to the outrageous extremes of some of his contemporaries when dealing with this tyrant, nor does he leave the role simple and undeveloped. He achieves a very fine balance in his treatment of Herod and his court, and it is this fine balance and his expert control over his material which, along with his literary and musical sophistication, give the Fleury plays about Herod their outstanding quality.

This paper will center on Herod as he appears in the two Fleury plays which deal with the Feasts of the Epiphany and the Holy Innocents.[8] The former opens with a Shepherds Play, followed by the appearance of the Magi, their summons to the court, and their interview with Herod during which the scribes give their evidence. This so angers Herod that his son must calm him before he dismisses the Magi, who then follow the star to Bethlehem, meeting the shepherds who are now on their way home. After the Adoration, the Magi are warned by an angel to return another way to avoid Herod. They return to the choir and the *Te Deum* is sung. The following play opens with processional entrances for both the Innocents and Herod. Then the Flight to Egypt is followed by news of the Magi's escape presented to Herod who is so angered that he attempts suicide. When he is prevented from this action, he orders the Massacre of the Innocents, after which the most moving section of the play, starring Rachel and her consolers, is presented. The play continues with the resurrection of the Innocents, the replacement of Herod by his son Archelaus, and the Return of the Holy Family, and it ends with the *Te Deum*. The scenes relevant to this study of the iconography of Herod will be considered under the following headings: the court, the Magi, the scribes, the soldiers, and Herod's suicide and death. In each instance, the Fleury plays will be described and then compared with other Latin dramas. Lastly, examples of Herod in the visual arts of France and England (where he appears most frequently at this time) will be considered in an attempt to appreciate the Fleury treatment of Herod the Great in relation to other depictions of this king in the twelfth century.

I

The Court. The Fleury playbook is unique in labelling its Epiphany play *Ordo ad Representandem Herodem.*[9] This title throws emphasis onto Herod and, by extension, his extraordinarily well populated court. When the Magi arrive in his country, Herod sends an *armiger* to question them; not satisfied with the information of this servant, he then sends *oratores* and *inter-*

pretes, whom he addresses as *inquisitores,* to examine them further; finally he sends the *armiger* to them again to bring them into his presence. Thus the Magi are questioned and fully identified for Herod and his court three times. During the interview, Herod turns to yet a different group of people, *symmistae in habitu juvenili,* who are requested to fetch the scribes for him. The evidence of these men so angers him that his young son Archelaus makes an appearance and, after soothing his father, offers himself as his avenger. Herod's last appearance in this play is, in fact, with his son as they wave their swords in anger behind the Magi.

In the following play, Herod is ceremonially presented with his scepter in the court while the antiphon *Super solium David* is sung, neatly contrasting this "foreign" king who sits on the throne of David with the new-born King, son of Joseph, *fili David,* whom the angel addresses in the very next line. A messenger brings news that he has been deceived by the Magi, whereupon Herod is only prevented from suicide because he is surrounded by attendants who restrain him. Then an *armiger,* who seems more a soldier than a messenger, receives the command to massacre the children. At the end of the play, Archelaus is shown succeeding Herod as king, emphasizing the power of the court and causing Joseph to withdraw into Galilee rather than to return directly. Through its title, then, the Fleury play throws emphasis onto Herod, and through the introduction of these various characters prominence is given to his court. Even before the action reaches the court, the Magi are seen questioning the citizens of Jerusalem about the new-born King of the Jews before they speak with the present king of the Jews. Thus the country as well as the court is included, and a sense of numbers and importance is given.

This is not always the case in other Epiphany plays. In the simplest *Officium Stellae* such as that of Besançon, only the Magi appear, following the star and presenting their gifts.[10] In the eleventh-century play from Nevers, they meet Herod but no court attendants are present.[11] They gradually make an appearance: Strassburg (c.1200) provides messengers and attendants,[12] and Compiègne (eleventh-century) includes the scribes.[13] Other plays are still more complex. Bilsen (twelfth-century) has much "stage business" with three different messengers rushing around, threatening the Magi, boasting of Herod as king of the whole world, and running into court one after the other to tell their news to the king.[14] Arnold Williams sees this as a means of building up suspense,[15] while Karl Young sees "a touch of unusual animation, possibly of humour"[16] in the excited "Rex! Rex! Rex!" of the second messenger. The eleventh-century Freising play has even more elaborate roles for the court messengers and soldiers who deal with the Magi and scribes under Herod's orders as well as an indication of the citizens of Jerusalem whom the Magi question.[17] Both of these plays also open with choral processionals during which Herod enters and ascends his throne in much greater splendor than he does in the Fleury Massacre play.[18] Thus the seemingly unusual treatment of Herod's entrance in Fleury is not original with this playwright, nor is the introduction of his son, Archelaus, who also appears in a twelfth-century play from Montpellier where he pompously greets Herod and urges violence against the child.[19] But the Fleury plays maintain a decorum and dignity that is sometimes wanting in the other plays. The ultimate exaggeration in this tendency to expand the roles of people in the court comes in the thirteenth-century Benediktbeuern play when the outrageous Archisynagogus becomes Herod's chief counsellor. The Fleury plays avoid any unseemly or exaggerated action at the court.

In the visual arts the tradition of representing Herod as a powerful monarch in a courtly setting was well established by the twelfth century. He first appears in the fifth-century mosaics of Santa Maria Maggiore in Rome, nimbed and garbed in the robes of a Roman emperor, guarded by armed attendants, advised by scribes, and served by soldiers ready to carry out his commands. In Carolingian and Ottonian art he is also presented as an emperor, seated on a raised, bejewelled throne, holding a scepter and suitably attended. In some instances, such as the ninth-century ivory book cover for the Lorsch Gospels now in the Vatican Museum, Herod, seated on the left of the bottom panel interviewing the Magi, is given equal prominence with the Virgin Mary, who is seated on the right of the same panel, holding the Christ Child, and receiving the same Magi. A great many twelfth-century manuscripts and sculptures continue the tradition of presenting Herod as the king or emperor of a powerful court, but at the same time new motifs were introduced which reflected the same interest revealed in the drama in Herod as an angry, violent, evil tyrant. These motifs first appear in depictions of his meeting with the Magi.

II

The Magi. The coming of the Magi was the most popular of all events depicted in Christmas/Epiphany art and drama. Their meeting with Herod, based on scripture, was a natural extension of the developing Magi cycles of the eleventh and twelfth centuries. At the same time, it offered great dramatic opportunities. Arnold Williams thus points out that "the appearance of the Magi at Herod's court afforded a chance for spectacle—think of it, four kings on stage at once—and Herod is the first villain in the drama of Western Europe."[20] In the Fleury play, Herod's reception of the Magi is of great interest especially when compared with other plays of the period. It is a mean between two extremes. He is neither a paragon nor a demon.

The Fleury Magi enter in the traditional manner from different directions, commenting on the bright star which they are following. When they meet, elaborate rubrics explain precisely how each one is to greet the other two individually with the phrase "Pax tibi, frater" and then to give the kiss of peace to each of them before proceeding to Jerusalem. In most other plays, Herod is informed by rather precocious messengers of their arrival in his country, but in the Fleury play, in spite of his large court, he takes the initiative in sending out an *armiger* to question the strangers. When they are finally brought into the presence of Herod, the Magi fully and elaborately identify themselves for the third time in the play, each time making special mention of the star. They are received graciously by the king who decides to make further inquiries. He asks a question which is not in scripture but which seems to have originated in an earlier Magi play from Nevers:[21] "Si illum regnare creditis, dicite nobis." In response, the Magi show him their mystical gifts as evidence of their faith in the new-born king. Herod turns away from them then to consult his scribes for corroborating evidence and to talk to his son about possible courses of action before dismissing the Magi with the canonical request that they return and inform him about the Child. As the Magi leave the court, the rubrics explain that the star, which had stopped shining in Herod's presence, now reappears to lead them to Bethlehem. Herod and his son, seeing this, shake their swords after them in a most unkingly manner. Although this is his last appearance in the play, he is not forgotten. As the Magi proceed to the manger they discuss the power of the babe, born in a stable between an ox and an ass (in contrast to Herod's opulent court), and they quote Balaam on his Jewish ancestry (in contrast to Herod's "foreign" lineage); when they are warned by the angel at the end of the play, they make a highly unusual response: "Deo Gracias. Surgamus ergo uisione moniti angelica, et calle mutato lateant Herodem que uidimus de puero." Karl Young suggests that this speech "expresses their readiness to outwit Herod"[22] and indeed the rubrics also bring attention back to him by stating that the Magi escape safely "non vidente Herode." Certainly the villainous nature of Herod is suggested by such lines, but in the presence of the Magi, Herod is a dignified, gracious, and regal monarch in the Fleury play.

Several of the details in the Fleury presentation of the Magi with Herod can be strikingly illuminated when compared with other plays. Let us consider first the Pax, or kiss of peace. This is an eminently suitable greeting for the Magi, but one cannot but feel that other playwrights go to extremes when they extend the use of this greeting to Herod himself. In the Compiègne play, the Magi greet each other with the Pax and then at court they greet Herod in the same way. The twelfth-century Montpellier play goes even further in that Herod seems to take the initiative in greeting each king with a kiss and then ceremoniously seating them, the first on Herod's right, the second beside the first, and the third on Herod's left. Herod shows extraordinary patience in this play when the Magi, instead of waiting for Herod to speak, break protocol by asking why they have been summoned; then, when he formally greets them, two of them speak in a totally foreign-sounding language. In contrast to this princely behavior, we are given an outrageously rude and arrogant Herod in other plays. In the Freising play, Herod insolently (and ironically) refers to his visitors as those "externos tyrannos"; he haughtily demands to know where they are from, addressing each king in rude, abrupt language: "Tu mihi responde," "Tu ai, unde es?" and "Tu tertius unde es?" The most extreme example of his rude reception of the Magi comes in the Bilsen play. Angered by the Magi's explanation of the star, Herod brandishes swords in their presence and demands a statement of faith in the new king; so enraged is he when the Magi then show him their gifts that he orders them to be thrown into prison; later they are recalled and abruptly quizzed (as they were in Freising). Dissuaded from killing the Magi by his *armiger,* Herod returns their gifts and sends them off with his hypocritical request that they report back to him. It becomes quite clear that when compared with such exaggerated versions of Herod's meeting with the Magi, the Fleury play manages to avoid extremes. It chooses a "middle way" which is powerful, yet dignified.

Twelfth-century art, like the drama, was bold and inventive in portraying Herod's evil. However, the meeting of the Magi with Herod was treated rather conventionally in the visual arts, as it was, indeed, in the Fleury play. Two motifs are of interest when comparing the development of this scene at Fleury and in the arts—the star and the sword. Let us first consider the star, which in the twelfth century appears appropriately enough in painted glass as well as in manuscripts.

The apocryphal disappearance of the star over the palace of Herod, referred to in the Fleury play, was well known at this time, and indeed the absence of the star over scenes at the court was a popular, if negative convention for indicating the evil of Herod. Thus the standard iconography in twelfth-century Magi cycles included a star in the scene of the Journey of the Magi but not in their meeting with Herod. Most of these cycles occur in manuscripts within cycles of the Infancy of Christ or the Life of Christ which became so popular at this time as a preface to the Psalter. One of the surviving leaves of an English Psalter, produced at Canterbury around 1140, shows this iconography. This large leaf, now preserved in British Library Add. MS. 37,472, contains twelve scenes covering events between the Annunciation to the Shepherds and the Death of Herod. Herod appears twice within the Magi cycle, which begins with the Magi, all crowned and mounted, pointing up to a large star in the sky. In the next scene, they appear before Herod, who sits under an arch listening to them as one points up to the sky, though no star is there, while the other two point to Herod.[23] The same iconography can be seen in a similar Psalter leaf in the Bibliothèque Nationale, MS. lat. 8846, also painted at Canterbury not long before 1200 and directly influenced by the earlier leaf.[24] Again the star appears above the Magi as they travel to Jerusalem, but not when they meet King Herod, who is a lively figure holding a scepter and sitting in an animated pose with legs crossed in an exaggerated fashion. The better-known Winchester Psalter,[25] with its prefatory cycle of thirty-eight full-page miniatures (each page containing two or three registers), also reflects this standard iconography of the missing star in its scene of the Magi with Herod. One king points upward while the others (one holding a scroll) gesture to Herod, whose scepter, incidentally, has been replaced by a sword which lies unsheathed across his lap (see below). In all other respects this scene is conventional.

There are some interesting examples in twelfth-century art, nevertheless, of the star actually shining over Herod. One occurs in a panel of painted glass from the Etienne window of the Cathedral at Châlons-sur-Marne, now preserved in the Treasury of the Cathedral (the Museum of French Monuments) where it was installed in 1957. This was a narrative window of the Infancy of Christ[26] and the relevant scene is Herod meeting the Magi. He is presented as a king, crowned and enthroned, with his right hand raised toward the three Magi standing before him. One of the Magi holds a scroll (as in the Winchester Psalter) and all of them gesture towards a star which appears in the center of the panel above them. Attention is directed to the star rather than to Herod. This is further emphasized by the presentation of the Magi as astrologers rather than kings; they wear skull caps instead of the more typical twelfth-century crowns.[27] Another example of this unusual iconography occurs in a twelfth-century painted glass window in Canterbury Cathedral, second window in the north choir aisle.[28] This window has been restored but for the most part is still arranged in its original typological order. A fairly complete Magi cycle is included. At the top of the window, in the center, the three Magi appear on horseback; they all gesture to and look up at a large star at the top of the panel. Just below this panel we see the Magi before Herod, who is crowned but looks pensive as the Magi, also crowned, speak and gesture towards a star which again appears above their heads above an arc of heaven.[29] Both of these examples showing the star shining in the presence of Herod are highly unusual, and both appear in glass. Perhaps the eminent suitability of the motif for the medium was irresistibly attractive to the glaziers and those who designed the windows. It does not seem to be a case of the telescoping of scenes together.

The second motif from the Fleury play which finds expression in contemporary art is the new Herod who brandishes a sword at the Magi. One example from the Winchester Psalter has already been cited, and although several examples can be found it is unlikely that they outnumber the representations of Herod holding a scepter (Herod holding a sword while ordering the Massacre of the Innocents, on the other hand, became standard iconography). This motif certainly became popular at this period, but whether the artist chose the scepter or the sword seems to have been a matter of personal choice. In two closely related Psalters painted in the twelfth century, both motifs appear. The first, the Copenhagen Psalter produced in Northern England about 1170, shows the Magi before Herod who holds a floriated scepter.[30] The later Psalter, Gough liturg. 2 in the Bodleian Library, was executed around 1200.[31] Although it has a longer cycle of pictures, the Life of Christ cycle is closely dependent on the Copenhagen Psalter; in fact they have thirteen scenes in common which are almost identical in composition.[32] The Magi before Herod is among the common scenes, and yet in the later Psalter Herod holds a sword rather than a scepter, although one of the Magi has been given a scepter. Even when an artist was copying this scene, then, he could choose either the sword or the scepter for Herod to hold.

The sword was also introduced in other, more subtle ways. For example, the early twelfth-century St. Albans Psalter,[33] which includes a full Magi cycle among its forty-three full-page illuminations of the Life of Christ, presents Herod interviewing the Magi; he sits on a raised throne gesturing to the Magi while behind him stands an attendant, a small figure holding a large sword. Herod, in a most unusual iconographic detail, has a book on his knees. A telescoping of two scenes into one has taken place here. The artist, instead of showing Herod's interview with the scribes separately or including the scribes in the interview with the Magi, has omitted them altogether and transferred their book to Herod. And so Herod the king is seen consulting the prophecies himself, as he does in the drama, although in the St. Albans Psalter he is evidently discussing them with the Magi in a lively conversation rather than throwing them to the ground in a fit of rage. The little sword-bearer of this manuscript becomes more prominent in a little-known but interesting manuscript, Emmanuel College MS. 252^{2}, where the Magi meet an unusual Herod.[34] Crowned, he sits on the left on a cushioned bench facing the Magi but has one leg drawn up so that his foot actually rests on the bench and his knee is close to his chest, a most casual and unkingly posture. One hand is raised in gesture to the Magi (or perhaps it is pointing up to the sky), and the other is hooked into the neck of his garment in a rather peculiar way. He holds nothing, but sitting at his feet is a serious, scowling sword-bearer with a very prominent naked sword, hilt upwards, balanced on his knees. This sword in fact separates Herod from the Magi who stand on the right. The fierce-looking little sword-bearer in the middle of the picture is indeed the center of attention.

Herod holds the sword himself and becomes a much more menacing figure in the sculptural decoration of the late twelfth-century (c.1180-90) Church of St. Trophimes in Arles. He appears in a Magi cycle on a frieze across the capitals of the west front of the church. Proud and menacing, he is accompanied by armed guards, and he also has a huge sword laid across his knees as he entertains the Magi. This scene is reminiscent of the Herod in the plays from Freising, Bilsen, and Montpellier where he brandishes his sword at the Magi, but it should be remembered that in the more conservative Fleury play it is more likely that he carried a scepter, waiting until the Magi had left before taking out his sword.

One even more daring detail was introduced into French sculpture to indicate the evil of Herod during his interview with the Magi. The Cathedral of St. Peter at Poitiers shows a winged, horned devil perched on Herod's throne, giving him bad advice while he talks to the Magi. Maillard describes the scene: "Hérode, placé à un angle saillant du tailloir, est encore accosté d'un démon, ayant des cornes au front et de grande ailes, qui pose un pied sur le trône et, ainsi juché, souffle ses conseilles. Les trois mages, debout, couronnés, vêtus de longues robes, disent à Hérode la date à laquelle l'étoile leur apparue."[35] This devil, in this scene, is a twelfth-century imaginative innovation which makes the iconography of Herod the Great more vivid and dramatic. Such devils, however, appeared more often during Herod's questioning of the scribes, a scene which we must now consider.

III

The Scribes. The scribes, whom Herod summons after interviewing the Magi, enjoy an unprecedented period of popularity in the art and drama of the twelfth century. Of seventeen extant Epiphany plays from the eleventh and twelfth centuries, thirteen contain parts for the scribes, the Fleury playbook being one of the most complete. The rubrics of this play are fairly precise in indicating the scribes' appearance, the books they carry, and their actions in searching for the prophecy. They are ostentatiously summoned by young courtiers, with whom they are in sharp contrast, for they are bearded and are reverently carrying their books of the prophets. At Herod's command, they turn the pages for a while as if looking for the prophecy; finding it, they point it out to the unbelieving king while the chorus sings it. Herod then snatches the book away from them and in a fit of rage throws it to the ground. This superbly dramatic action involving the degradation of the holy books of the Jews was the playwrights' contribution to the *Herodes iratus* tradition, already fully developed by patristic writers. The earlier play from Freising had first introduced this action for Herod; later the Bilsen play had Herod examine the books himself before handing them back to the scribes. And in the play from Montpellier the scribes are summoned by Herod's "bishop," giving them greater religious importance, while Herod himself examines their book before dashing it to the ground. The Fleury play, however, gives the fullest explanation of his actions, and instead of having Herod turn abruptly to dismiss the Magi after this fit of rage, the playwright uses the tumult caused by Herod's anger at court to introduce Herod's son at this point to soothe his father and promise revenge. Thus the appearance of the scribes, their pointing out the prophecy, and the consequences of their action are all given prominence in the Fleury playbook and other drama of the twelfth century. Their role in liturgical drama can be perhaps more fully appreciated when one realizes that they do not appear at all in the later English mystery cycles. Their prophecies are spoken by the Magi; only the Chester cycle retains a "doctor" to quote and explain the "prophets," and this is made a source of some humor as Herod defies "that ould villard Jacob" and the other "dotardes" who have been quoted.

The art of the twelfth century gave the same prominence to the scribes as the drama. They enjoyed a brief period of popularity at this time and then faded away almost entirely. They never appear alone but always with Herod and usually in a scene with the Magi, but they can be found in sculpture, painted glass, and manuscript illumination. They first appear on the west doorway, the Portail Royale, of the Cathedral of Notre Dame in Chartres (c.1145-55)[36] in a frieze running across the jamb capitals showing events from Christ's Infancy. They are included in the scene which represents Herod's interview with the Magi, sitting beside Herod but turned away from him, consulting a book. A second portrayal of a similar scene on a much larger scale is found on the upper lintel of the tympanum of the St. Anne Portal, west front of Notre Dame Cathedral in Paris (c.1165).[37] The right side of the lintel is devoted to Herod as he asks the Magi and his scribes about the birthplace of Christ. He sits in the center, facing directly front. He is crowned and sits in a pose similar to earlier Carolingian and Ottonian emperor-portraits, knees apart, feet together, and resting on a dais. He has a scepter, and leans both hands on his knees, elbows out defiantly as he listens to the scribes beside him, towards whom he inclines slightly. The scribes are two little old men seated on a bench to Herod's right, huddled over a book which they earnestly consult. On Herod's left the three crowned Magi stand in a row holding their staffs (or scepters). A third but highly original example of the scribes in French sculpture can be seen beside the St. Michael portal on the north side of the Cathedral of St. Peter at Poitiers (mentioned above). Maillard describes the scene where they appear with Herod: "Sur l'angle saillant qui est au centre du tailloir, on voit Hérode, assis sur un trône, tourné vers le droite; il se penche pour écouter attentivement l'explication de la prophétie, relative à la venue du Messie, qui lui est faite par deux hommes sur un banc et tenant des livres; tandis qu'il écoute, un démon, vêtu d'une cotte courte, lui insuffle ses mauvais conseils au moyen d'une trompe."[38] Herod leaning over to hear the scribes is much the same as the scene at Notre Dame, Paris, but the last detail, describing the devil, dressed in a short coat, whispering evil advice in Herod's ear through a little trumpet, is a new and exciting element in this representation. This is the first appearance of such a devil and it possibly reflects a new role for the devil in twelfth-century thought.

The scribes also appeared in painted glass. Contained in the central chapel of the ambulatory of the Abbey Church of St. Denis was a window depicting the Infancy of Christ. Abbot Suger may have determined the iconographic program for this window, of which only fragments survive.[39] One of these fragments is a panel showing a crowned king sitting on a throne, holding a floriate scepter in his left hand, with his right hand raised in a gesture of greeting or conversation as he turns slightly to the left. A slightly mutilated inscription survives across the lower part of this panel, identifying the king as [HE]RODES. Beside Herod, on the right of the panel, two scribes sit on a bench, their heads inclined towards each other as they pore over an inscribed book. Grodecki points out that the condition of this glass is excellent and that it is all original except for a few pieces in the drapery of the scribe on the right.[40] However, this panel was not meant to be complete in itself, an independent representation of this first interview of Herod with his scribes; Herod is turned away from the seated figures and has his hand raised as if he were talking to someone in front of him who, of course, should be the three Magi. This very panel of the Three Magi before Herod was discovered in a house in Paris in 1957;[41] the kings walk towards the right, the first raising his hand in a gesture of conversation, matching Herod's gesture. There is an inscription but it is mutilated with only the beginning remaining: [MA]GI VENIUNT. This small rectangular medallion would have been placed beside the main medallion of Herod with his scribes in the Infancy window, as can be seen by Grodecki's plan of the original window. Herod is thus given great prominence in this window, forming one of only seven scenes that were represented in the central medallions. Herod and his scribes appear in the central medallion rather than the three Magi who have come to worship Christ.

The St. Denis scene of the Magi before Herod and his scribes may have been the direct source for the same scene in the painted glass window of the Infancy of Christ at the west end of the Cathedral in Chartres. Chartres, like St. Denis, has two panels for this scene; in one panel the three Magi approach, one behind the other, the first one with his hand raised in a gesture, while in the second panel Herod is seated, crowned and holding a scepter, and gesturing towards the Magi as two men sit behind him on a bench with heads inclined towards each other as they pore over an open book. The iconographic scheme is the same for both windows, although in Chartres the Magi approach from the right side instead of from the left as they do in St. Denis. Representations of Herod the Great in twelfth-century glass remained much more standard and traditional than those in frescoes or sculpture. No devils or swords were introduced until the thirteenth century.[42] However, the scribes were included in the earliest windows at St. Denis and Chartres, although they were excluded in later centuries.

Some of the most interesting depictions of Herod's scribes in twelfth-century art appear in the two Psalter leaves from Canterbury, mentioned above. The number of scribes increases dramatically and they become the center of attention. British

Library Add. MS. 37,472 includes a scene with Herod after he has met the Magi in which he is entertaining a large group of Jews who appear before him wearing their traditional caps. They seem to be discussing a long scroll which is held by Herod and the foremost Jewish scribe. This scroll must be the prophecy of Micah which the scribes identify for Herod in the Gospel and in the liturgical drama. Behind them in this rather crowded scene stand the three Magi, who are listening to what is being said. The Paris Infancy leaf, Bib. Nat. MS. lat. 8846, shows an interesting development of this scene and indeed is unique iconographically. Herod sits enthroned, crowned and with a scepter as usual, but he is confronted by a large group of twelve Jews (in caps) and scribes who are trying to persuade him to believe their prophetic books. One scribe, seated in the foreground, holds an open book, the prophecy of Micah; another, seated closest to Herod, is in lively conversation with him while a third holds up an astrolabe for him to see. This is an extremely apt but unique choice of attribute for the scribes here, for it was an instrument used for measuring the altitude of stars (Herod asks the Magi about the star they followed). Given the emphasis on the star in all Epiphany plays and the continued emphatic reference to it in the Fleury play, this appearance of the astrolabe in the visual arts, presented by the scribes, is highly suitable. Thus twelfth-century writers and artists treated the scribes of Herod's court with a good deal of originality and liveliness, which unfortunately was lost in later centuries.

IV

Soldiers. In the iconography of the Massacre of the Innocents, the soldiers play the most important part, receiving orders from Herod, performing their bloody business, and sometimes showing the results to the king. The Fleury Herod play is unusual in that it ends with the return of the Magi to their own countries (i.e., the choir); no messenger rushes to Herod with news of their escape as in most other *Officium Stellae* which include the order for the Massacre, given to a soldier. The only soldier in Herod's crowded court is the *armiger,* who seems to be mainly a messenger. The Fleury manuscript, of course, has a separate play for the Massacre, and although the proportion given to Herod and his court is quite small, it is significant. His *armiger* plays a more subtle role—ceremoniously presenting the scepter to him at the beginning, then informing Herod that he has been deceived. This news leads Herod to shout his Sallustian line, "Incendium meum ruina restiguam," and to snatch a sword to try to commit suicide rather than, as in all other extant plays, to order the Massacre. His *armiger* is among those who prevent him from this act of madness, but he is also the first to suggest that Herod vindicate his wrath by having the children killed by the sword. Herod's last act in the play is, in fact, to hand over his sword to the *armiger* giving the order for the Massacre, which seems to have been presented in a formal, stylized way before the major portion of the drama, the lament of Rachel, takes place.

One of the main points of interest in dramatic scenes involving Herod and his soldiers is: Who first suggests the Massacre? In the Fleury play, as in other *Officium Stellae* plays that end with the Massacre such as those from Freising and Compiègne, it is the soldier/*armiger* who introduces the idea, with Herod quickly consenting. In the play from Montpellier Herod's "dukes" wave their swords in the air, joined by Archelaus, inciting Herod to give the order.[43] The fact that Herod himself does not take the initiative in giving the order was made much of in later mystery cycles where Herod was presented as weak-minded, erratic, and easily manipulated by his advisors. In only one Latin play, the thirteenth-century *Ordo Rachelis* from Freising,[44] does Herod actually take the initiative for ordering the Massacre, and even here he commands that only the "rex novus" be destroyed; he changes the order after his enthusiastic soldier suggests that all the children be included.

The emphasis in the liturgical drama is more on the anger of Herod, the *Herodes iratus* of *Matthew* 2.16, than on his violence. One of the strikingly original and apt contributions to this tradition, included in the Fleury *Massacre,* is the use of the quotation from Sallust as an expression of Herod's explosive anger. The Strassburg play ends abruptly with this classical line; the Freising *Officium Stellae* gives the line to Herod when he hears that he has been deceived by the Magi; but the Fleury *Massacre* has Herod say this line as he tries to stab himself, imitating the actions of *Ira,* a fine touch of literary sophistication.

In the visual arts, the soldiers in the scene of the Massacre of the Innocents hold prominent swords as they drag children from their mothers and mutilate them. Herod himself may hold a scepter or a sword as he gives the order. Twelfth-century artists were the first to give him a sword in this scene, and their depictions are often lively and imaginative. One example will suffice—a particularly bold and arrogant Herod from the capital frieze of the Portail Royale of Chartres Cathedral. He sits in the center of an exceptionally large Massacre scene (including ten mothers and eight soldiers), "his legs crossed, his drawn sword held upright, his left arm aggressively akimbo, his cloak blown about as if by a hostile wind; he has a broad face with high cheekbones and an elegant moustache, a physiognomy of unforgettable insolence, matching his striking posture to perfection."[45] He is already the archetypal model for all wicked kings of later medieval art in this superb portrayal. In the same way, the Fleury Herod contains in essence all the seeds for later dramatic developments of this angry tyrant-king.

Although the visual arts of the twelfth century never went to the lengths of the fifteenth century in showing Herod himself massacring children,[46] they did introduce twisting, ugly soldiers and, in the Winchester Psalter, one grotesque monster to help carry out Herod's orders.[47] In the Massacre scene of this manuscript, fol. 14, Herod sits on a cushioned throne on the left, holding his naked sword point up with his left hand, while pointing with a crooked finger at the Massacre in front of him. His face is painted very dark, a technique which became popular later for depicting evil characters. Behind him stands a soldier in chain mail, holding a lance; in front of him stands another, stabbing a child he holds by the arm as he turns back to hear Herod's orders. But this figure is eclipsed by a gigantic, grotesque, negroid monster which is biting into the body of a child he has impaled on his sword. This astonishing creature is the supreme expression of all the evil of the Massacre and of Herod who orders it.

This monster may very well be unique, but his closest relative, the devil, having been introduced into Romanesque art in the eleventh century, soon found an ideal associate in the Herod of Massacre scenes. The devils who make tentative appearances while Herod interviews the Magi and consults his scribes also appear in Massacre scenes, urging him on to do evil and violent deeds. The Poitiers sculpture includes a winged devil whispering in Herod's ear during the Massacre; a capital in the cloisters of Moissac shows two devils with Herod, one on his shoulder and one at his feet;[48] the English Emmanuel College MS. 252[2] also introduces a little devil standing on the back of his neck. In the thirteenth and fourteenth centuries these devils become much more lively and prominent, but they are introduced into the iconography of Herod the Great in the twelfth century as a concrete example of his association with evil and madness. In the contemporary drama too evil is emphasized, yet controlled in plays such as the Fleury *Massacre*. Here the fine control and restraint is of the utmost importance.

V

Herod's Suicide and Death. The Fleury play is unique in introducing Herod's attempted suicide into liturgical drama; it was also the first play to show his death. This is all accomplished in the rubrics: "Tunc Herodes, quasi corruptus, arrepto gladio, paret seipsum occidere; sed prohibeatur tandem a suis et pacificetur." Herod, in a moment of madness, seizes a sword and tries to kill himself, but is restrained by his attendants. His only comment here is the line from Sallust, mentioned above, subtly shifted to this new context. The whole scene is in stark contrast to what precedes and follows: Joseph's gentle address to Egypt as the Holy Family approaches and the procession of Innocents, dressed in white, following the Lamb and praising God.

The attempted suicide of Herod is not merely an imaginative fiction of the Fleury playwright; it was an historical fact, first presented by Josephus,[49] much discussed in patristic writings, and known in the twelfth century through such encyclopedic histories as the *Historia Scholastica* of Petrus Comestor.[50] But the Fleury version is not the attempted suicide of these sources, which described a desperately ill and aged Herod lying in bed in agony and trying to end his misery by plunging a fruit knife into his breast. This play has Herod seated on his throne in majesty, healthy and powerful, enjoying the pomp and ceremony of his court. By this time, his anger was proverbial (note the many plays in which he brandishes his sword), and the Fleury playwright extended this anger to the ultimate act of madness, suicide.[51] This is thus the first time that Herod's suicide is presented in medieval dramatic literature, and it is portrayed as an act of madness and anger.

At the same time, Herod's suicide was also presented in the visual arts, which seem to have followed historical accounts and patristic commentary more accurately. The two large twelfth-century Psalter leaves, already referred to above in relation to Herod's meeting with the Magi and the scribes, both include the suicide-death of Herod. The great iconographical innovation of these leaves is in fact in the last picture of each showing the Death of Herod. In the British Library MS. (Add. 37,472) he lies in bed with a coverlet over him; with his right hand he stabs himself in the chest (or throat). His soul issues from his mouth and is seized by a demon above his head. Behind the bed are two figures: one carries a sword upright and seems to be an attendant, the other offers to Herod a round object. This object is the apple which Herod asked for in order to get the fruit knife which he used in his attempted suicide, according to Josephus. The miniature gives a slightly inaccurate version of the episode, however. According to Josephus, Herod did try to commit suicide by stabbing himself with a fruit knife, but was stopped by his cousin, Achiabus, who happened to be nearby. Herod did not die until five days later. Jacobus de Voragine, in the *Golden Legend,* gives this story in his chapter on the Holy Innocents,[52] but at the very end he adds the version of Remigius, given in *In Originali super Matthaeum,* which claims that Herod's suicide attempt was successful. The representation on this Psalter leaf could be following Remigius' version or, more likely, it is the result of telescoping the major related details—suicide and then death—into a single miniature. The suicide and/or death of Herod was illustrated in later English manuscripts, notably the Holkham Bible Picture Book, but Add. MS. 37,472 is the first known example in English work.

In the Paris leaf, Bib. Nat. MS. lat. 8846, the Death of Herod is almost the same composition as in the earlier, related British Library manuscript. However, in the Paris leaf, Herod still wears his crown; also the demon snatching his soul has increased considerably in size and has become quite a lively, dramatic figure. One of the men behind Herod's bed holds the same round object in his hands—the apple. Because his hands are covered with cloth, usually a sign of reverence (priests are usually shown holding the host with covered hands), Leroquais interpreted this figure as a priest offering Herod the sacrament, which he refuses.[53] This interpretation is to be questioned, however, as iconographically improbable because the figure is not tonsured, and as far as I know there is no literary source for this subject at all. Herod was never considered a candidate, as Pilate sometimes was, for heaven or salvation in any patristic or liturgical writings or in any of the apocryphal books.

The Fleury play is accurate in indicating that Herod's suicide attempt was unsuccessful. At the end of the play, while the (slain) Innocents rise again in response to the angel's call and proceed, singing, to the choir, a new and separate scene is introduced, again in the rubrics: "Dum hec fiunt, tollatur Herodes et substituatur in loco eius Filius eius, Archelaus, et exaltetur in regem." This presumably was acted out in mime and is immediately followed by the angel's message to Joseph: "Ioseph, Ioseph, Ioseph, fili David! Revertere in terram Iudam, defuncti sunt enim qui querebant animam pueri," from *Matthew* 2.20. The playwright is following the Vulgate closely. However, the Gospel of Matthew refers only fleetingly to the death of Herod and other enemies of Christ. As this is essential information in order to motivate the Return from Egypt, the playwright presented the action in mime, not providing any new dialogue for the death of Herod or the enthronement of Archelaus, but including this event in order to explain the Return from Egypt in its dramatic sequence.

The Fleury play is the first to present the death of Herod. It does so in a formal, dignified fashion which can be fully appreciated when compared with the thirteenth-century Benediktbeuern version of the same event, which in that play is gruesome and horrible. Again it is described in the rubrics: "Postea Herodes corrodatur a vermibus, et excedens de sede sua mortuus accipiatur a Diabolis multum congaudentibus. Et Herodis corona imponatur Archelao filio suo." He is not simply removed from his throne and replaced by Archelaus as in Fleury. In the Benediktbeuern version, some of the more macabre details of his sickness and death, first given by Josephus, dwelt on by patristic writers, and emphasized by Petrus Comestor in the twelfth century and Vincent de Beauvais in the thirteenth, are presented in drama for the first time. In the *Historia Scholastica,* Comestor described him:

> Nam febris non mediocris erat, prurigo intolerabilis in omni corporis superficie, assidius vexabatur colli tormentis, pedes intercutaneo vitio tumuerant, putredo testiculorum vermes generebat, creber anhelitus et interrupta suspiria, quae ad vindictam Dei ab omnibus referebantur.

Comestor interpreted Herod's vile, disgusting death as the direct vengeance of God for the Massacre. The Benediktbeuern playwright thus disregarded historical time and had Herod die immediately after the Massacre rather than several years later. In the play, Herod is not only eaten by worms, but when death takes him devils snatch his soul with great jubilation, as they did in the twelfth-century Psalter leaves. One can see in comparing these two dramatic versions of the death of Herod in liturgical plays that the Fleury play, as always, treats its material with restraint and solemnity throughout.

VI

The Fleury Herod plays have been widely praised by a great variety of critics. In this paper we have limited our observations to Herod and his court and then compared the Fleury treatment with other liturgical drama and contemporary art in France and England. Through such an approach it becomes overwhelmingly clear that the Fleury plays are complex and sophisticated in composition and characterization; they introduce new scenes upon occasion, they improve the motivation and timing of Herod's acts, and they include the newest developments of contemporary twelfth-century drama that contribute to the growing tradition of the biblical *Herodes iratus* and *Herodes turbatus*. At the same time, however, the playwright exercises a fine control over his material, presenting it with the dignity and solemnity to be expected within the confines of the medieval church walls. When transcribing the music for the two Herod plays in the Fleury manuscript, William Smoldon was impressed with this same quality. He compares the music for these plays with the common "pool" of material in the Magi scenes of other plays and concludes that "whatever occasional parallels can be traced in Fleury's musical settings they seem to reflect an original mind and are the most satisfactory and polished among the surviving Christmas material."[55] The music, like the text, is often original and polished, satisfactory because it is supremely appropriate. The Fleury play does not go to the extremes of the Freising play which has Herod express his volatile character by throwing the Magi into prison or the Benediktbeuern play which has his dying body covered with worms and his damned soul snatched by a rejoicing devil. One is left with a new appreciation of the propriety of the Fleury plays and the judicious handling of their material. At the same time, it can be said that Herod was given certain traits of personality and his dramatic role was greatly increased. Scenes involving Herod became quite lively and displayed a great range of interpretation: he greets the Magi ceremoniously but shakes his sword at them when they leave; his anger makes him throw the books of the scribes on the ground and try to commit suicide. He may rant and rage more in the English mystery cycles, but almost every action in those later plays is foreshadowed by the treatment he is given in the Fleury play and in other music-dramas of the eleventh and twelfth centuries. Indeed, although Herod did more ranting and raving on the pageant wagons and in the streets of later medieval England, his dramatic character was already well developed in the Latin liturgical drama of the Church in the eleventh and twelfth centuries when his action was confined to the choir and nave of the sanctuary. The Fleury *Playbook* Herod plays represent the very best of this genre.

NOTES

1 Karl Young, *The Drama of the Medieval Church* (Oxford, 1933), II, 29.

2 O. B. Hardison, Jr., *Christian Rite and Christian Drama in the Middle Ages* (Baltimore: Johns Hopkins Press, 1965), p. 226.

3 See *The Play of Herod,* ed. Noah Greenberg and William Smoldon (New York: Oxford Univ. Press, 1965); Fletcher Collins, Jr., *The Production of Medieval Music-Drama* (Charlottesville: Univ. Press of Virginia, 1972); David Bevington, ed., *Medieval Drama* (Boston: Houghton Mifflin, 1975).

4 Young, II, 29-101. On p. 92, he suggests that the tradition of violence for Herod culminates in the Freising play, but this is in fact one of the earlier plays. One cannot agree with Young's chronological explanation of the growing sophistication of these plays. Nevertheless, his texts are still accepted as the standard ones and will be referred to throughout this paper. The *Ordo ad Representandum Herodem* is included in Young, II, 84-89, and the *Ordo ad Interfectionem Puerorum* appears in Young, II, 110-13.

5 Greenberg and Smoldon, p. vii.

6 Collins, *Production,* p. 135.

7 Grace Frank, *The Medieval French Drama* (Oxford, 1954), p. 34.

8 Critics differ as to whether these plays should be considered as one unit or as separate. E. K. Chambers, *The Mediaeval Stage* (Oxford, 1903), p. 50, found it impossible to believe that the play on the Massacre was performed a week earlier than the Herod play, as the church calendar would suggest. Greenberg and Smoldon performed and edited them as one unit. Fletcher Collins, although he discusses them as a unit, recognizes the difficulty of reconciling the dramaturgy of the two plays and doubts that they were even written by the same playwright (p. 136). Richard Axton, *European Drama of the Early Middle Ages* (London: Hutchinson, 1974), also states that the "two plays were probably not performed consecutively" (p. 80), although he too discusses them as a unit.

9 One other Norman-French play from Sicily labels its *Officium Stellae Versus ad Herodem Faciendum.* See Young, II, 59.

10 Young, II, 37-40.

11 Young, II, 50-51.

[12] Young, II, 64-67.

[13] Young, II, 53-56.

[14] Young, II, 75-80.

[15] Arnold Williams, *The Drama of Medieval England* (East Lansing: Michigan State Univ. Press, 1961), p. 24.

[16] Young, II, 82.

[17] Young, II, 93-97.

[18] The Bilsen play includes the same antiphon, *Super solium David*, after the opening chorus of hexameters, but the rubrics indicate that Herod ascends the throne whereas in the Fleury play he is already seated on the throne.

[19] Young, II, 68-72.

[20] Arnold Williams, p. 23.

[21] Young, II, 50-51.

[22] Young, II, 91.

[23] Plate 3. Herod's other appearance is with the scribes. See below.

[24] Plate 4; see especially V. Leroquais, *Les Psautiers Latins des bibliothèques publiques de France* (Mâcon, 1940-41), II 78-79. Leroquais dates this manuscript in the thirteenth century, but later authorities put it at the end of the twelfth century. See C. M. Kaufmann, *Romanesque Manuscripts 1066-1190* (London, 1975), p. 94.

[25] London, British Library, Cotton MS. Nero C.IV. For a reproduction see Francis Wormald, *The Winchester Psalter* (London, 1973).

[26] For reproduction see the Princeton Index of Christian Art.

[27] Gilberte Vezin, *L'Adoration et le Cycle des Mages* (Paris, 1950), p. 100.

[28] B. Rackham, *The Ancient Glass of Canterbury Cathedral* (London, 1949), dates this glass c.1200, but Madeline Caviness has recently established the date as 1220.

[29] In one very unusual illumination in the *Hortus Deliciarum,* Herod himself points to the star as he talks with the Magi.

[30] Copenhagen, Royal Library, MS. Thott 143 2°. For description, see Kaufmann, Cat. No. 96 and color frontispiece.

[31] Oxford, Bodleian Library, MS. Gough Liturg. 2 (S. C. 18343). For description, see Kaufmann, Cat. No. 97, and also Otto Pächt and J. J. G. Alexander, *Illuminated Manuscripts in the Bodleian Library* (Oxford, 1973), III, No. 290.

[32] Kaufmann, 121.

[33] Hildesheim, Library of St. Godehard. For reproduction, see O. Pächt, C. R. Dodwell, and F. Wormald, *St. Albans Psalter* (London, 1960).

[34] Plate 5. See also M. R. James, *Catalogue of the Western Manuscripts in the Library of Emmanuel College* (Cambridge, 1904), pp. 150-52.

[35] Elisa Maillard, *Les Sculptures de la Cathedrale de Saint-Pierre de Poitiers* (Poitiers, 1921), p. 82.

[36] See Adelheid Heimann, "The Capital Frieze and Pilasters of the Portail Royale, Chartres," *Journal of the Warburg and Courtauld Institutes,* 31 (1968), 73, for date.

[37] See Willibald Sauerlander, *Gothic Sculpture in France, 1140-1270,* trans. Janet Sondheimer (London, 1970), p. 405, for date.

[38] Maillard, pp. 79-80; see also Pl. XII.

[39] Louis Grodecki, "Les Vitraux de Saint-Denis. L'Enfance de Christ," *De Artibus Opuscula XL,* ed. Millard Meiss (New York, 1961), I, 170-86, claims that fragments from all three of the windows mentioned by Suger survive.

[40] Grodecki, p. 181.

[41] The glass is now in the Musée de Cluny.

[42] In the thirteenth-century windows of Lyons, Herod is accompanied by a devil as he orders the Massacre of the Innocents.

[43] In a thirteenth-century play from Laon, Archelaus alone urges Herod to the Massacre. See Young, II, 103-06.

[44] Young, II, 117-20.

[45] Heimann, p. 80.

[46] See the East window of St. Peter Mancroft Church, Norwich.

[47] See note 25, above.

[48] Jean Chagnolleau, *Moissac* (Arthaud, 1951), numbers this column 37. It is in the east gallery.

[49] Josephus, *The Jewish War* and *Jewish Antiquities,* in *Josephus,* trans. Ralph Marcus *et al.,* Loeb Classical Library (London, 1927-63).

[50] See *PL,* CXCVIII, cols. 1541-1689.

[51] This is the traditional act of *Ira* in Prudentius' *Psychomachia.*

[52] Jacobus de Voragine, *Legenda Aurea,* ed. Th. Graesse (1890; rpt. 1969), Cap. X, "De Innocentibus," pp. 62-66.

[53] Leroquais, I, cxv. The British Library leaf is reproduced and discussed by M. R. James, "Four Leaves of an English Psalter," *Walpole Society,* 25 (1936-37), 1-23 and Pl. III. The Bibliothèque Nationale leaf is reproduced in Plates 4, 7.

[54] *PL,* CXCVIII, col. 1546.

[55] Greenberg and Smoldon, p. 79.

Liturgical Dramaturgy and Modern Production

Cynthia Bourgeault

In this paper I wish to speak not only as a scholar but as a director, and to consider this dramatic entity called liturgical drama. What kind of an art form is it? What makes it tick? While I have attempted to ground the following reflections in solid scholarship, they have emerged primarily out of several years of actual experience in the production of this drama, most of it gained in collaboration with the University of Pennsylvania Collegium Musicum and its director, Mary Anne Ballard. A particular focus of our production activity has been the Fleury Playbook, and this focus will be reflected in my comments in this paper, although three non-Fleury plays have also been represented in our repertory: the Beauvais *Daniel* and *Peregrinus* and the Rouen *Officium Pastorum*.

My controlling interests are thus quite practical. Over and above those essential considerations of scholarly accuracy, I am concerned with yet another dimension: what will work? For work these plays will. Time and again I have seen them come alive, evoking a depth and power of response far out of proportion to their modest dramatic contours. Because of this power, which seems to be inherent in the nature of the drama itself, effective scholarly inquiry and practical production must both begin at the same point, with what George Steiner in his splendid study on translation, *After Babel*, refers to as faith in "the hermeneutic motion":[1] the conviction that the art form is intended to communicate expressively and a commitment to making that communication happen. Anything less is a form of cheating.

I do not mean, however, to suggest the opposite extreme: a laying on of stylish gimmickry in order to achieve effect. Lavish costumes, swollen medieval "orchestras," psychedelic lighting effects, or the creation of extraneous new characters to provide modern commentary are also forms of cheating, all the more regrettable because they are so unnecessary. What is called for instead is simply an attempt to discover the "living core" of this idiom, and then to re-create it as simply and honestly as possible.

I

Dramatic Modality. From the outset it is necessary to bear in mind that liturgical drama is a unique dramatic genre whose characteristics differ from all other forms of drama, even those of its closest neighbor, cycle drama. Liturgical drama rests on three pillars: theater, music, and liturgy. The three are of equal structural weight; a successful production requires a sensitivity to the innuendos in all three areas.

The recognition of this multi-dimensional nature of liturgical drama has been a relatively recent achievement of scholarship. The early days, in which the plays were regarded primarily as *literature,* have now fortunately given way to a greater sensitivity to the whole, W. L. Smoldon having argued valiantly that we give full consideration to the music, Fletcher Collins urging us to see the plays as theater. Liturgy, however, remains the curiously neglected member of this triumvirate, and one whose crucial role in the drama needs to be further explored if we are to understand fully the unique art form we are dealing with.

For more than forty years, ever since the publication of Karl Young's monumental *The Drama of the Medieval Church*, scholarship has been preoccupied with the boundary line between liturgy and drama. The reason for this preoccupation is undoubtedly to be found in that even more compelling puzzle: the question of the origin of the drama. Through a precise definition of boundaries it would seem possible to ascertain what is and what is not drama and hence to establish as clearly as possible that point in time at which the drama began. For Young the key issue was *impersonation*, a criterion which encouraged the fixing of broad and unbreachable boundaries—particularly so between Mass and drama. Because of "the impossibility of there being impersonation in the liturgy of the Eucharist,"[2] he was obligated to conclude that "the Mass has never been a drama, nor did it ever directly give rise to drama."[3]

More recent scholarship, spearheaded by O. B. Hardison, Jr., in his *Christian Rite and Christian Drama in the Middle Ages*

(Baltimore, 1965), has attempted to reverse this direction. In emphasizing the similarity rather than the discontinuity of ritual and drama, Hardison manages, as is his intention, to incorporate most of Christian liturgy, including the Mass itself, under the heading of "genuinely dramatic" and thus to extend far backwards in time the beginnings of drama. And yet in a curious way Hardison still feels the need to slip in a very low-key boundary between "ritual" and "representational" drama—a distinction which, for all his protestation, is not very far removed from Young's "impersonation." More seriously, from a theological standpoint, Hardison's work is based upon a very forced and "literary" interpretation of the liturgy, fashionable among certain liturgiologists of a generation ago but now increasingly fallen into disfavor.[4] Liturgy and drama *are* different, both qualitatively and historically, and despite Hardison's brilliant and fascinating perceptions of kinship, Young's understanding, though more stolid, is by far the more accurate.

The real problem with all this boundary-fixing activity, however, is that it misses the point, obscuring that which from a functional standpoint is the central motion of liturgical drama, *the playing against a boundary*. My own conviction, which I will attempt shortly to demonstrate, is that the medieval playwrights/liturgists sensed very well the difference between liturgy and drama. It was not ignorance but conscious delight which caused them to take as their starting point—as, in fact, the modality of the drama itself—a deliberate weaving back and forth between liturgy and drama, out of the ritual, into the representational, and back again. Liturgical drama "opens" to liturgy and "closes" to drama; this motion is the basic breathing of the play itself, building tremendous creative tension and energy.

In all plays this "breathing" is noticeable, in some far more markedly than in others. It is sustained in four ways:

1. In *liturgical borrowings*.

Recent scholarship on the liturgical drama has seen a vigorous outpouring of musicological contributions, of which one of the major benefits—particularly in a work such as Smoldon's *The Music of the Medieval Church Dramas* (London, 1980)—is to document chapter and verse just how much of liturgical drama is based upon pre-existent chant material. Even though the point is made, however, I am not sure that we moderns can fully grasp its dramatic impact; the monastic ambience is simply no longer there. For the medieval monk, geared into his familiar routine of Mass and Office, each chant had its own place, its own liturgical resonance. It was not merely a "pre-existent melody" to be identified by *Incipit* and CAO number, but an old friend. Perhaps the closest contemporary parallel would be if one were to encounter, woven into the score of a modern Broadway musical, the words and melody of "Old Hundredth" or the *Sursum corda.* The effect would be an immediate anchoring in the dimension of liturgy, an activating of the "worship" responses. So too in liturgical drama.

2. In *processionals*, where the play suddenly leaps "out of character" into festival celebration. This happens most obviously in the final *Te Deum*, in which all players join together in praise of God, but there are many other instances as well.

In *Daniel* there are at least a half-dozen such festival processionals. One of these, the opening *Astra tenenti*, incurred the particular displeasure of Smoldon because in his opinion it gave away the entire plot. "The text is a quaint example of medieval insensitivity to dramatic suspense," he complained.[5] Here, however, Smoldon misses the point, for the concern of the playwright is not so much with plot as with celebration. The purpose of the *Astra tenenti*, with its broad and reflective overview of the history of Daniel, is to dedicate the entire play *Ad honorem tui Christe* (as we are told in the very first line). This point becomes even clearer when, as Daniel is summoned to Darius' court, the whole ensemble sings *Congaudentes*, a conductus in honor of Christ and the Christmas season in which the play was performed. In terms of the drama *per se,* this digression makes no sense whatsoever; in terms of the drama as liturgical festival, however, it is at the heart of the whole undertaking. Practically speaking, processionals in liturgical drama seem more often to be there for liturgical than for dramatic reasons; as in the liturgy itself, their purpose is to establish a climate of participatory celebration.

3. In *prayers and proclamations*, which frequently take on a larger than life quality, pointing beyond the limits of the theatrical artifice. Euphrosina's prayer in the Fleury *Filius Getronis* or Daniel's in the lion's den; the angelic proclamation in the *Officium Pastorum* or the shepherds' beautiful *Salve virgo* at the manger: these and other such instances transport the play—for their duration at least—directly into the sphere of worship.

4. In *liturgical paraphrase and innuendo.* Instances of these

are scattered throughout the repertory, adding depth and resonance to the dramatic action. In *Filius Getronis* Marmorinus' elaborate "priestly" ablutions before the meal amount to a highly sophisticated parody of the communion rite, intended to emphasize the grotesqueness of the pagan court. In *Peregrinus* the dramatic climax arrives in the imitation of the central liturgical act, the breaking of the bread. In *Visitatio Sepulchri* the display and folding of the linens at the empty tomb paraphrase the folding of the corporal at the conclusion of the Eucharistic celebration. These liturgical nuances are further reinforced by such factors as the church building itself, the use of liturgical vestments and properties (as so many of the rubrics specify; this point will be discussed in more detail when we come to a consideration of costuming), and, in plays such as the *Officium Pastorum*, a conception of the whole drama within the framework of "officium" rather than "ludus."

I do not wish to imply that this liturgical/dramatic commingling is of equal strength in all plays. The Rouen *Officium Pastorum*, for example, is far more obviously "liturgical" than the Fleury *Tres Filiae*, a play which operates almost entirely within the confines of dramatic space as we now understand it. Looking at the whole *corpus* of liturgical drama, however, we find that it displays an overwhelming tendency to cross back and forth between liturgy and drama; this tendency is not an aberration, but the very nature of the art form. The essence of liturgical drama is the movement from self-contained dramatic time (history) into liturgical time and space *(locus sacer)* and back again—a kind of dynamic current, as between a positive and negative pole, which generates tremendous energy.

I have spoken earlier of this movement as the "breathing" of the play. The art of the director is to discover this breathing, at whatever rate it exists, and to enable it to happen through a careful attention to the play's modality and to its areas of transition and interplay. Most of the lifeless productions I have seen are so because not enough breathing room has been allowed.

II

Characterization. It is a common prejudice of modern theater people that medieval drama is dramatically naive. This prejudice often results in a self-fulfilling prophecy in which characters are played woodenly and the play's dramatic potential is held rigidly in check. To stage liturgical drama successfully, it is necessary to take it absolutely seriously as theater. When one does, one discovers that the repertory abounds in acting tour de forces, requiring a depth of concentration and emotional involvement equal to that found anywhere in theater.

Nevertheless, there are a few important qualifications, most of which stem from this fluctuating dramatic modality we have just spoken of. Much of what we moderns judge as "naive" is really our inability to perceive the liturgical play's modulation into celebration and to deal accordingly. Modern theater is heavily—perhaps exclusively—character oriented, its entire dramatic weight rising or falling on the strength of its character-revealing episodes. For the liturgical dramatist, characterization is certainly an option, but it is only one option among several, and not necessarily the best one. In any case, the kind of intense, highly individualized role-building that modern actors almost instinctively seek out is only occasionally appropriate and can actually become counter-productive.

A case in point can be made with the Rouen *Officium Pastorum*; here this modern predilection for characterization at any cost leads even as shrewd a theater man as Fletcher Collins, Jr., to miscalculate. In his discussion of this play in *The Production of Medieval Church Music-Drama* Collins suggests that the shepherds be played humorously, individualized with an eye to gentle parody.[6] He reasons that such an approach will create dramatic interest.

And yet, it is clear that this individualization works against the best interests of the play. When one sticks strictly with the text, the assertion of parody, even gentle parody, becomes difficult to support. Nowhere is there a hint of the clowning and misunderstanding which characterizes the later cyclic shepherds' plays. (Rouen's unique specification of five shepherds, in fact, suggests that the playwright is thinking more in terms of a chorus than of individualized personalities.) Moreover, if such clowning is introduced and allowed to get out of hand, the director eventually paints him/herself into a corner, and is left with the necessity of an awkward "conversion" scene at the manger before the singing of the graceful *Salve virgo*.

If one approaches the Rouen play strictly within its own modality, however, it rapidly becomes apparent that the dramatic motivation of the shepherds lies not in their humor but in something quite different. They proclaim; their energy is kerygmatic. In both of their lyric numbers, *Pax in terris* and *Salve virgo*, there is considerable theological and poetic felicity at work, hardly "in character" for rustic bumpkins. Thus, rather than filling up what is perceived as "dead" space with a contrived attempt at humorous characterization, the trick is to create a climate in which the shepherds can authentically proclaim.

I am aware that what I am saying may sound puzzling. Yet I have seen actors achieve that delicate balance of centeredness and detachment which allows liturgical drama to happen, and the goal, difficult though it may be to put into words, is well worth working toward. A simple and effective beginning point is to introduce actors to that basic convention of medieval staging, the *platea* or "place." Most actors are at first wretchedly uncomfortable with the whole concept of the medieval "offstage," which requires them to sit—just sit—in their place in plain sight of everybody. They try desperately to fill the vacuum with distracting counter-ripples of "staying in character." Gradually, however, they begin to learn that this time is an intensely valuable "neutral zone" in which they can learn to shift gears smoothly within the shifting modalities of the play.

When it comes to actual methods of acting, the question frequently arises as to whether a "stylistic" or "naturalistic" approach is more appropriate. Frankly, I see no real conflict: the two can be effectively combined.

Liturgical drama is intensely pictorial, and a bit of stylization goes a long way, particularly in the minor roles where there is no room for extensive individualization. The repertory of stylized actions can be borrowed in part from liturgical gesture, but more from the age-old stock-in-trade of mime and situation comedy (e.g., the wisemen in our *Daniel* brought down the house by miming a heated scholarly debate as to the meaning of the handwriting on the wall). Symmetry is also an effective principle of stylization which works particularly well with characters whose real import lies in their sameness rather than in their individuality: midwives, magi, comforters, counsellors, soldiers, etc. To balance or mirror the action on two halves of the playing area creates a satisfying visual coherence and sonority.

Such gentle stylization, however, by no means precludes the need for robust, "three-dimensional" acting. Although naturalistic acting in the strict Stanislavsky sense is inappropriate for reasons we have already seen, *natural* acting is not only appropriate but mandatory, particularly for the major characters. I recall a production I once saw in which the iconography of medieval gesture had been studiously researched so that every dramatic exchange was sonorous and ceremonial. The play, unfortunately, was the Fleury *Visitatio Sepulchri*, and the near-hysterical joy of Mary Magdalene's meeting with her risen lord in the garden fell flat—and with it, the play. Emotional encounter, wherever it happens, *must* be portrayed, and stylized gesture is simply not a "real" enough tool.[7] My own tastes in characterization, then, are for a blending of graceful stylization of the minor characters with a more natural and vigorous playing of the major roles.

Characterization arises naturally out of the need to communicate. Surprising as it may seem, actors who take upon themselves as a serious responsibility the communication of their Latin text are in fact remarkably well understood, even by non-specialist audiences. The gesture and inflection suggest themselves naturally out of the text itself and add sweep and power.

The art, all in all, is one of concentration and fluidity. The poet Wallace Stevens, in his poem "The Snow Man," speaks of beholding "Nothing that is not there and the nothing that is." In many ways this cryptic phrase captures the essence of characterization in liturgical drama. To understand precisely how much character is there, to play that character to the limits of its emotional range (but no further), to be guided by a loyalty to the overall design of the play and to allow this design to transmute but not diminish the emotional reality of the characterization: this is to experience the richness and subtlety of the liturgical dramatic art.

III

Staging. I will make my prejudice clear from the start: I vastly prefer to stage liturgical drama in a church because of the tremendous dramatic possibilities inherent in the building itself. If a church is not a possibility, the next choice is a neutral or even highly modern building, one whose space is inherently interesting and well defined—as, for example, the circular glass foyer of a local art museum which over the years housed many of our Collegium Musicum productions.

What will *not* work is a proscenium theater. The underlying dramatic concepts are too different and work at cross-purposes, the "self-containedness" of proscenium theater conflicting directly with the need of liturgical drama to spill over into participatory celebration. On those occasions where the Collegium has been required to perform in a proscenium theater, we always play before the curtain and in the aisles.

Assuming that one is using a church, the first task in staging is simply to go sit in the building to "feel out" its space. In most churches the following associations will naturally suggest themselves:

altar: sacred space. For the appearance of Christ; for sepulchre or manger.
pulpit: proclamation. Also, a location which is elevated and somewhat removed from the main flow of the action: a natural spot for angelic appearances.
aisles: congregational space. For processions and dramatic actions intended to underscore the immediacy of the play or to evoke participatory response.

There is, of course, give-and-take. Sometimes an altar will be too far back, sometimes a pulpit too far to the side or impossible to light. But insofar as one can get the basic energies of the building working, the play is already well on its way. Once a few non-negotiables have been nailed down, the rest of the staging will fall together naturally, with chancel and crossing providing the main playing areas. Balconies, baptismal fonts, side chapels, and alcoves all offer great opportunities to the imaginative director.

Sedes. Medieval theatre is *sedes*-oriented; scenes are made horizontally rather than consecutively. Given the overwhelmingly naturalistic bent of modern theater, it is surprising how easily this convention is accepted. As has been mentioned already, that great phobia of modern actors—"you mean I just *sit* there?"—rarely becomes obtrusive if handled well, and the audience very accommodatingly shifts its attention to wherever the action is.

Nevertheless, I have long been uncomfortable with a too mechanical or inflexible concept of *sedes*. The fixed "tents" of place and scaffold theater seem somehow out of place in liturgical drama, wasteful of space and disruptive of the real dramatic fluidity possible. Too often such *sedes* bottle up the action, rendering it stilted and overly stylized.

An extreme case in point is the Fleury *Conversion of St. Paul,* a play which Collins and others have considered to be virtually unperformable.[8] And if one takes the stage directions at face value, it is. The play calls for an unwieldy "tale of two cities" set, involving three *sedes* in Jerusalem (Saul's house, Barnabas' house, the high priest's chamber), four in Damascus (Judas' house, Ananias' bedroom, the high priest's chamber, a wall), and also the road on which Christ makes his appearance. Such a plan seemed to tie up the chancel horribly—not to mention the awkwardness of having Ananias lie abed for half the play. Rather than abandoning the play, which does have some very good dramatic moments, we hit upon the alternative of freeing up the action through a much more flexible approach to *sedes*.

Our staging involved those four basic quadrants of the church: chancel, altar, pulpit, and aisles. Around these four poles the various *sedes* were cycled and recycled in a continuous motion. The two high priestly *sedes* were positioned at either side of the chancel and elevated slightly so as to be out of the main playing area. The chancel itself then became a kind of neutral territory upon which the various encounters could unfold. During the course of the play it served as Saul's house, the road, Judas' house, and Barnabas' house. Ananias' house was positioned in the pulpit and later doubled as the wall from which Saul was lowered. Christ sang his thunderous *Saule, Saule, quid me persequeris?* from the altar, while the aisles served as the route for Saul's march from Jerusalem to Damascus and later as his escape route from Damascus back to Jerusalem. This staging scheme worked well, transforming a dramatic white elephant into a crisp and compact play which we were able to tour successfully with a minimum of set and properties.

My observations on *sedes*, then, are as follows:

1. They can be flexible, and sketched with the barest of strokes. There is really little need for elaborate or permanent "tents"; liturgical *sedes* work best by innuendo.

2. They can overlap and be recycled.

3. And finally, one must not be reluctant to widen the area and play in the aisles as well as the chancel. There are some risks involved, of course, but not nearly so many as one might think. What is lost in sight lines is more than made up in the intensity of audience involvement and the added dramatic sweep. There is much rubric evidence to suggest that liturgical drama was originally performed in the midst of its audience and that the intimate proximity of the audience is in fact central to the total impact of the drama. At any rate, a director should not hesitate

to "think big" and, where it seems appropriate, to use the entire church as a playing area.

IV

Processionals. One senses in liturgical drama a processional orientation. The majority of the plays feature a journey: to the manger, to the sepulchre, to the inn at Emmaus, to Damascus, to and from Daniel's house, to and from Excoranda. Moreover, one discovers in directing these plays that the processionals seem to require space. The number of verses in most processional pieces ranges upward of a half dozen, suggesting travel music to cover a fair distance; the director who refuses to wean him/herself from a proscenium "safety zone" is forced to troop round and round in a very small area, bottling up the action.

Processionals are in fact a tremendously effective way to claim and widen space as well as an exciting way to build audience involvement. There are three situations in which full processionals (or processional-style action involving movement the full length of the building) seem particularly appropriate:

1. Clearly, at the beginning and end of the play, where processional music has either been provided in the manuscript or editorially appended.
2. For long journeys or ones with excitement or "large" movement: the race to the tomb in the Fleury *Visitatio*, Saul's escape from Damascus, the summoning of Daniel to the Babylonian and Persian courts, the invasion of Darius' army, the Magi's following of the star, the journey to the inn in *Peregrinus*.
3. For "holy journeys" where the movement is essentially from unsanctified to sanctified space, culminating in a direct revelation of the Christian Mystery. I am thinking particularly of *Visitatio Sepulchri, Officium Pastorum, Ordo Stellae,* and *Peregrinus*. In these plays the movement from the rear of the church to the altar area represents a "centering down," a repeating in play of a primary liturgical action which carries tremendous power.

V

Set, Properties, and Lighting. It took many years before I could verbalize my instinctive distaste for chancel drama *per se*. I finally realized that it had to do with my discomfort at seeing items such as sofas, lamps, and decanters introduced into the church where like alien objects they detracted from the already powerful dramatic integrity of the building. This same reaction is at work in my attitude towards set and properties in liturgical drama.

It takes imagination to realize just how little is really required and how much of it is already easily at hand in the church building. An ecclesiastical chair functions perfectly well as court or crèche; for less elegant (or more temporary) *sedes*, one can do very well with small wooden stools. Backdrops are almost always unnecessary.

Scene-making, then, becomes an art of graceful choreography, requiring very little in the way of actual set changes. In *The Conversion of St. Paul* the scene at Judas' house is created by having Judas enter with a small stool and tenderly help the blinded Saul to take his seat. In *Officium Pastorum* the midwives, clad in full-sleeved dalmatics, make their scene with the shepherds by stepping aside and extending their arms to reveal the Virgin and Child. The effect is as strong as anything that could be achieved with elaborate staging and set.

Lighting is a modern blessing and can work effectively within the basic *sedes* orientation of liturgical drama to dim a stage area which is no longer of primary importance or to direct attention to an unexpected new area. Nevertheless, good taste must prevail. Since many shows must be performed in daylight or in churches with woefully inadequate lighting facilities, my own rule of thumb is never to stage anything in such a way that its effectiveness depends entirely upon special lighting effects. The action must stand on its own; lighting may then be used to highlight. Anything more than this seems to be an unjustifiable use of modern gadgetry.

VI

Costumes. Appropriateness in costuming is a more complex matter than might first meet the eye. At stake is more than merely the monetary factor (lavish budgets resulting in sumptuous effects); the real question is which tradition is to be normative for costuming, the iconographic or the liturgical? Fletcher Collins displays a strong preference for the former, documenting his influential *The Production of Medieval Church Music-Drama* with many rich illustrations from medieval illuminations and stained glass windows. On the other hand, given the established circumstances of plays being performed within the context of the liturgy and by actors whose primary role is as members of the liturgical community, it seems far-fetched to imagine costumes which, at play's end, would necessitate elaborate costume changes before the resumption of the liturgy—as would certainly be the case with costumes copied too scrupulously from the iconographic tradition. That historic first account in the tenth century *Regularis Concordia* clearly envisions a recycling of liturgical properties and vestments which is marvellous in its simplicity and ingenuity:[9]

> While the third lesson is being read, four of the brethren shall vest, one of whom, *wearing an alb* as though for some different purpose, shall enter and go stealthily to the place of the "sepulchre" and sit there quietly, *holding a palm in his hand*. Then, while the third respond is being sung, the other three brethren, *vested in copes* and *holding thuribles in their hands*, shall enter in their turn and go to the place of the sepulchre, step by step, as though searching for something. . . . [italics mine]

The resolution of this dilemma is most helpfully found in the question of artistic intent. For those plays rich in liturgical ambience or closely tied to the liturgy—as with the *Regularis Concordia* or the *Officium Pastorum*—it seems wise to use liturgical vestiture as the norm for costuming. With plays whose liturgical associations are not so prominent—as with *Daniel* and the Fleury Playbook—one has more leeway to draw upon the rich legacy of medieval artwork. The point is, however, that such decisions should be a matter of conscious choice between two viable traditions whose precise interrelationship in the liturgical drama still awaits definitive research.

VII

Music. The first musical decision confronting the would-be producer of liturgical drama is whether to use a published edition or to try a hand at one's own transcription.

Of the published editions, the most important are: W. L. Smoldon's versions of the *Planctus Mariae, Visitatio Sepulchri, Peregrinus,* and *Officium Pastorum* (on rental only from Oxford University Press); the New York Pro Musica's versions of *The Play of Daniel* and *The Play of Herod* (the former based on a transcription by Rembert Weakland, the latter in collaboration with W. L. Smoldon); and Collins' transcription of sixteen plays of the repertory in his *Medieval Church Music-Drama* (Charlottesville, 1976). Each edition has its strengths and weaknesses.

The major weakness of the Pro Musica editions is the excessive interpolation. Entire pieces, both instrumental and vocal, are imported into the score, and the drama is fitted out with ornate instrumental accompaniment. To a lesser degree the same objection holds true for Smoldon's editions, although his orchestration is limited to organ and bells and he is quite scrupulous in noting his editorial changes.

Collins' collection, containing only the single-line melodies, is in that sense more faithful to the original. The problem with this edition, however, is its lack of adequate editorial markings in the scores themselves—an omission which makes it frustrating to doublecheck such matters as accidentals, key transpositions, and the interpretation of specific ligatures. Another potential difficulty lies in Collins' strong preference for the mensuralization of the play melodies, an interpretation with which not everyone will agree.

The alternative is to attempt one's own transcription. This is an option, incidentally, which has only very recently become easily available to American scholars. In the past the difficulty of obtaining primary sources made such a route inaccessible to all but the very determined. With the assembling of the splendid microfilm archive in liturgical drama at the Hill Monastic Manuscript Library in Minnesota,[10] however, it seems likely that this option will become an increasingly attractive one.

The major advantage of doing one's own edition—aside from the opportunity it provides to get to know the play quite intimately—comes in being able to satisfy one's own tastes with regard to rhythmic interpretation. Without becoming too complex about a subject over which much blood has already been spilt, let me briefly sketch the parameters. On the one hand, there is a school of thought which would prefer to hear the plays entirely in free rhythm. The problems with this approach are (1) that it tends to impart a rather static quality to the drama, and (2) that there are any number of items in the repertory whose metrical patterns are so pronounced and regular that even when left unmensuralized they tend to fall into rhythm. Consider, for example, the opening lament in the Fleury *Vistatio:*[11]

Heu! pius pastor occi-dit quem culpa nulla infe-cit.

On the other hand, there are those who would push hard for mensuralization. If a rhythmic pattern can be detected (or imposed), no matter how far-fetched, it is employed. The problem with this approach is that it places severe strain on word and phrase sense, creating lines which are virtually impossible for the performers to deliver dramatically. Moreover, it tends to impart an overall monotonous or "sing-song" quality to the drama.

To my mind, there is little question that liturgical drama utilizes a combination of mensural and non-mensural items. The effect is dramatically as well as musically satisfying, providing welcome contrast in pace and mood. My own preference is to limit mensuralization to rhymed items which show clear and regular metrical patterns.

Within the general category of mensuralization, there are of course a variety of ways to go about it, as a comparison of the editions of Smoldon, Collins, and the Pro Musica will quickly reveal. The would-be transcriber is plunged into waters which are still largely uncharted and in which the tides of passion run high. Though there seems to be emerging a scholarly consensus that the rhythmic modes, devised for polyphony, ought not to be grafted indiscriminately onto monophonic melodies,[12] more than enough conundrums still remain: the acceptability (if ever) of duple meter, the rhythmic interpretation of certain ligatures, and—perhaps most vexing—the question of how to handle the situation when individual word accent and poetic line go at cross-purposes, as in the opening hymn of *Peregrinus: Jesu nostra redemptio/ amor et desiderio*—Je-śu nos-tŕa re-demp-ti-ó, *or* Jé-su nós-tra re-démp-ti-ó? Collins, for example, has a strong preference for aligning accented word syllables with downbeats, as in the latter solution, while others feel equally strongly that the regularity of the poetic line is the paramount consideration. In an area in which few definitive standards have yet been established, perhaps the most that can be said is that a rhythmic interpretation is acceptable if it maintains both musical and dramatic sense.

Instrumentation. The appropriateness of using instruments in liturgical drama has created a lively controversy in recent years. The reality of the recent performance situation is that it has been instrumental ensembles, not vocal ensembles who have taken the lead in the recovery and popularization of these plays. Modern audiences, trained to expect instruments, are delighted to hear them and invariably wander up at intermission for a closer look. Instruments can be of considerable practical value as well: they do help to anchor pitch and to provide musical variety, particularly in lengthy processional numbers.

Over and against these considerations, however, must be set the weight of historical evidence, which indicates clearly that liturgical drama was intended to be performed *a capella* or with instrumentation limited to organ and bells—with only a very few striking exceptions.[13] The practice of scoring these dramas for medieval "orchestras," tempting though it may be, is historically indefensible.

VIII

Throughout this study the word which has been constantly recurring is "fluidity," and fluidity does indeed seem to be the essence of the liturgical art form. The fluidity is felt in the undulating melodies of the chant, in the delicate interplay between liturgy and drama, in characterization, and in set. Liturgical drama is an art of gesture, of understatement, of a graceful austerity which intensifies the real dramatic power.

And what of this art today? In the final chapter of his book Smoldon briefly sketches the decline of liturgical drama, lamenting that this subtle art form, "born before its time,"[14] was more and more eclipsed by the earthier dramatic energies of the late Middle Ages. But if liturgical drama was indeed born before its time, there are clear recent indications that its time at last has come. A vigorously renewed interest is in evidence on both the scholarly and performance fronts, signalled on the one hand by such milestones as the establishment of the HMML archive, on the other by the plethora of recent productions and the appearance of a whole new periodical, *Medieval Music-Drama News*,[15] to keep track of them all.

To be sure, the liturgical drama will perhaps always be a rarified art form, and in mounting it for modern audiences certain amenities—such as providing a translation or at least a summary of the action—are essential. But it is an art form that *will* communicate if performed with skill and conviction. Nearly thirty years ago the New York Pro Musica discovered this extraordinary communicative power in its pioneer productions of *Herod* and *Daniel*; even today revivals of those productions still play to sell-out audiences. My own experiences have been more modest but no less intense. Time and again, but perhaps most profoundly in the Easter plays, I have watched audiences visibly moved by a dramatic power and immediacy far beyond their expectations. They are caught off guard; caught up: not only are the centuries bridged, but something else happens. One pauses to marvel at this and to ponder what deep vein of ritual awareness and experience, largely lost in our culture, may again be being tapped in these productions.

NOTES

1 George Steiner, *After Babel* (London, 1975), Chapter 5.

2 Karl Young, *The Drama of the Medieval Church* (Oxford: Clarendon Press, 1933), I, 84.

3 Ibid., I, 85.

4 I discuss these concerns further in "The Aesthetic Dimension in the Liturgy: A Theological Perspective for Literary Historians," *University of Toronto Quarterly*, 52 (1982), 9-19.

5 W. L. Smoldon, *The Music of the Medieval Church Dramas* (London: Oxford Univ. Press, 1980), p. 235.

6 Fletcher Collins, Jr., *The Production of Medieval Church Music-Drama* (Charlottesville: Univ. Press of Virginia, 1972), p. 124.

7 For this reason I am in full agreement with Collins' comments on the stage directions for the Cividale *Planctus Mariae* (ibid., pp. 94-96), which seem to him suspiciously wooden, as if provided by someone not intimately connected with the play.

8 Ibid., p. 175.

9 Quoted from O. B. Hardison, Jr., *Christian Rite and Christian Drama in the Middle Ages* (Baltimore: Johns Hopkins Univ. Press, 1965), p. 193.

10 For an inventory of the holdings of this archive, see *The EDAM Newsletter*, 5, No. 1 (Fall 1982), 19-44.

11 Quoted from E. de Coussemaker, *Les drames liturgiques du moyen age* (Rennes, 1865), p. 178.

12 For a brief but informative survey of the state of the art, see Fletcher Collins, Jr., *A Medieval Songbook* (Charlottesville: Univ. Press of Virginia, 1982), pp. x-xii.

13 The most conclusive study of this subject is by Edmund A. Bowles, "Were Musical Instruments used in the Liturgical Service during the Middle Ages?" *The Galpin Society Journal*, No. 10 (May 1957) and No. 12 (May 1959).

14 Smoldon, p. 418.

15 *Medieval Music-Drama News*, edited by Fletcher Collins, Jr., and issued by Medieval Institute Publications, began publication in 1982.

Appendix

Introduction to Orléans, Bibliothèque Municipale MS. 201

The inclusion of plates which illustrate the Fleury *Playbook* in its entirety, made possible through the courtesy of the Bibliothèque Municipale d'Orléans and the Hill Monastic Manuscript Library, will provide at hand a convenient facsimile of the entire section of MS. 201 containing the medieval dramas (pp. 176-243). Along with this section, the pages immediately prior to and following the *Playbook* have been shown for comparison.

The Orléans manuscript is, in fact, a compilation of separate manuscripts which at some time, most probably in the sixteenth century, were bound together. The manuscript contains three sections characterized by three distinct types of compositions, written in quite different hands and bound in sections, each with its own subject matter and stylistic variation. Furthermore, each section forms a relatively complete volume in itself. The first, pages 1-175, contains a series of homilies primarily dedicated to the Virgin Mary. These follow approximately the order of the liturgical calendar and end abruptly in the middle of a sermon. The style of the sermons is quite complex, usually drawing allegorical lessons from scriptural citation. A very cramped and condensed hand is employed, using many abbreviations, especially when familiar scripture is being cited. Given the small size of the manuscript (6 3/4 x 5 5/8 inches) and the cramped nature of the writing with its heavy use of abbreviations, it is clear that this section of the manuscript is intended for a single reader and is not likely to have been designed as a service book.

The second section of the Orléans manuscript, the collection of plays studied and reproduced here, is more carefully and artistically produced. While the writing is small, it contains few abbreviations, and the music is quite precisely aligned with the text underlay. Occasional blue and red coloration is employed decoratively, and bold vertical red lines separate prose rubrics from the musical verses. While again the size of the manuscript argues strongly against any kind of use as a book to be shared by a group of singers, the musical notation is easily readable even from a distance, which could argue for its use by a sort of dramatic director or even by a principal singer. However, since the rubrics in some plays call for rather elaborate staging by a large cast, including a chorus, it is at least doubtful that the manuscript in its present form would have served in the latter capacity. Resemblance of some of the music-dramas to others from widely disparate sources points to the comprehensive nature of the collection, to an academic rather than a practical interest in setting them down.

The final section of the manuscript is quite short, containing but two pieces, both of them sequences and both in a hand and musical style quite different from those of the plays which precede them.

Attempts to see a unified purpose in the manuscript have strongly influenced previous descriptions of it. Solange Corbin's well-known attribution of the *Playbook* to the monastery of St. Lomer in Blois depends in large part on her assumption that all three parts of the manuscript, and especially the last two sections, are written on the same type of vellum. A quite different view concerning the Orléans MS. 201 is provided by Père Lin Donnat of the Abbaye St. Benoît-sur-Loire, whose remarks concerning his first hand examination of the manuscript are quoted here with his kind permission in English translation provided by Fletcher Collins, Jr.:

> *Orléans MS. 201 is a small volume, 162mm x 144mm, written on parchment, bound in worn leather, its fur-side out, over wooden panels. One readily observes that this is a composite manuscript. It begins with two sermons on the Virgin, which are separated by a Lenten sermon. The second sermon on the Virgin breaks off abruptly at the bottom of page 175. All gatherings are of four leaves, except the fifth which has nine.*
>
> *After this section of the manuscript there are found, on pages 176-243, the famous liturgical plays, written on a quite different kind of parchment: of much better quality, supple and white like that of the illuminated manuscripts of the thirteenth century. The writing therein is similarly more artistic: the capitals have the long stems and blue volutes characteristic of the thirteenth century. The music is meticulously written on four red staff-lines, the notation generally well-formed and distinct. This ensemble of features has nothing in common with the preceding pages.*
>
> *There follows in the manuscript, to make a gathering of four pages, in a parchment different from that of either of the two preceding sections of sermons and plays, a parchment more crude, stiff, and yellow. These pages contain a hymn to St. Lomer, in a different calligraphy, one rather heavy and closer to the fourteenth-century style. The music is presented without staff-lines but with clef signs [C and F], a different notational system from that used in the liturgical plays. Staffed but without notation, a*

> *hymn in honor of the Virgin concludes MS. 201.*
>
> *These particulars clearly demonstrate that MS. 201 is not a homogeneous whole, that it is more what librarians call a miscellany, a* recueil factice, *for which only the binding provides unity. The condition of the manuscript accounts for the cut-off of text at the bottom of page 175, at the end of a gathering; for the different grades of parchment; and for the difference in the style of musical notation employed in the hymn to St. Lomer. This impression of disparity is intensified by the fact of an insertion of a small section of pages in a 50mm x 50mm [2 x 2 inches] format, sewn into the middle of one of the gatherings, and containing biblical texts unrelated to the adjoining sermons.*
>
> *In view of these manuscript conditions, can one make anything more than coincidence of the presence of the St. Nicholas plays in the same manuscript as a hymn in honor of St. Lomer? Their meeting here seems almost certainly occasional, to be credited to the happenstance of later binding.*

A few comments may be in order concerning the preparation of the photographs that were utilized for the plates. Though the negatives were somewhat uneven in quality, fairly sophisticated techniques were attempted in order to produce the best photograph possible, but at times text obscured by blotches or dark areas could not be entirely restored. The beginning and ending pages as well as pages 207-08 of the *Playbook* have been illustrated from a different set of photographs supplied by Fletcher Collins, Jr. Comparison of these plates with those of the Tintori-Monterosso edition reveals, we believe, a superior facsimile. Nevertheless, no black and white facsimile of this manuscript can replace examination of the manuscript itself. The major purpose has here been to produce a useful facsimile which can be consulted in conjunction with the studies in this volume and with the texts as edited by Karl Young in his monumental *Drama of the Medieval Church.*

The contents of the *Playbook* section of MS. 201 may be conveniently summarized in the chart on the following page. The chart is keyed to the edited texts of the individual plays in Young's *Drama of the Medieval Church* (*DMC*). For editions of the music, see the survey by Clyde Brockett, above, pp. 58-59, fn. 1, to which may be added the practical edition of the *Visitatio Sepulchri* prepared by W. L. Smoldon for Oxford University Press and another practical edition, containing the *Ordo Representandum Herodem* and *Ad Interfectionem Puerorum*, prepared by Dr. Smoldon and Noah Greenberg under the title *The Play of Herod: A Twelfth-Century Musical Drama* (Oxford Univ. Press, 1965).

Play	Page Reference in *Playbook*	*DMC*
1. *Tres Filiae*	176-82	II, 316-21
2. *Tres Clerici*	183-87	II, 330-32
3. *De Sancto Nicolao et de Iudeo (Iconia)*	188-96	II, 344-48
4. *Filius Getronis*	196-205	II, 351-57
5. *Ordo ad Representandum Herodem*	205-14	II, 84-89
6. *Ad Interfectionem Puerorum*	214-20	II, 110-13
7. *Visitatio Sepulchri*	220-25	I, 393-97
8. *Peregrinus*	225-30	I, 471-75
9. *Ad Representandum Conversionem B. Pauli*	230-33	II, 219-22
10. *Resuscitatio Lazari*	233-43	II, 199-208

Index

Abelard 9, 106, 114
Achiabus 138
Adam 83, 92, 98, 106
AD INTERFECTIONEM PUERORUM (ORDO RACHELIS) 1, 4-5, 12-13, 20, 50-52, 64, 70, 73-76, 86-88, 93, 97, 121, 124, 134-43, 163-64
AD REPRESENTANDUM CONVERSIONEM B. PAULI 5, 13, 53, 55-56, 58, 64, 70-71, 76, 94, 99, 152-53, 155, 164
Adam of St. Victor 110
Adeodatus 46-47, 76-77, 93, 98
Advent 60, 97, 113-14, 118
Aelred of Rievaulx 104-05
Agareni 93
Agno sacrato ("To the hallowed Lamb") 51-52, 74
Alleluia 38, 60
Ananias 94, 99, 153
Anselm of Canterbury 106, 114-15, 117, 119
antiphons 38-40, 47, 49-51, 59-60, 113, 120, 142
antiphonaries 4
Apollo 77, 93
Aquilèa Cathedral 68, 96
Aquinas, St. Thomas 118
Archelaus 50, 71, 74, 122-24, 131, 135, 139
Archisynagogus 124
Ardens est Cor 60
Astra tenenti 147
Auerbach, Erich 110
Augsburg 68
Ave Regina coelorum 60

Axton, Richard 141

Balaam 126
Ballard, Mary Ann 144
Barnabas 55-56, 153
Bautier, R.-H. 32
Beauvais 5, 31, 62, 64, 97
Bede 111
Beckerman, Bernard 62
Benediktbeuern MS. (including plays) 11-12, 14, 21, 24, 63, 71, 95, 116, 124, 139-40
Berland, Dom Jean-Marie 34
Bernard of Clairvaux 101, 104, 109, 113-14, 116, 118
Bethlehem non est minima 50, 58, 60
Besançon 123
Bevington, David 1, 96-97
Bibliothèque Nationale, MS. Lat. 1020 27; MS. Lat. 11331 9-10; MS. Lat. 8846 (Paris Infancy Leaf) 127, 133-34, 138-39, figs. 4, 7
Bilsen 123, 126, 130-31, 142
Bischoff, Bernhard 24
Blois, Church of Notre-Dame de Bourgmoyen 31; *see also* St. Laumer, Abbaye
Bodel, Jean 8
breviaries 4, 6
British Library, MS. Add. 22,414 (Hildesheim) 7-9; MS. Egerton 2615 (Beauvais) 5; Add. MS. 37,472 (Canterbury Psalter) 127, 133-34, 138-39, fig. 3

Campbell, Thomas P. 76, 80

Canterbury Cathedral 128
Canterbury Psalter *see* British Library Add. MS. 37,472
Carmina Burana *see* Benediktbeuern MS.
Caviness, Madeline 142
Châlons-sur-Marne 128
Chambers, E. K. 141
Chanson de Roland 100
Charlemagne 83
Chartres, Cathedral of Notre Dame 131, 133, 136
Chester cycle 131
Chrétien de Troyes 100
Christ, Jesus 53, 58, 63, 68, 70, 73-75, 78-79, 81, 83-87, 89, 97, 100-17, 120-21, 125, 127-28, 132, 152-53, 155
Christmas 2, 8, 11-12, 60, 69, 76, 86, 88, 93, 99, 125, 140, 147
Chronica sive historia de duabus civitatibus 83, 95-96
Cicero 104, 117
Circumcision, Feast of 5
Cividale 160
Clement of Alexandria 101
Cohen, Gustave 1, 81
Collins, Fletcher, Jr. 1, 59, 80-81, 97-99, 103, 121, 141, 145, 149, 152, 155-58, 160, 162-63
Commemoratio brevis 36
Compiègne 123, 126, 135
conductus 74, 147
Congaudentes 147
Constantes estote 60
CONVERSIO SANCTI PAULI *see* AD REPRESENTANDUM CONVERSIONEM B. PAULI
Copenhagen Psalter 129
Copiosae karitatis 33, 49
Corbin, Solange 1, 26-33, 80, 116, 162
Coussemaker, E. de 28
Curtius, Ernst 107

Damascus 76, 94, 99, 153-54
Daniel 147, 154
DANIELIS LUDUS (Beauvais) 5, 71, 95, 144, 147, 150, 154, 156, 159
Darius 147, 154
Davis, Colonius 55-56, 61
Davril, Dom Anselme 30
deBoor, Helmut 2, 15
DE SANCTO NICHOLAO ET DE QUODAM IUDEO (ICONIA) 5, 13, 19-20, 40-45, 49, 78, 91-92, 164
devils 106, 108-09, 117, 120, 132, 136-38, 140, 143
disciples 76, 79, 85-86, 103
Dolan, Diane Marie 80
Donnat, Père Lin 28, 162
Donovan, Richard B. 26, 33
Dulcitius, of Hrosvitha 9
Dümmler, Ernst 8

Easter 2-4, 8, 11-12, 20, 60, 62, 65, 85-88, 96-97, 99, 113, 118
Easter Monday 39
Easter Sepulchre 78
Ecce [Salve] Agnus Dei 60
Einhardt 83
Elders, Willem 13
Elevatio 69
Emitte agnum, Domine 60
Emmanuel College, MS. 252[2] 129, 136, figs. 5-6
English mystery cycles 131, 141
Epiphany 69, 86, 122, 125, 130, 134
Euphrosina 46-49, 59, 76-77, 93, 98, 147
evangelary 4
Eve 93, 98, 106
Excoranda 48, 76-77, 93, 154

FILIUS GETRONIS 12-13, 33, 45-47, 49, 71, 75-78, 82, 93-94, 97, 147-48, 164
Foakes, R. A. 80
folk drama 19
Fontevrault 32
Frank, Grace 121
Freising 124, 126, 130-31, 135, 140
Fulgentius 83
Fuller, John Bernard 9

Gallicanus, of Hrosvitha 9
Gardiner, F. C. 96
Gaude Maria Virgo 51, 88
Getron 12, 46, 48, 76-77, 93
Gevaert, François A. 35
Girardus of Cluny 60

Gloria in excelsis 69
Glossa Ordinaria 111
Golden Legend, see Legenda Aurea
Gombrich, E. H. 80
Gough Psalter 129
Greenberg, Noah 121, 141, 163
Gregory the Great 108, 116-17
Grodecki, Louis 133, 143
Guiette, Robert 25

Hardison, O. B., Jr. 14-15, 22, 84, 145-46
Hartker 60
Herod 1, 5, 32, 50-51, 64-66, 69, 71-77, 86-88, 120-43, figs. 5-7
Hilarius 9-11, 13-15, 34, 89, 91, 95, 97-98
Hildegard of Bingen 10
Hildesheim 7-9, 11-12, 15, 90, 92, 95, 98
Hill Monastic Manuscript Library 157-59, 161
HISTORIA DE DANIEL REPRESENTANDA (Hilarius) 9-10
Holkham Bible Picture Book 138
Holloway, Julia Bolton 80
Holy Innocents 4, 73-74, 78, 87-88, 122, 138-39, 143, fig. 6
Homilies 27, 161-62
Hortus Deliciarum 142
Hrosvitha of Gandersheim 9
Hugues de Sainte-Marie 31-32, fig. 1
hymns 57, 74, 120, 162-63

ICONIA SANCTI NICHOLAI (Hilarius) 9-10, 91, 98
In sapientia disponens omnia 56
Innocents, plays of *see* Slaughter of the Innocents, plays of
Iudeus 45, 49, 78, 91

Jauss, Hans Robert 24-25
Jerusalem 70, 76, 94, 123-24, 153
Jesus junxit 40
Job 117
Jones, Charles W. 8-9
Joseph 51, 73, 75, 88, 123, 137, 139
Joseph, fili David 51, 60
Josephus 137-39

Laon 143
Langosch, Karl 1
La Porte, Jean 26
Lauds 33, 49, 60
Lazarus 5, 13, 35, 57, 78, 89, 97, 100-18
Leclercq, Jean 116, 118
lectionaries 4
Legenda Aurea, by Jacobus de Voragine 118, 138
Lent 113
Leroquais, V. 28, 138, 142
Lesne, Émile 31
LI JUS DE SAINT NICHOLAI (Jean Bodel) 8
Liber Usualis 36-37, 46, 59
Lipphardt, Walther 2, 4, 20-21, 24, 35
Lorsch Gospels 124
Lubac, Henri de 111
LUDUS DE REGE AEGYPTI (Benediktbeuern) 11
Lyons 143

Magi 49-51, 53, 64, 69-73, 75-76, 86-88, 122-37, 140, 150, 154, figs. 3, 5
Magnificat 10, 39
Maillard, Elisa 130, 132
Mane prima sabbati 56, 118
Marmorinus 46-47, 75-77, 93, 98, 148
Martha 97-98, 103, 105, 107-08, 110, 112, 116-18
Mary Magdalene 53, 65, 68, 77-78, 81, 85, 89, 92, 98, 102-05, 107-08, 110, 112, 114, 116-18, 151, fig. 2
Mary, Blessed Virgin 27, 29, 32, 73, 75, 87-88, 155, 161-63, fig. 1
Mass 6-7, 21, 49, 60-64, 68, 145-47
Matins 5, 10-11, 17, 37, 49, 64-65, 69
McGuire, Brian P. 115
Medieval Music-Drama News 159
Micah 134
mime 73
missal 4, 6, 28, 30
Montpellier 124, 126, 130-31, 135
Morrison, Karl F. 99
music 35-61, 97, 146-47, 156-59, 162
musical instruments 158-59
musical notation 27-28, 36, 55, 60, 156-58, 162-63
musical style 13-14, 35-61, 156-59 3

Nevers 123, 125
New York Pro Musica 156, 158-59
Norton, Michael 59
Notker Balbulus 52

O Christe pietas 33, 49
Office 6-8, 21, 147
OFFICIUM PASTORUM (Rouen) 144, 147-49, 154-56
OFFICIUM STELLAE, Plays 4, 7, 12, 64, 120-21, 123, 134-35, 154
OFFICIUM STELLAE VERSUS AD HERODEM (Sicily) 141
Oratio Sancti Nicolai 42
ordinals 4
Ordinarium 28
ORDO AD REPRESENTANDUM HERODEM (Play of Herod) 1, 5, 32-33, 49-50, 53-55, 58, 60, 69-73, 76, 82, 86-87, 97, 121-43, 156, 159, 163-64
ORDO RACHELIS (Freising) 124, 126, 131, 135, 140
ORDO VIRTUTUM, of Hildegard of Bingen 10
O regem coeli 60
Orléans, MS. 129 27, 30
Orléans, diocese of 30
Orosius 83
Otto of Freising 83, 95, 99

Paris, Cathedral of Notre Dame 132-33
Paris Infancy Leaf, *see* Bibliothèque Nationale, MS. Lat. 8846
Pax in terris 150
PEREGRINUS 1, 5, 12-13, 38-39, 49-50, 53-55, 58, 64, 79, 85-86, 96, 148, 154, 158, 164
PEREGRINUS (Beauvais) 95, 97, 144, 148
PEREGRINUS (Benediktbeuern) 11
PEREGRINUS (Le Mans) 55
Petrus Comestor 137, 139
Pharisees 109-11
Philip I 32
Pilate 138
Plaimpied 32
PLANCTUS MARIAE 156, 160
Plautus 19
Play of Herod, *see* ORDO AD REPRESENTANDUM HERODEM
Poitiers, Cathedral of Notre Dame 130, 132, 136
prayers 147
processionals 4
processions 70-76, 80, 84, 124, 147, 154
Prudentius 143
Purdy, Rob Roy 117

Quem queritis 67, 84
Quem vidistis pastores 60
Qui sunt hi sermones 39, 54, 59
Quid tu virgo 52

Rachel 52, 64, 74, 87-88, 93, 122, 135
Raising of Lazarus, *see* RESUSCITATIO LAZARI
Raoul de Tortaire 31
Remegius 138
Regino of Prüm 36
Regularis Concordia 6, 33, 63, 96, 156
RESUSCITATIO LAZARI 1, 10, 13, 29, 55-57, 64, 78, 82, 88, 99, 100-19, 164
Revertere in terram Judam 31, 60
Riga 19
Rome 124
Roth, Stephan 4
Rouen 31
rubrics 8, 63, 68, 70, 72, 76, 79, 84, 96-98, 125, 130, 137, 139, 148, 162
Rudick, Michael 111

St. Aignan 30
St. Albans Psalter 129
St. Augustine 80, 82-84, 93, 111, 115
St. Benedict 29-30, 32
St. Benoît-sur-Loire 1, 6, 64
St.-Denis 60
St.-Denis, Abbey Church of 132-33
St. Jerome 111
St. John 68
St. Laumer 27-30, 162-63
St. Laumer (Lomer), Abbaye, in Blois 6, 26, 28-32, 162
St. Lazare, Church of 29-30
St. Martial de Limoges 31, 70
St. Maur-les Fossés 60
St. Nicholas 1, 7-9, 12, 28-30, 33, 35, 40, 42, 45-46, 48, 51, 60-61, 75-78, 90-93, 98, 163

St. Nicholas, liturgy of 5, 8, 17, 20, 41, 49
St. Paul 5, 35, 55-56, 61, 76, 94, 99, 152-54
St. Peter 68
St. Peter Mancroft Church, Norwich 143
St.-Solenne de Blois 31
St. Thomas 55, 85
St. Trophimes, Church of, at Arles 130
Sallust 135, 137
Salve festa dies 55, 86
Salve virgo 147, 149-50
S. Maria Maggiore, Church of, in Rome 124
Sapientia, of Hrosvitha 9
Satan 101, 108
Saul, *see* St. Paul
Schlauch, Margaret 111
schools 8-9, 19
scribes, of Herod 50, 73, 122-23, 129-34, 141-42
Seckau 24
Secundum quod dictum est 60
sequences 13, 27-28, 30, 74, 89, 97, 120
Shakespeare, William 26, 62
shepherds 34, 50, 64, 69-70, 72-73, 76, 86-87, 122, 127, 149
Simon 78, 97, 103, 107-08
Slater, Ann 62
Slaughter of the Innocents, plays of 4, 72-76; *see also* AD INTERFECTIONEM PUERORUM
Smalley, Beryl 111
Smoldon, William L. 35, 40, 44, 51-54, 56, 59-61, 140-41, 145-47, 156-59, 163
Southern, Richard W. 100, 102, 106, 113-115, 119
SPONSUS (St. Martial) 113
Stanislavsky, Konstantin 150
Stanzaic Life of Christ 117
Statuit ei Dominus 46, 49
Steiner, George 144
Stevens, John 35
Stevens, Wallace 151
Sticca, Sandro 103
Strassburg 123, 135
Styan, John 62
Suger, Abbot 132, 143
Super solium David 123, 142
Surrexit Dominus de sepulchro 54, 60, 84
Surrexit enim sicut dixit 60
Sursum corda 147
SUSCITATIO LAZARI (Hilarius) 9-10, 89, 97
Synagogue 111-12

Te Deum laudamus 3, 5, 8, 10, 17, 37-38, 42, 49, 51, 65, 88, 94, 122, 147
Terence 18
Tertia dies 38, 50, 54, 58
Tintori, Giampiero 1, 163
Tolle puerum et matrem 51, 60
tonaries 36, 38
Tortaire, Raoul de 31
TRES CLERICI 7, 12-13, 41-42, 49, 77, 92, 164
TRES CLERICI (Hildesheim) 7
TRES FILIAE 5, 7, 12-13, 33, 35, 40, 45, 47, 49, 78, 90, 99, 148, 164
TRES FILIAE (Hildesheim) 7-8
tropers 4
tropes 65
Tydeman, William 64, 80-81, 97

Vah! Perii! 44
Venite adoremus eum 60
Vespers 11, 33, 49
Vézelay 32
Vincent of Beauvais 139
Visitatio offices 15-16
VISITATIO SEPULCHRI 1, 3-7, 12-13, 17, 35, 52-55, 64-65, 67, 69, 72, 75, 81, 84, 86, 92, 96, 148, 151, 154, 156-57, 163-64, fig. 2
Vitalis of Blois 19
Vos qui in pulvere estis 60

Warning, Rainer 25
Weakland, Rembert 156
Williams, Arnold 73, 124-25
Winchester Psalter 127-28, 136
Woolf, Rosemary 18-21, 117
Worcester Antiphonal 60-61

Young, Karl 2, 4, 7-9, 14-15, 22, 24, 28, 70, 73, 80, 97-99, 121, 124, 126, 141, 145, 163

1. Triforium capital at Fleury. Hugues de Sainte-Marie kneeling before the Virgin and Child and offering a gift of one of his books.

2. Custer LaRue in the role of Mary Magdalene in the Fleury *Visitatio Sepulchri* as performed at the Abbaye St. Benoît-de-

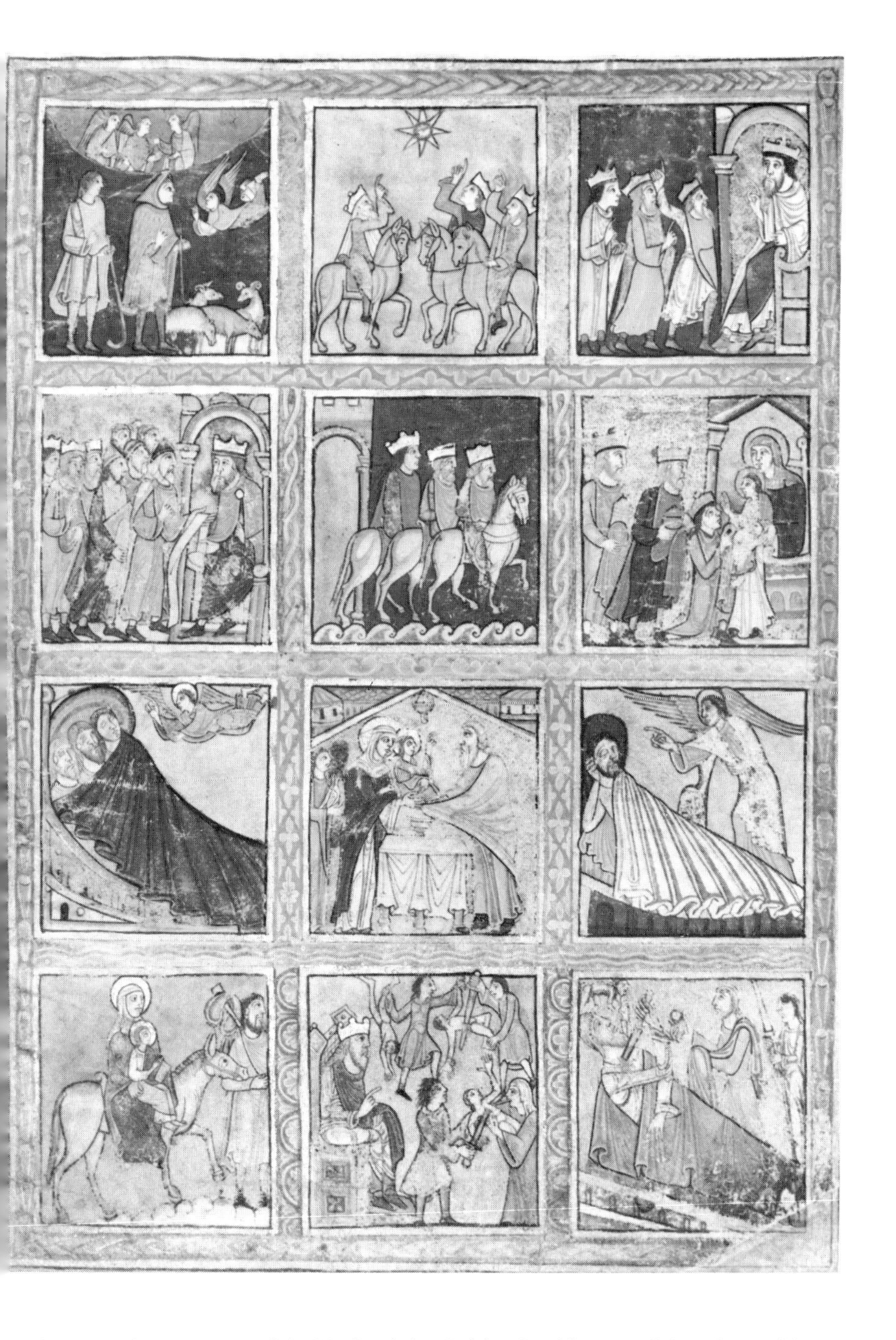

3. Scenes from the story of the Magi and the Nativity. Leaf from English Psalter. British Library Add. MS. 37,472. By permission of the British Library.

4. Scenes from the early life of Christ. Psalter. Paris, Bibliothèque Nationale MS. lat. 8846.

5. The Magi meet Herod (seated, at left). Cambridge, Emmanuel College, MS. 252[2], fol. 8[r].

6. Massacre of the Innocents, with Herod (seated, at right) looking on. Cambridge, Emmanuel College, MS. 252^2, fol. 9^r.

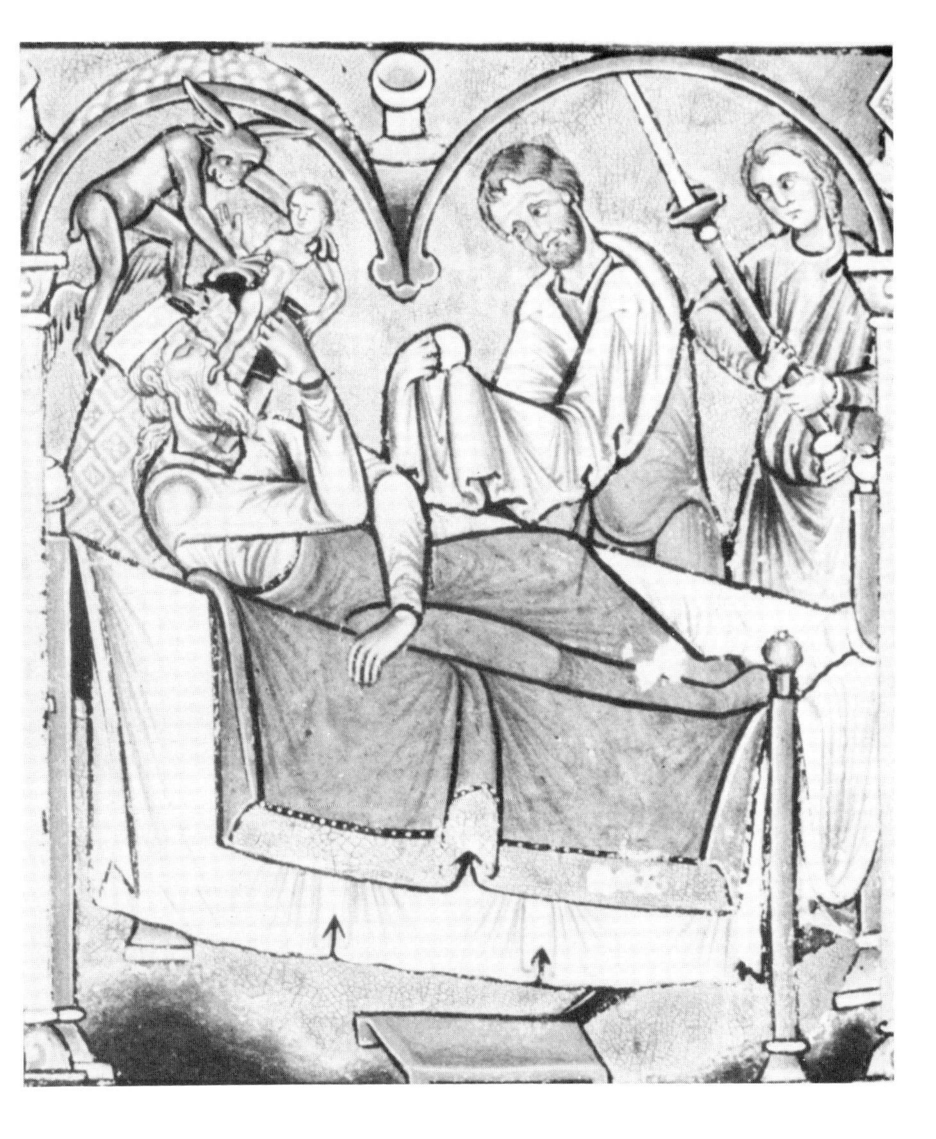

7. Death of Herod. Detail of Paris, Bibliothèque Nationale MS. lat. 8846.

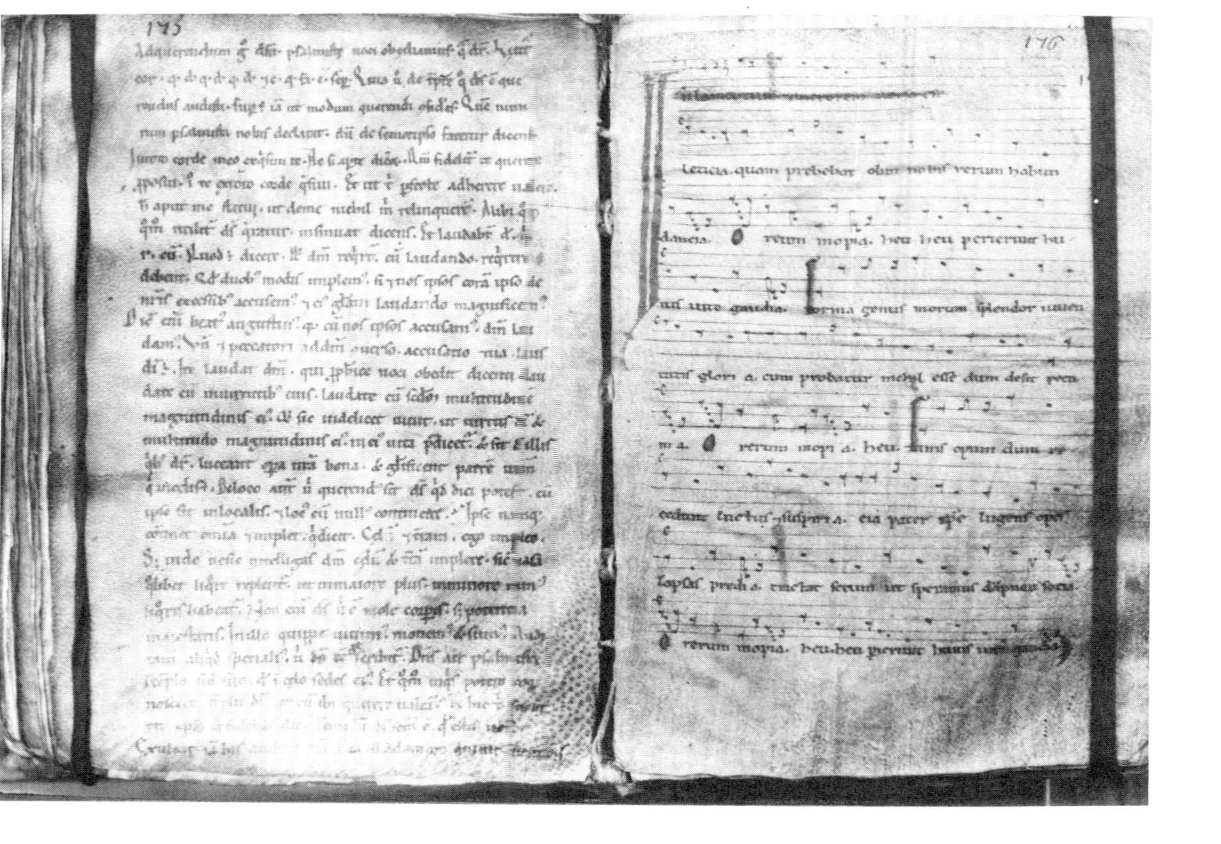

8. Orléans, Bibliothèque Municipale MS. 201, pp. 175-76. The Fleury *Playbook* begins on page 176. Photograph courtesy of Fletcher Collins, Jr.

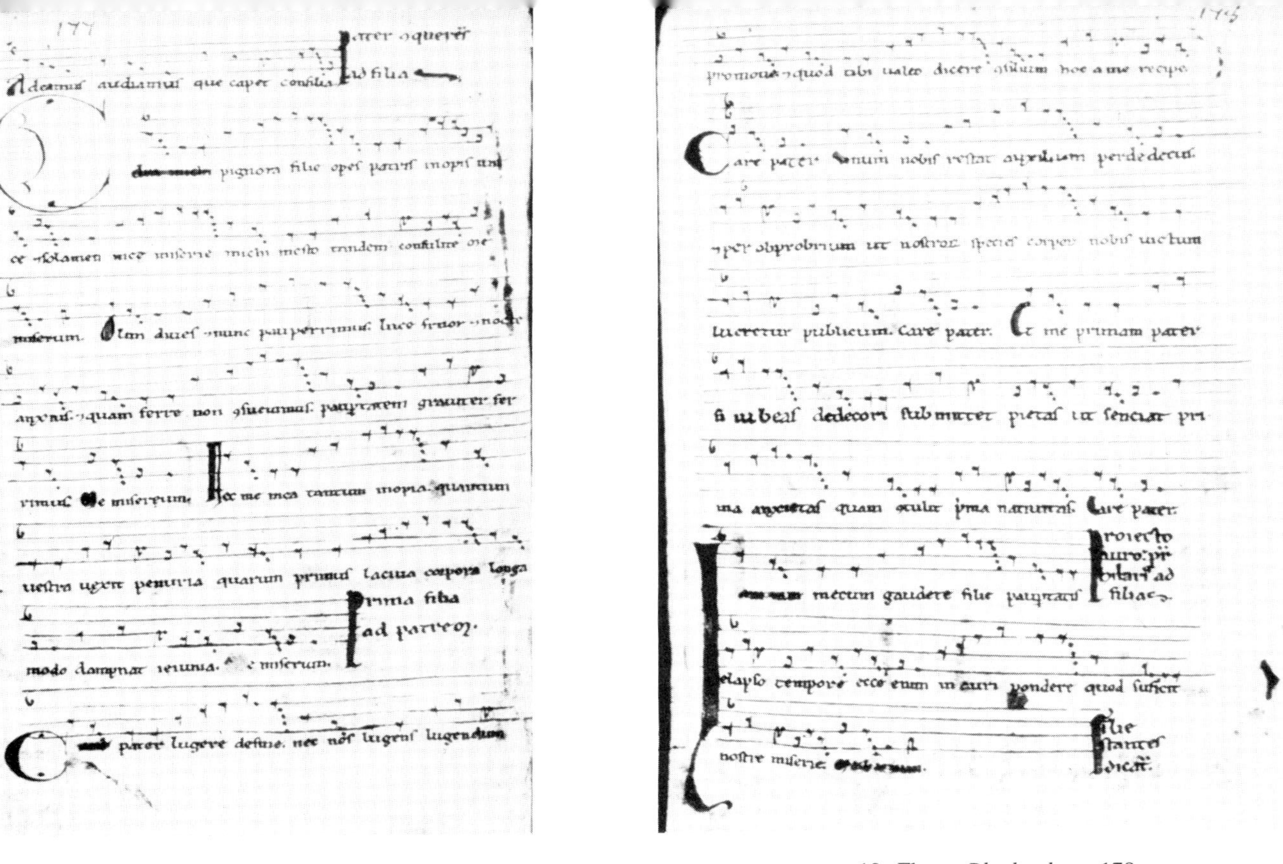

9. Fleury *Playbook*, p. 177.

10. Fleury *Playbook*, p. 178.

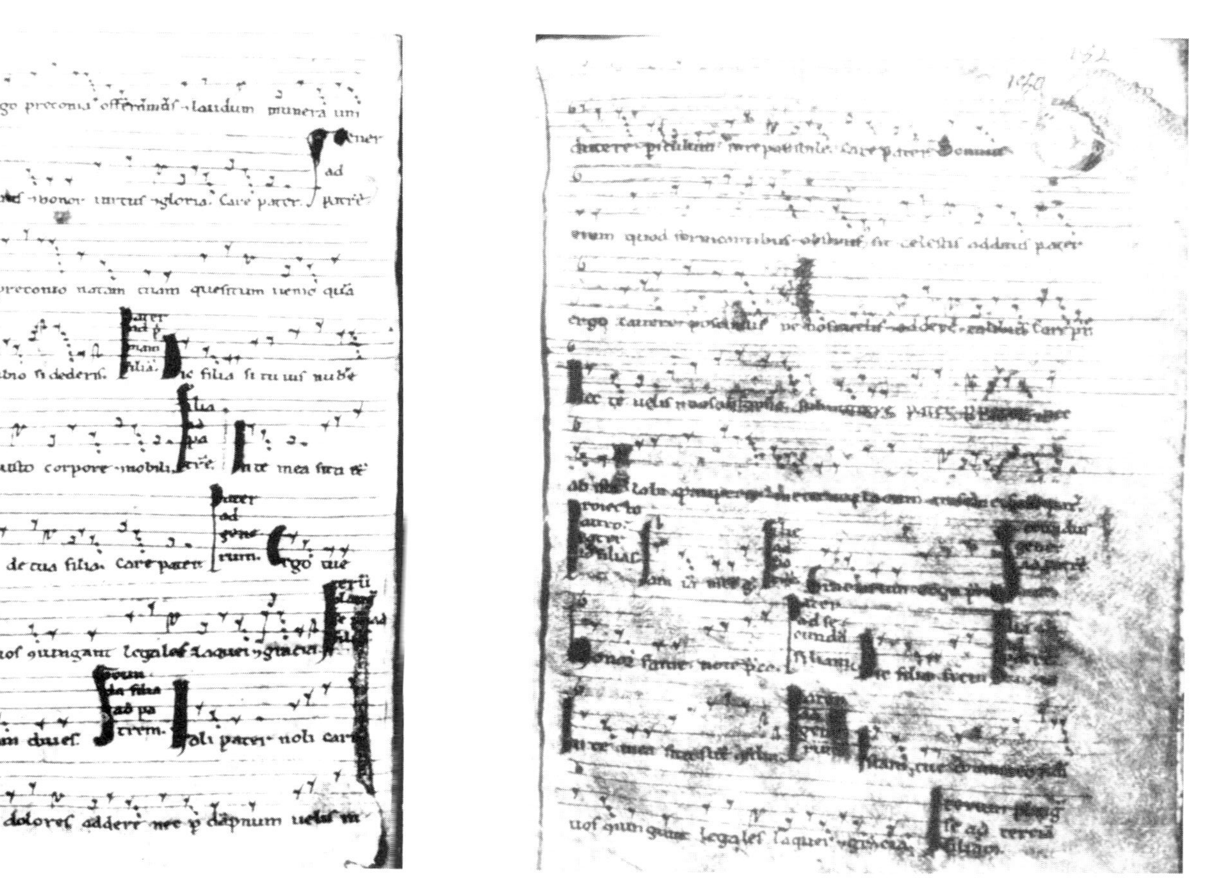

11. Fleury *Playbook*, p. 179.

12. Fleury *Playbook*, p. 180.

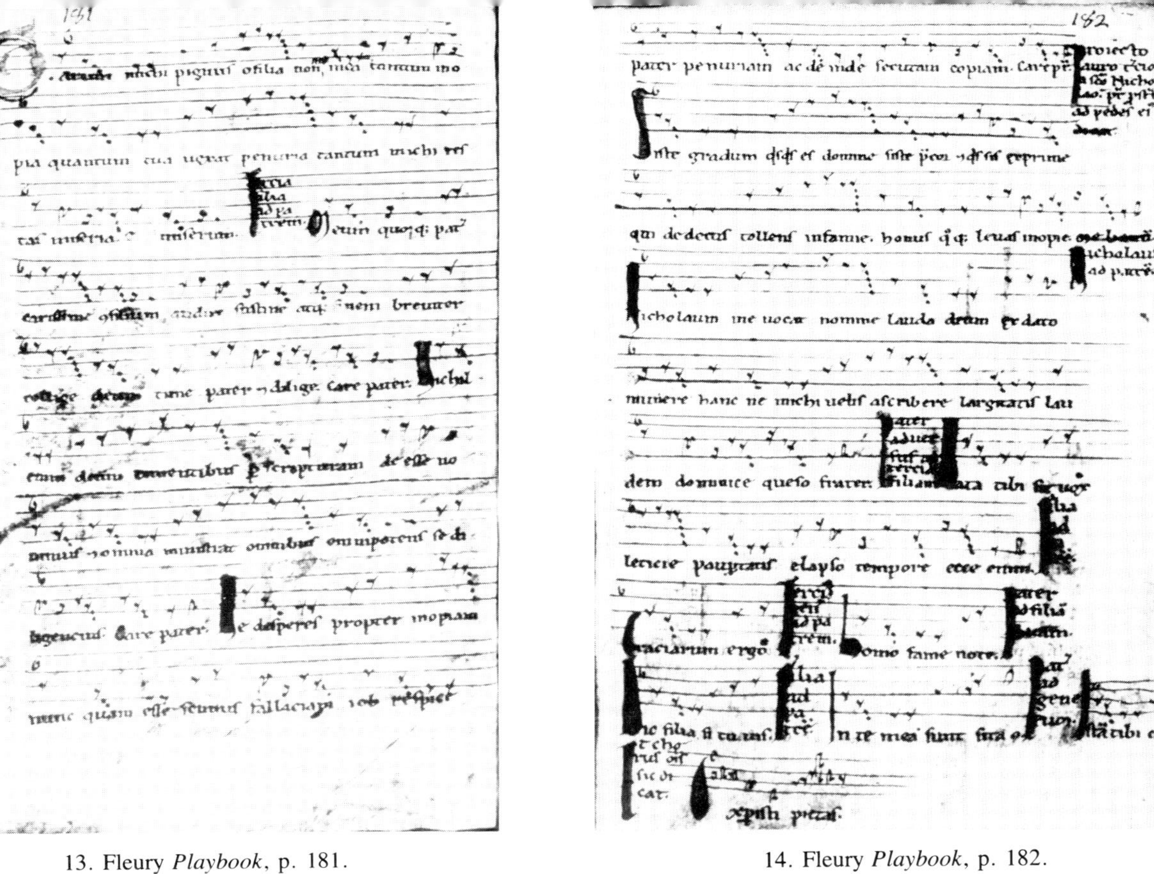

13. Fleury *Playbook*, p. 181.

14. Fleury *Playbook*, p. 182.

15 Fleury *Playbook*, p. 183

16 Fleury *Playbook*, p. 184

17. Fleury *Playbook*, p. 185.

18. Fleury *Playbook*, p. 186.

neqwora quam machari fecit potuimus

[M]iserere nostri te petimus. nam te sanctum dei

cognouimus. nos ... scelus abhominabile non

est tamen inpdonabile. Nicho-la-us [M]ortuorum as

ferte corpora. contrita sunt uestra pectora.

... resurgent per dei graciam. Vos ...

[O]racio sci Nicho-lai ... quentis ueniam. [D]ie deus cuius sunt

omnia. celum tellus aer ... resur-

gant isti precipias. hos ad te clamantes au

[E]t post unus chorus di dicat. [T]e deum laud.

Aliud miraculum de sco nicholao. de quodam iudeo qui imaginem sci ap se absconditam pposse suo cotidie uenerabatur. ... dives ... tendens Sci Nicholai imaginem eius custode sue domus sine ... aliquid. Iterum fures cuncta que habebat furati sunt. Que sci nicholaus ei post modum restituit. furibus ... sci omnia referentibus. Iudeus ad scm Nicholaum.

[S]... dicta sunt ascripta tibi dei famule. ...

... tantur ceu uulgantur te post bustum ... Non e

sane quod non plane ... credam meritis. ... nam

... de te dant xpicole. ...

se se meritis asserunt copouere. ... qui luce caret

... dicunt ... morti ...

uiuos reddis ... surdos uoce ...

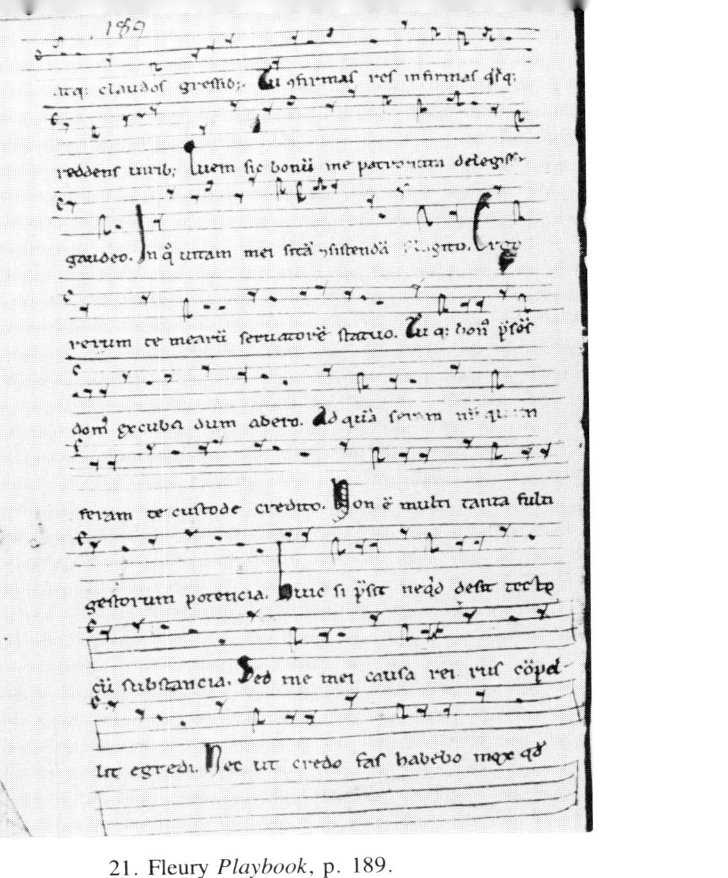

21. Fleury *Playbook*, p. 189.

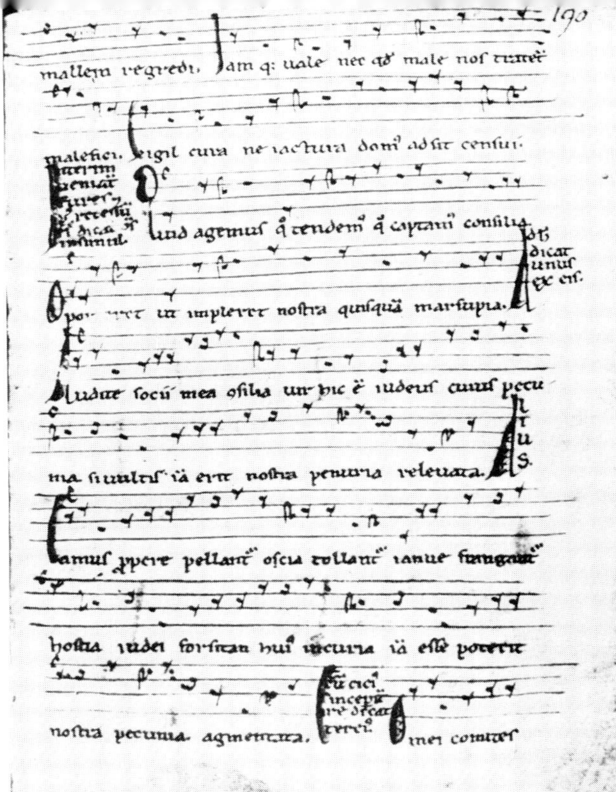

22. Fleury *Playbook*, p. 190.

191

ite fratuis nos qui pspicite ne [illegible] tur talis

caucius servat quia alius [illegible] oc quia metuit · [illegible]

eius est servata · [illegible] prius dicat. [illegible]cam istam

hinc tollite si potestis q̃. cerce qd si nescitis frangere

que sunt mea capite. [illegible] sos oportet

hanc archã frangere q̃. neqmus magni tollere · dicat

O quanta exultacio [illegible] marthe magno gaudio se reserat

noluit nobis aperuit. dicat [illegible] [illegible] perii

nichil e reliqui michi cur esse cepi? Cur mater cur

192

seue pater fove me tribuisti? Heu qd pervenit michi

pfuit aut generari? Cur natum parens assistere me

[illegible]debat? Que luctus michi que gemit nos pspiciebat?

Quod q̃rat in cunctã in crimen ob esse ruinã? [illegible] modo

dives eram nunc aut nulli egebat. Pollens argento p[illegible]

ciosis vestibus auro. Dum miser [illegible] moles est

pauperies. Iam latet ex habitu me post modo q̃ [illegible]

[illegible] Quod lentus [illegible] si fe[illegible] prius [illegible]

deceptor ego sane despiciebam. Hic ego qd nomen nichil

22. Fl[illegible] Pl[illegible] 191

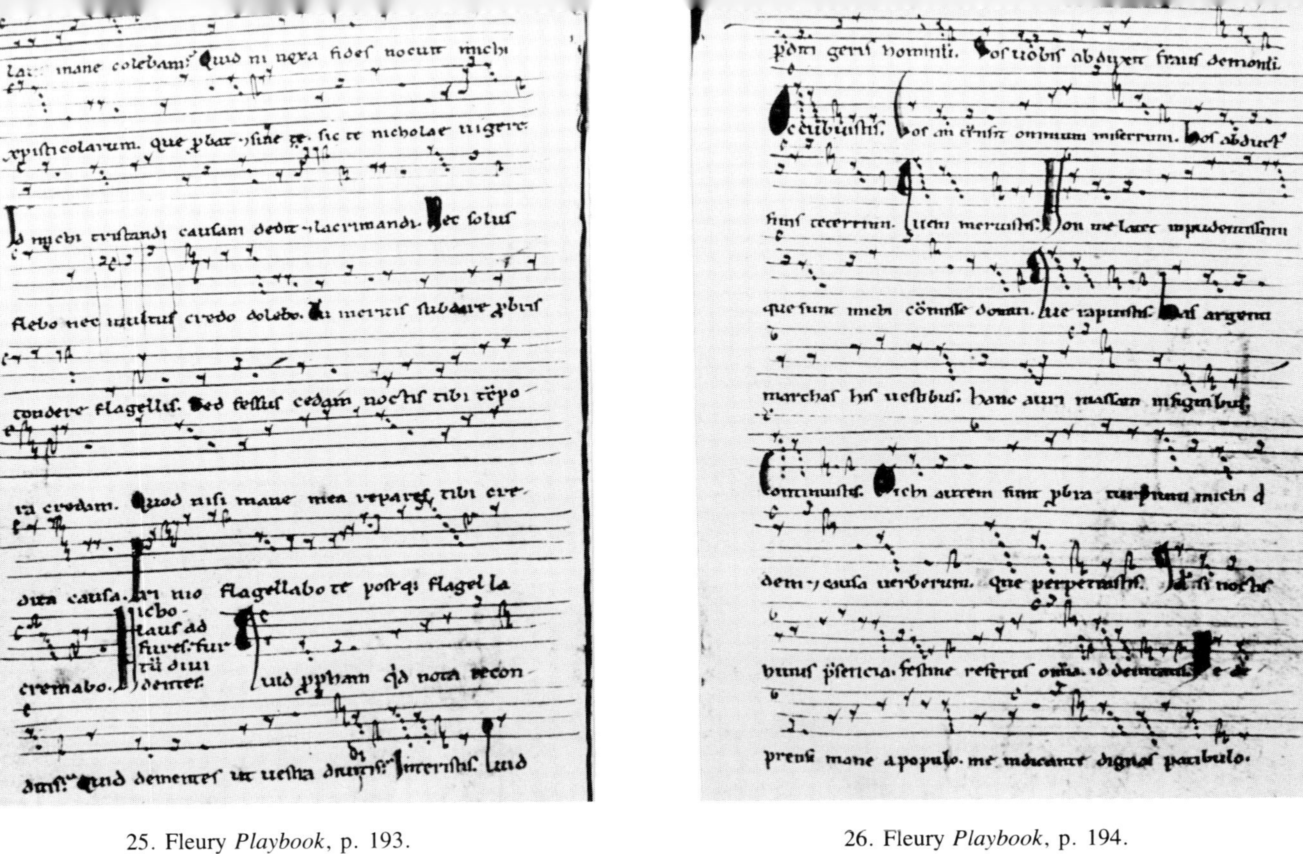

25. Fleury *Playbook*, p. 193.

26. Fleury *Playbook*, p. 194.

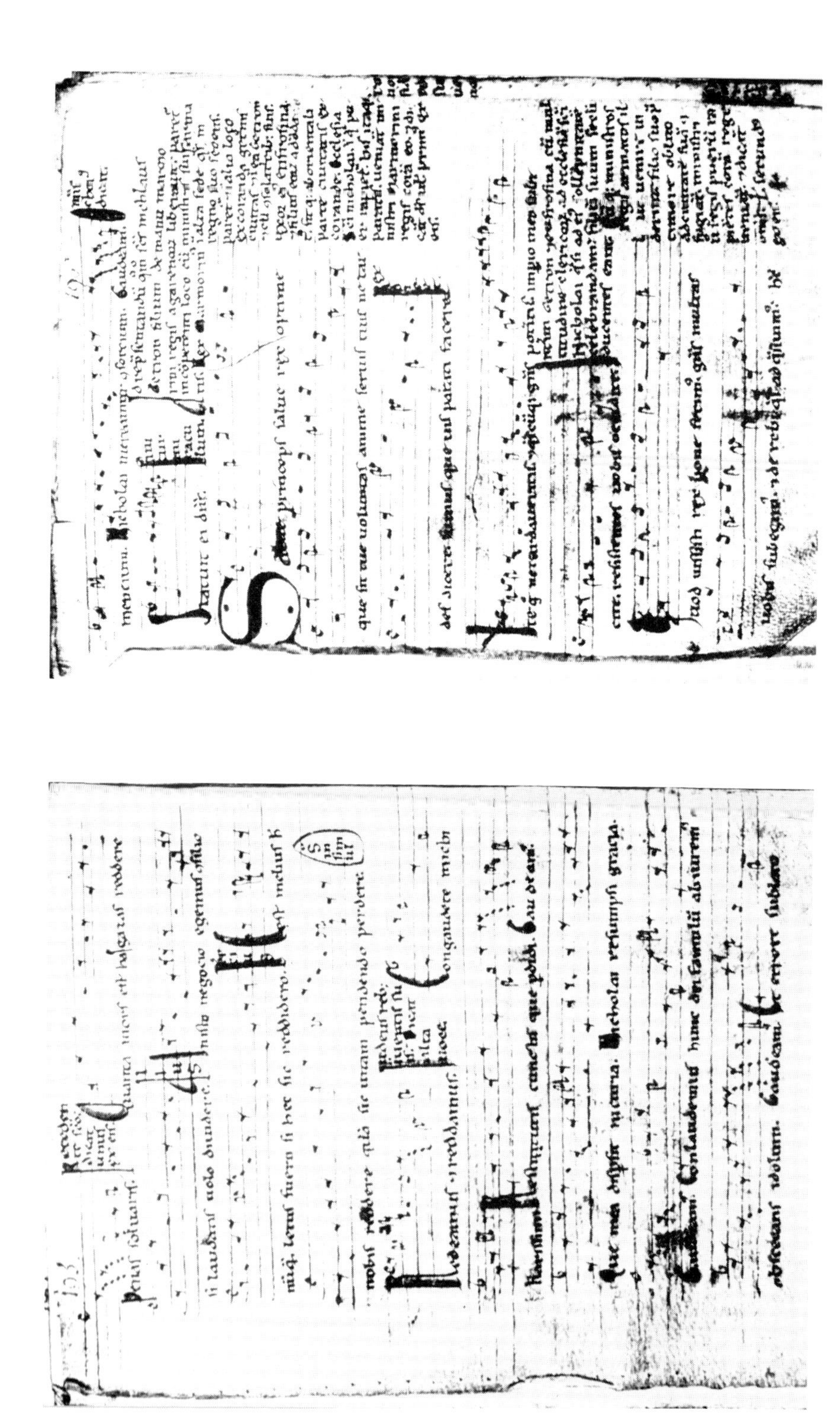

197

puerū uobis ād ducimꝰ. Puer iste multū laudabi

lis sensu prudens. genere nobilis. bene debet uīo

iudicio subiacere uīo impiō seruicio. Apollom q̄reg

omīa semp sit laus uobis q; gr̄a. q̄ secistis michi tā paruū.

subiugatas redditarias. Puer bone nobis edissere.

de q̄ t'ra. de q̄ sis gente. cuiꝰ uitu. gn̄s gens tue patre sūt

gentiles siue xp̄isticole. Decorando principālis poplo.

pater mr̄ Getron uocabulo. dm̄ colit cuiꝰ sunt maria

q̄ fecit nos. uos. omīa. Deus mr̄ apollo ē q̄ ē qui ne

fecit uerax. uboris & regit t'ras regnat in ethere illi

soli debemꝰ credere. Deus tuus mdax. malꝰ & stultꝰ cec

surdus mutus ē. tale dm̄ nō debes credere. q̄ nō potest se

ipsum regere. Noli puer talia dicere. dm̄ meū noli des

picere. nā si eū iratū feceris. euadere nesq̄. poteris.

Heu heu heu michi misere. q̄d agā q̄d q̄ā dicere

q̄ peccato meum pōere natū meū iulē inuere. Cur

me pat' infelix genuit. cur me mat' infelix abluit.

cur me nutx lactare debuit. morte michi cē nō fluit.

29. Fleury *Playbook*, p. 197.

30. Fleury *Playbook*, p. 198.

tand te iuuat si desolacio. noli flere pro tuo filio. summi

patris exora filium qui offerent ei consilium fili care

fili carissime. fili mee magna pars anime. sic es nobis causa tristi

cie. sic eras causa leticie. Ne desperes deo gratia cuius mag

na misericordia. illum e donauit puerum et reddet aut uel aut

alium. Operari in me spiritus. cur morans mi iterum. elle te

possum

fili necesse malle mori quam diu uiuere. tet dolor

desperacio. et nocet nec prodest filio. sed pete de tuis opibus

da clericis atque pauperibus. Nicholai roga clemenciam ut reddet

misericordiam. summi patris pro tuo filio. nec fateor tua peticio.

Nicholae pater sanctissime. nicholae deo carissime. siuis ut te

colam amplius fac ut meus uideat filius. Tu saluasti multos

in pelago. tres uiros amoris uinculo. preces mee precantis

audias. sic ille me certam facias. Non comedam carnem amplius

neque uino fruar ulterius. nullo modo letabor amplius. donec meus

rediret filius. Cara soror lugere desine. tue est nil prosit

lacrime. sed oret pro nostro filio. summi patris pietacio. Incitasti

no erit festiuitas. Nicholai que christianitas tota debet

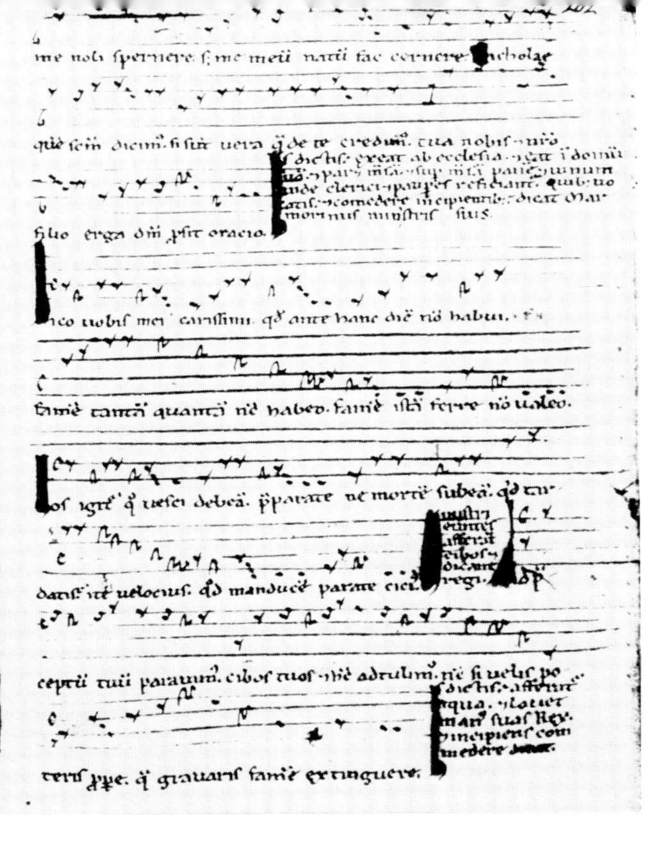

33. Fleury *Playbook*, p. 201.

34. Fleury *Playbook*, p. 202.

seruum modo fieri. unici inuesti dari pro se ipso. qd asserat mihi quam

Tunc intrat ... Gaudiosa suspirans ... ei dicat.

... filius. Heu heu heu mihi misero. uite

me nil desidero. unicus enim quia dum fuero / liberari nequaquam potero.

Ergo que causa suspiras taliter. suspirare te uidi fortiter. quod possit

suspirauerim. qd te noces aut unde queritis. Recordatus mei mi

serie mei patris. mee patrie. suspirare cepi. & gemere. unicus me

talia dicere. Annus unus expletus hodie. postquam seruus factus miserie.

potestati subiectus regie. fines mui ... patrie. Heu misselle

qd ita cogitas. qd te iuuat cordis anxietas. nemo potest te

Interea ueniat aliquis in similitudine Nicholai ... puerum ... apprehendat ... ponat ... unus de ciuibus ad puerum dicat

mihi tollere. quandiu te nolo uelim perdere.

Puer quis es ... tuis parere. cuius est decor largicio. ... uiti cum

recitamus. Hic uenio non ibo longius. sum Getronis unicus filius.

... Ille ad ... dicat.

Nicholao sit laus & gloria. cuius me reducit gratia.

Gaude Getron nec fleas amplius. extra fores stat tuus filius.

... ad osculandum ... dicat.

Nicholas laudat magnalia. cuius eum reducit gratia.

Deo nostro sit laus & gloria. cuius magna misericordia.

luctus nostros uertens in gaudium. nostrum nobis re

duxit filium. Sit quia pater noster propterea Nicholao lau

dei et gracie. Cuius erga deum oracio. nos adiuuet in hoc nego-
cio. Versus ordo ad representandum Hero-
dem. Parato Herode et ceteris personis.
tunc quidam angelus cum multitudine in
excelsis appareat. Quo viso pastores
perterriti. salutem annunciet eis. Ceteris
adhuc tacentibus.

Omnis copiose karitatis.

Nolite timere uos enim euuangelizo uobis gaudium
magnum quod erit omni populo quia natus est nobis odie saluator mundi in ciuitate dauid. et hoc uobis signum inuenietis infantem pannis inuolutum et positum in presepio in medio duum
animalium.

Et subito omnis multitudo cum angelo dicat.

Gloria in excelsis deo et in terra
pax hominibus bone uoluntatis alleluia alleluia.

Tunc demum surgentes cantent intra se. Transeamus et cetera. et sic et cedant usque ad presepe.
quod ad ianuas monas-
terii paratum erit.

Transeamus usque bethleem et uideamus

37. Fleury *Playbook*, p. 205.

hoc uerbum quod factum est. quod fecit dominus osten-
dit nobis.

Tunc due mulie-
res custodien-
tes presepe in-
terrogent pasto-
res dicentes.

Quem queritis pastores dicite.

Res-
pon-
deant
pasto-
res.

Saluatorem christum dominum infantem pannis inuolutum secundum sermonem angelicum.

Adest paruu-
lus cum maria matre eius de quo dudum uaticinando
Isaias propheta dixerat. ecce uirgo concipiet et pariet filium.

Tunc pastores pro-
cidentes
adorent in-
fantem dicen-
tes.

Salue rex seculorum.

Postea surgentes inuitent
populum circumstantem
adorandum infantem
dicentes. [illegible]

Venite. uenite. uenite adoremus dominum quia ipse est saluator noster.

Interim magi prodeun-
tes quisque de angulo
suo quasi de regione
sua. conueniant ante
altare et ad ortum
stelle. et cum appro-
pinquant. primus
dicat.

Stella fulgore nimio rutilat.

38. Fleury *Playbook*, p. 206.

Quem uenturum olim propheta signauerat

... stantes collaterales dicat dexter ad medium. Pax tibi frater. ille respondeat ... osculentur se se sic medius ad sinistrum. sic sinister ad dexter.

Salutacio cuique.

Ecce stella. Ecce stella. Ecce stella.

Procedente autem stella sequentes ... precedentem stellam dicentes.

...amus ergo inquiramus eum offerentes ei munera aurum, thus, et mirram. Quia scriptum didicimus. Ado...

...bunt eum omnes reges, omnes gentes seruient ei.

...icite nobis o ierosolimitani ciues ubi est expectacio gencium, ubi est qui natus est rex iudeorum quem signis celestibus agnitum uenimus adorare. dicens. ...

Herodes mittat ad armigerum ...

nouitas aut que causa subegit uos ignotas temptare uias

Quo tenditis ergo quod genus unde domo pacem ne huc fertis an arma.

Caldei sumus pacem ferimus regem regum querimus

quem natum esse stella indicat que fulgore ceteris clarior rutilat.

Viuat rex in eternum. Saluet te gratia mea.

Adsunt nobis domine tres uiri ignoti ab oriente uenientes nouum natum quendam regem querentes.

... inquisitores qui sunt inquirite regis auctore quos nostris ... fama reuoluit in auris.

Principes edicite regis

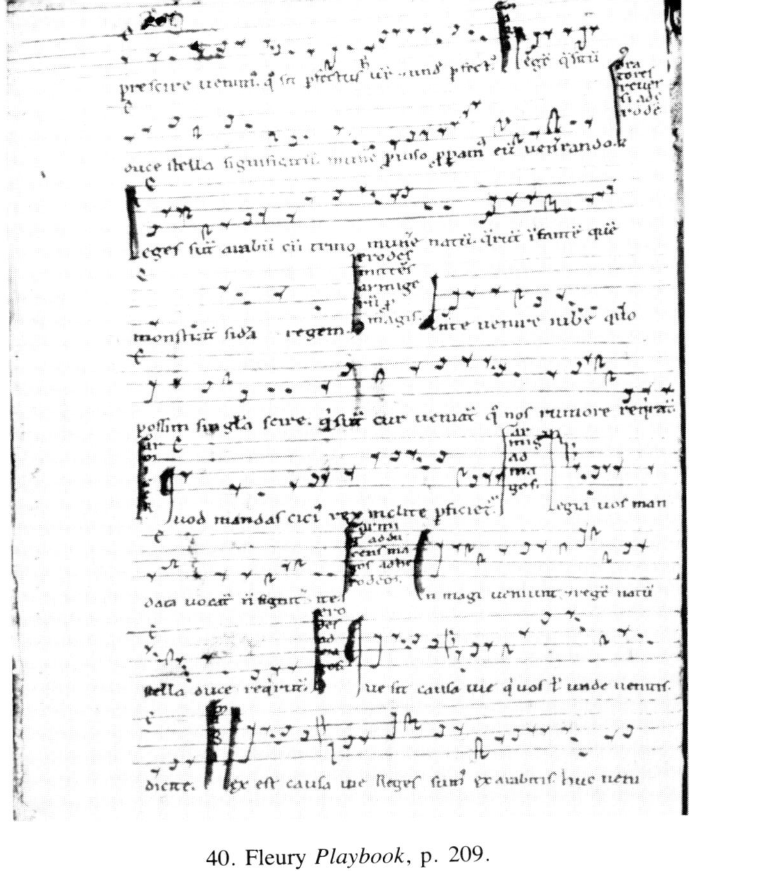

40. Fleury *Playbook*, p. 209.

41. Fleury *Playbook*, p. 210.

42. Fleury *Playbook*, p. 211

43. Fleury *Playbook*, p. 212

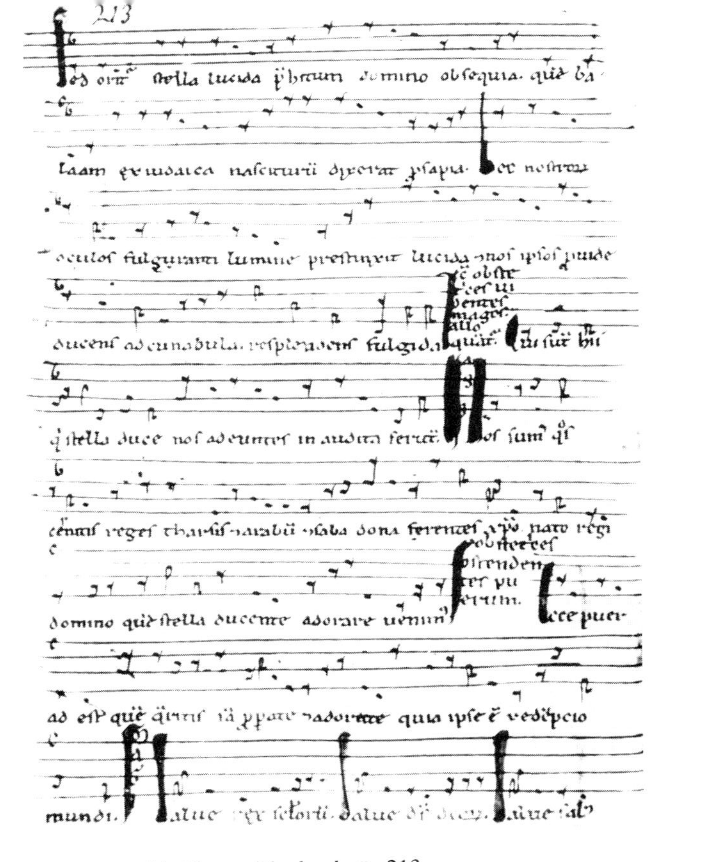

44. Fleury *Playbook*, p. 213.

45. Fleury *Playbook*, p. 214.

215

quam gloriosum est regnum ... matre agnum domini

sup solium dd. ... Ioseph. ioseph. ioseph. ioseph fili dd.

Tolle puerum matrem eius et vade

in egiptum et esto ibi usque dum dicam

futurum est enim ut herodes querat puerum ad perdendum eum

Quare noli flere. ... Ex meren-

tium tunc delusus es domine Magi viam redierunt aliam

Incendium meum ruina restinguam

Agno sancto pro nobis mortificato.

46. Fleury *Playbook*, p. 215

216

Splendorem patris splendorem virginitatis offerimus xpe

sub signo luminis isto. Multis iam modis in [illegible] herodes

Agno salutem cum xpo commorientis ... Discerne domine

vindicare iam dicta stricto mucrone iube occidi pueros

forte inter oculos occidetur xpe. ... Armiger gemme

pueros fac ense perire. ... Salve agnus dei salve

qui tollis peccata mundi alleluia.

natorum parentem ... Os qui in pulvere

eius [illegible] sclamates ... quare non defendis

47. Fleury *Playbook*, p. 216

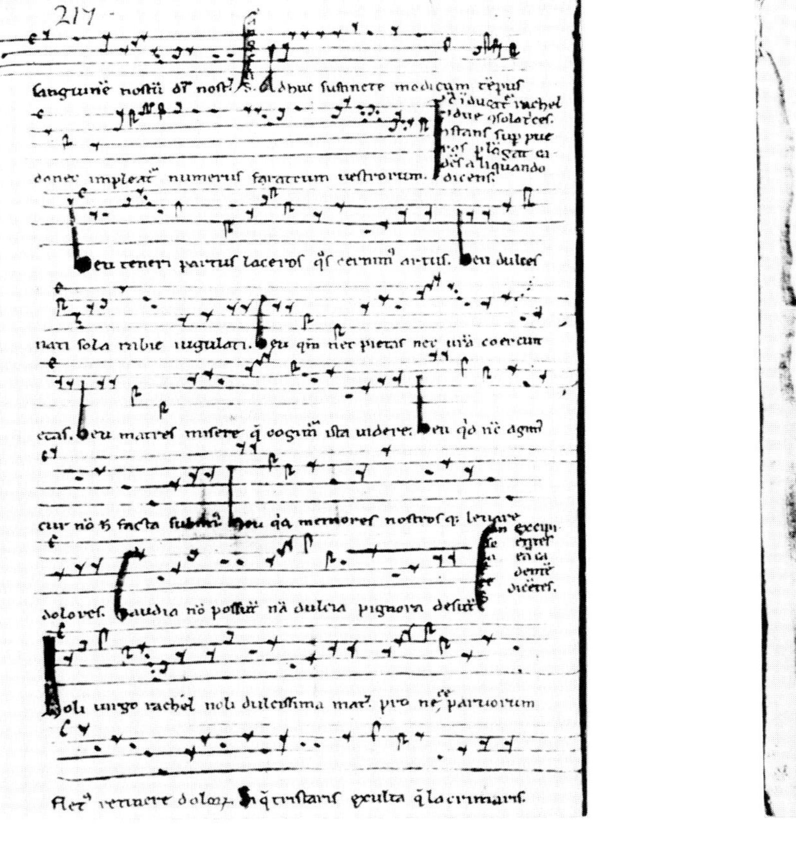

48. Fleury *Playbook*, p. 217.

49. Fleury *Playbook*, p. 218.

219

50. Fleury *Playbook*, p. 219.

220

51. Fleury *Playbook*, p. 220.

221

angippe qd solū qui fače. Venite deuota [illegible] onduitis aro

matū ungamꝰ corpꝰ sčissimū. Quo preciosa. Nardi uetet

sum actis ueniūt a chorū. [illegible] ad monumentū [illegible] cantent omēs simul.

cōmixtio ne putrescat ī tumulo. Cum beata. hunc [illegible] sum. Sed nequi

hoc patrare sine ad iutorio. Quis nō saxū hoc reuoluet ab monu

mēto. respondeat angelus sedens foris ad caput sepulcri uestitus alba deaurata mitra tectus caput [illegible] palmā ī sinistra. ramū candelarū plenū tenens ī manu dextera. & dicat moderata & admodū graui uoce

[illegible] hostio.

Quē queritis ī sepulcro o xpisticole. Ihm nazarenū crucifixum

Mulieres respondeant. Angelus.

o celicola. Quid xpisticole uiuentē queritis cū mortuis.

Non est hic surrexit sicut dixit ut discipulis. Mementote quid iā uob

locutꝰ est ī galilea. Quia xpm opportebat pati atq; die tercia resur

52. Fleury *Playbook*, p. 221.

222

Mulieres conuerse ad populum cantent.

gere cū gloria. Ad monumentū dñi uenimus gementes angelū

Tunc maria magdalene relictis duabus aliis accedat ad sepulcrū. In quod sepe aspiciens dicat.

dei sedentē uidimus & dicentē quia surrexit a morte.

Heu dolor. heu quā dira doloris angustia. Quod dilecti sim orbata

Deinde pergat [illegible] illos qui [illegible] [illegible] debet [illegible]

magistri presencia. heu quis corpus tā dilectū sustulit e tumulo.

Sustulerūt dñm meū & nescio ubi posuerunt eum. & monumentū

Illi autem [illegible] sepulcrū [illegible]

uacuū ī uenerū & sudarium cū sindone, repositum

[illegible] dicit. [illegible]

Surrexit credo [illegible] Sed [illegible] in sepulcro sudariū cū linteis.

[illegible] resurgentis ñ erat necessaria. [illegible] resurrectionis [illegible] Maria ad sepulcrū [illegible] dicat.

53. Fleury *Playbook*, p. 222.

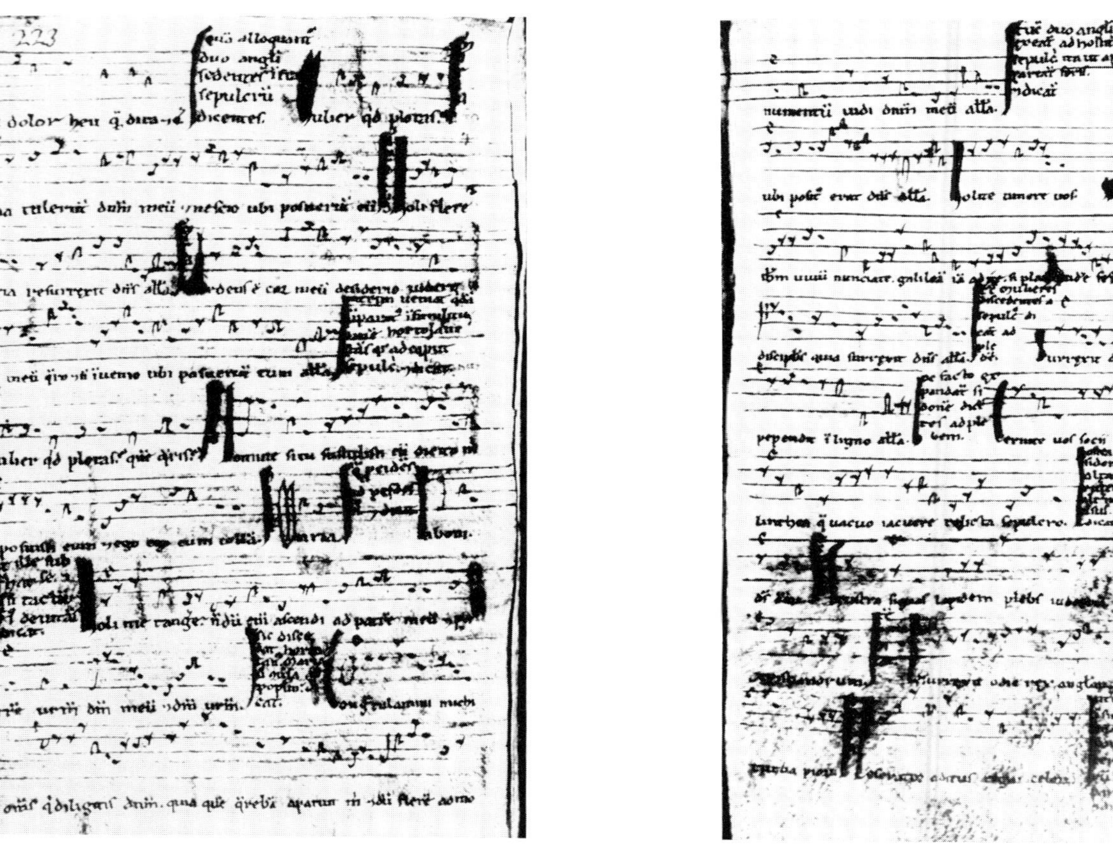

54. Fleury *Playbook*, p. 223.

55. Fleury *Playbook*, p. 224.

56. Fleury *Playbook*, p. 225.

57. Fleury *Playbook*, p. 226.

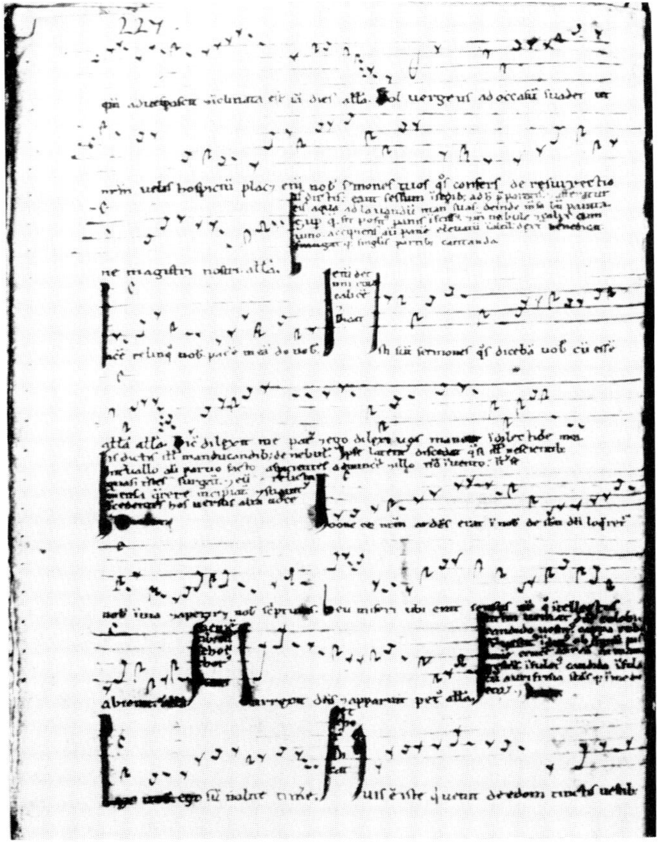

58. Fleury *Playbook*, p. 227.

59. Fleury *Playbook*, p. 228.

60. Fleury *Playbook*, p. 229.

61. Fleury *Playbook*, p. 230.

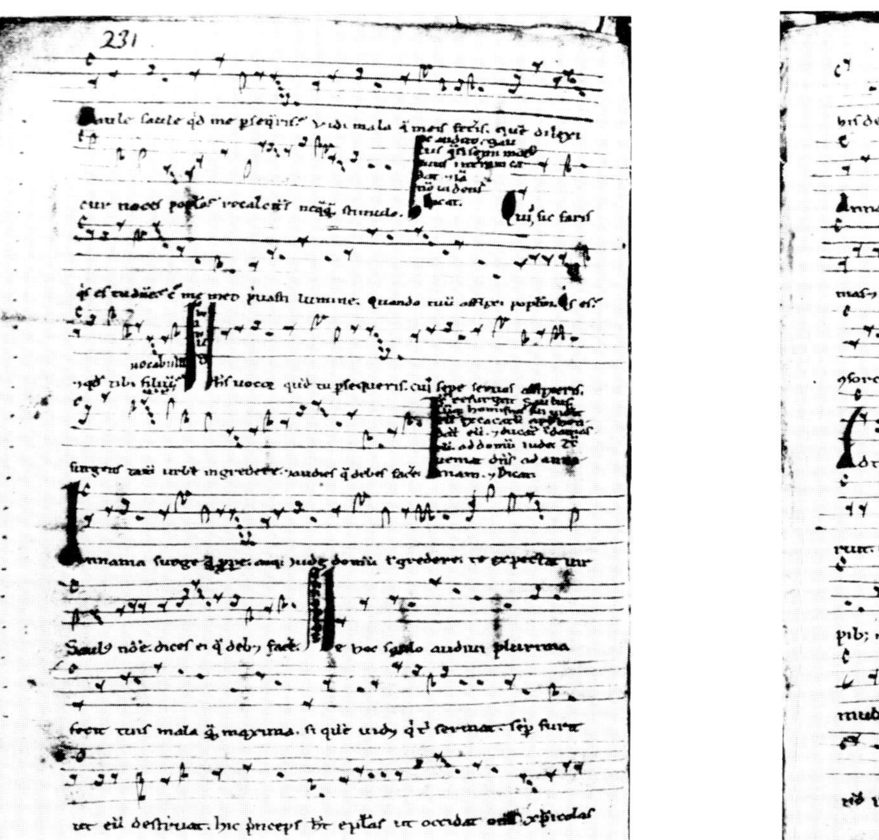

231

Saule saule qd me psequis? vidi mala ī meis fris. quē diligi
cur noces populis vocalem? [illegible] stimulo. Qui, sic faris
[illegible] es tu dñe? ego me meo pulsasti lumine. Quando tui afflixi populum [illegible] es?
[illegible] tibi filius [illegible] his vocat quid tu psequeris. cui sepe servus [illegible]
surgens tamen urbem ingredere. audies q̄ debes facere
Annania surge [illegible] iudas domum ingredere et expecta ut
Saulus nōe. dices ei q̄ debes facere. De hoc saulo audivi plurima
fecit tuis mala q̄ maxima. si quē vidi q̄ servat. [illegible]
ut eum destruat. hic princeps de cultas ut occidat [illegible]

62. Fleury *Playbook*, p. 231.

232

bus de causis hunc saulum timeo. ad hūc saulum ire nō audeo.
Annania surge velociter quere saulum fiducialiter, cui orat ut ve
nias ut eum videat faciat. hunc elegi meo servicio. hic elegi
glorie. hic elegi ut de me predicet et nomen meum clarificet.
Frater saule me misit dns ihc pater excelsi filius qui visio tibi apa
ruit ut venires ad te me monuit. Predicabit coram princi
pib; nomen eius secundum gentibus ut fit civis celestis patrie
multa feret pro xpi nomine
nō resipiscens. [illegible] cur corde [illegible] cur negas [illegible]

63. Fleury *Playbook*, p. 232.

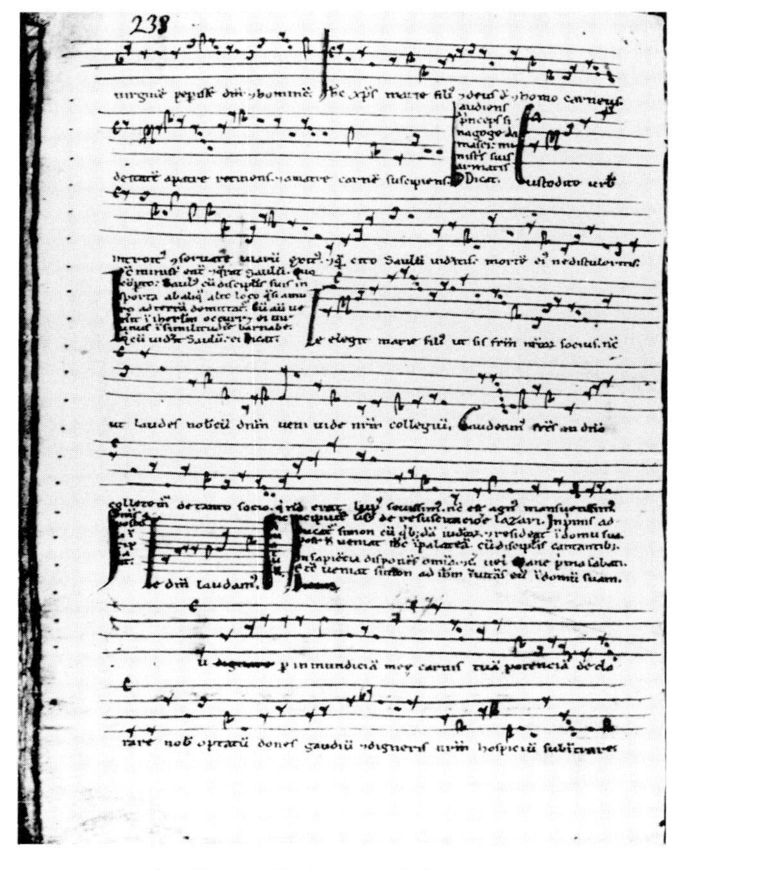

64. Fleury *Playbook*, p. 233.

65. Fleury *Playbook*, p. 234.

235

ab hac tangi. hospes di i hoc hospicio pedes ad ut caput oleo [illegible]

fudit pedes meos rigauit lacrimis caput meu unguentis [illegible]

t[illegible] dicat [illegible] ad [illegible] [illegible] [illegible]

[illegible] p[illegible]fudit. Dilexisti multu o femina tui flet[illegible] tua peccami-

na diluerit. illud enim oris confessio atque illa cordis conpunctio meruit enim

[illegible]. Surgat Maria ubi resideat. [illegible] ihc cum discipulis in desertum

abeat qui galilea. [illegible] paradiso [illegible] [illegible] locus ubi residerat.

[illegible] recedat iudei in quedam aliu locum [illegible]. ut in [illegible] lo-

co ueniat consolari duas sorores. [illegible] ipsius simonis [illegible] remoto.

[illegible] [illegible] betthania. [illegible] adueniat Martha. Lazar[illegible] au[illegible] et [illegible]

[illegible]. [illegible] sic dicat [illegible].

[illegible] soror hunc miserabilem esse reor inmedicabilem morbum

[illegible]. ut germano reddat sanitatem orando [illegible] [illegible] nostri

[illegible] ipse solus nunc [illegible]. nunc solus est consolacio. [illegible] abest.

[illegible] corporaliter quamquam potencialiter presens adsit. [illegible] [illegible]

66. Fleury *Playbook*, p. 235.

236

tam et id nuncium [illegible] et auxilium. [illegible] [illegible] in

[illegible] mox [illegible] nunc [illegible] se dabit. [illegible] nil [illegible]

lateat nunc tam legatum uideat. actualem [illegible] et [illegible]

[illegible] nobis [illegible] presencia corporalem [illegible] ad

[illegible] legati [illegible] presentes dicite hoc mandatum.

[illegible] rogamus ut nos exaudiat [illegible] sanare ueniat in-

firmantem. [illegible] noscat quanta tristicia sit repleta fua [illegible]-

milia pater bonum ut uirtute sue potencie [illegible] recedat

tante tristicie [illegible] bon[illegible]. [illegible] ihu [illegible] [illegible]

67. Fleury *Playbook*, p. 236.

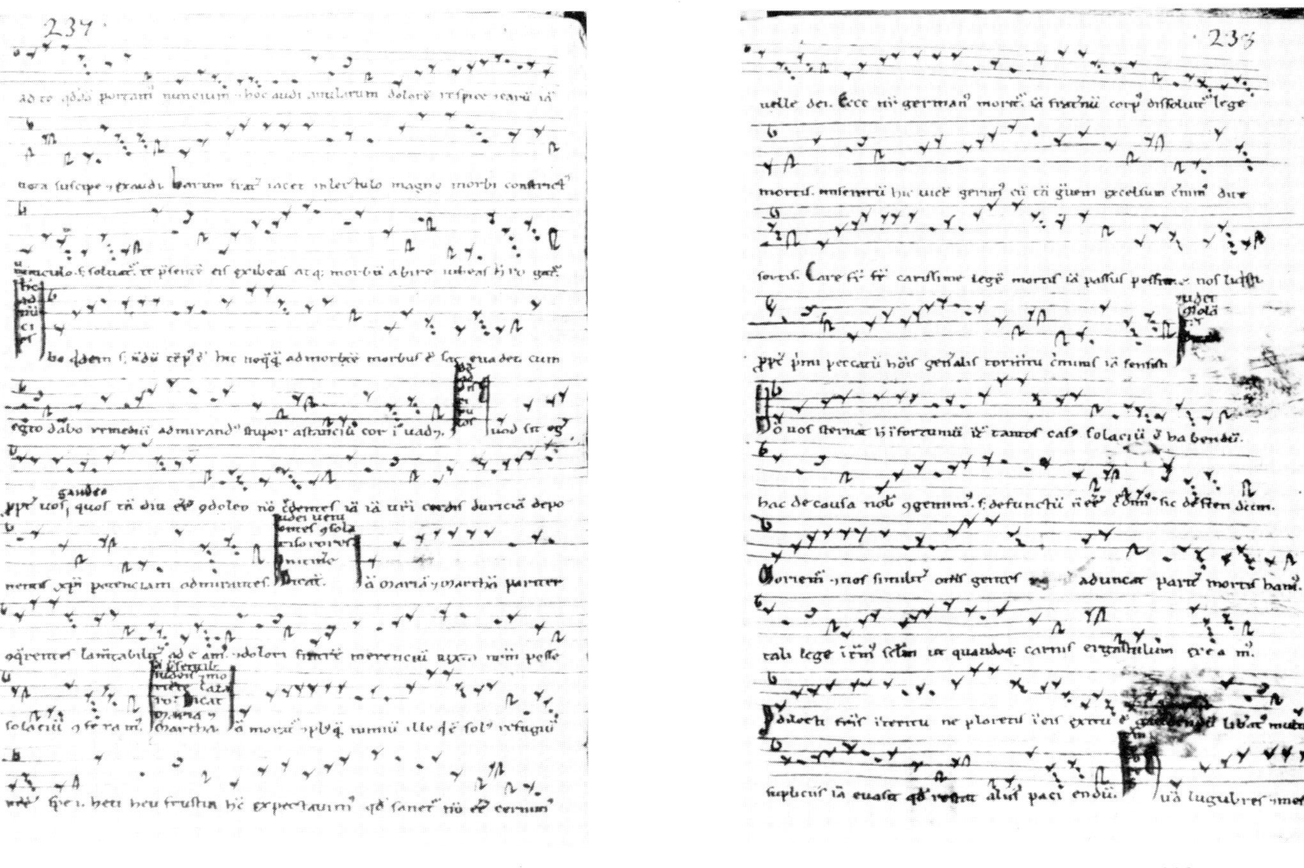

68. Fleury *Playbook*, p. 237.

69. Fleury *Playbook*, p. 238.

70. Fleury *Playbook*, p. 239.

71. Fleury *Playbook*, p. 240.

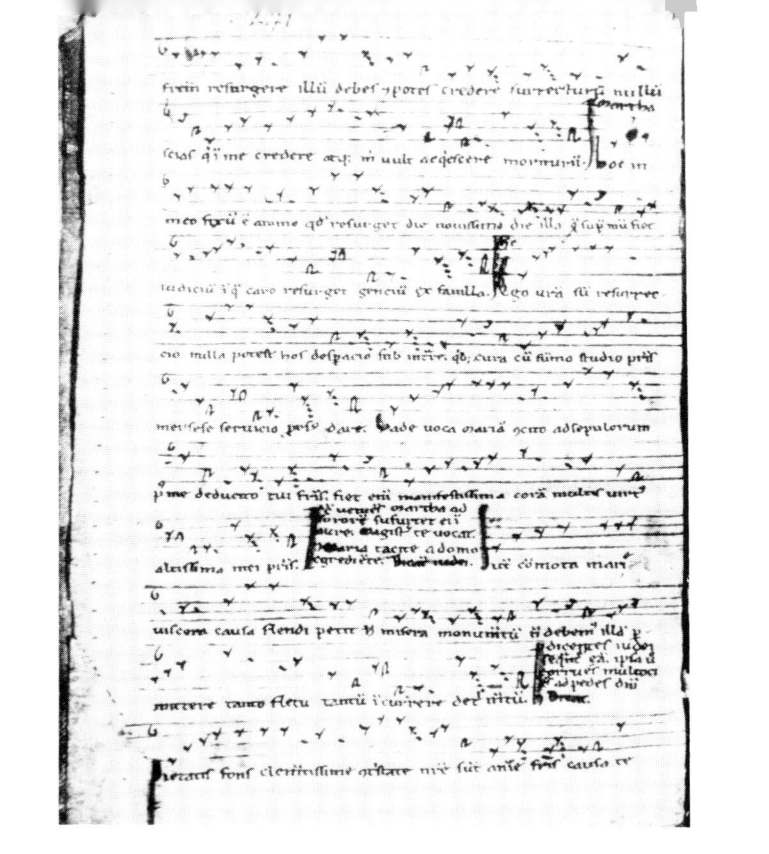

72. Fleury *Playbook*, p. 241.

73. Fleury *Playbook*, p. 242.

74. Orléans, Bibliothèque Municipale MS. 201, pp. 243-44. The Fleury *Playbook* concludes on p. 243. Photograph courtesy of Fletcher Collins, Jr.